"Once again, Koulopoulos looks to the future, describing some of the most critical trends that will affect our lives. In this compelling book, he also suggests what we should do about the changes ahead, suggesting the future is already here."

—**Jim Champy**, New York Times Bestselling Author
of Reengineering the Corporation

"*Gigatrends* points a way forward that is both optimistic and practical. A must-read glimpse into the future for leaders trying to build a better world and navigate the dramatic changes to come!"

—**Andrew Winston**, Sustainability Strategist and Bestselling Author
of *Net Positive*

"Tom is a true futurist and visionary whose understanding of major themes in the evolution of technology should be carefully considered by any business leader that wants to look over the horizon."

—**David Friend**, CEO, Wasabi

"For decades the authors have used their clear-eyed vision to create, drive, and guide healthcare, transportation, and all of the service THINGS that float around the heads of those of us struggling valiantly to get closer to the people we are trying to serve. They have led by creating and guiding the change that is upon us. Visionaries before their time, preaching the gospel about the seismic shifts that we are now experiencing with things like chatbots and generative AI long before everyone else had the temperament to pay attention, they are doing it again. With *Gigatrends* they seek to bring the rest of us to the light, once again, with concrete currency. Follow them and get there faster."

—**Karen M. Shields**, Former Chief Operating Officer for Healthcare.gov

"With *Gigatrends*, Koulopoulos and Palmer provide essential—even urgent—perspectives on what our digital future holds for us. Highly recommended."

—**Anthony M. Amore**, *New York Times* Bestselling Author
of *The Art of the Con*

GIGATRENDS

Also by Thomas Koulopoulos

Revealing the Invisible: How Our Hidden Behaviors Are Becoming the Most Valuable Commodity of the 21st Century

Reimagining Healthcare: How the Smartsourcing Revolution Will Drive the Future of Healthcare and Refocus It on What Matters Most, the Patient

GIGATRENDS

SIX FORCES THAT ARE CHANGING THE FUTURE FOR BILLIONS

THOMAS KOULOPOULOS
and **NATHANIEL PALMER**

Post Hill
PRESS

A POST HILL PRESS BOOK

Gigatrends:
Six Forces That Are Changing the Future for Billions
© 2024 by Thomas Koulopoulos and Nathaniel Palmer
All Rights Reserved

ISBN: 978-1-63758-980-9
ISBN (eBook): 978-1-63758-981-6

Cover design by Conroy Accord
Interior design and composition by Greg Johnson, Textbook Perfect

Post Hill Press
New York • Nashville
posthillpress.com

Published in the United States of America
1 2 3 4 5 6 7 8 9 10

To Mia and Adam:
With you rest my greatest hopes and dreams for the future.
—TK

To Nathaniel and Amelia:
You are forever my most important lens on the future.
—NP

"Every few hundred years throughout Western history, a sharp
transformation has occurred.... In a matter of decades, society
altogether rearranges itself—its worldview, its basic values,
its social and political structures, its arts, its key institutions.
Fifty years later a new world exists. And the people born into that
world cannot even imagine the world in which their grandparents
lived and into which their own parents were born.
Our age is such a period of transformation."

—PETER DRUCKER

Contents

Introduction 1

Chapter 1 Why the Future Is so Hard to Predict 17
How Emergent Systems Are Redefining Our Future   23
Of Clocks and Clouds   27
The World's Largest Clock Problem   28
Unsolvable   30

Chapter 2 The Future of Population: Demographic Disruption . . . 40
The End of Population Pyramids   41
Scaling the Skyscraper   45
The Power of Influence   51
The Last Generation   53
The Third Act   55
The High Cost of Aging   58
At the Edge of Immortality   60
DEMOGRAPHIC DISRUPTION TIMELINE   63

Chapter 3 The Future of Healthcare: Ambient Care 66
Healthcare Tomorrow: A New Standard of Care   66
Healthcare Today: Nobody Is At Fault, Yet Everybody Is to Blame   68
Teetering on the Edge   70
A New Narrative   78
The Healthcare Disruptors   82
AMBIENT CARE TIMELINE   107

**Chapter 4 The Future of Work: Digital Workers
and Digital Ecosystems** 110
The Legacy of Detroit's Whiz Kids   112
Digital Workers   119
What is a Digital Worker   123
Productivity at a Standstill   127
The Digital Worker Ecosystem   130
Driving Out the Friction   139
Digital Ecosystems   140
DIGITAL WORKERS AND DIGITAL ECOSYSTEMS TIMELINE   149

Chapter 5 The Future of Transportation: Mobility as a Service . . 151

The Road to Autonomy   155
Factors Driving the Shift to MaaS   161
Closing the Gap   165
A Wildly Distributed Future   168
A Radical New Vision of Transportation   170
MOBILITY AS A SERVICE TIMELINE   172

Chapter 6 The Future of Identity: Your Digital Self 175

The Identity Flaw   176
Not for Us, But from Us: Our Digital Self in the Era of Surveillance
    Capitalism   177
Our Data, for Our Benefit Not Theirs   183
Identity Beyond Web2   184
Self-Sovereign Identity: Ownership of Your Digital Self   186
Origins of Self-Sovereign Identity   189
The State of Self-Sovereign Identity   191
Self-Sovereign Identity in Healthcare   195
Digital Identity for Emerging Markets and Vulnerable Populations   197
Digital Identity, E-residency, and the Digital Nomad Visa   199
The End of Passwords: Behavior as Identity   201
Every Soldier Is a Sensor   206
Protection Against the Rising Threat of Deepfake Technology   207
The Next Trillion Dollar Market Opportunity   209
Identify and Fraud   210
Cashing In On Your Identity   212
Your Meta Identity   217
YOUR DIGITAL SELF TIMELINE   220

Chapter 7 The Future of Things: Hyper-dematerialization 224

From Scale to Scope   228
Digital Ecosystem   229
Digital Twins   230
Reusable Resources   231
Shifting Gears   232
Powering the Four Billion Left Behind   235
The Smart Grid   238
Why Access to Electricity Is Especially Critical to Vulnerable Populations   246
Solar Power Will Continue to Decline in Cost   248
Exporting the Sun   250
Energy Drives Growth and Entrepreneurship in Emerging Markets   251
Our Last Mission   252
Combating Food Insecurity: The Next Green Revolution   253
Precision Agriculture   255

Edge Case Innovations in Agriculture   257
Manna From Heaven: Turning Air Into Food   258
A Global GI Bill: How Hyper-dematerialization Enables 1 Billion New
    Innovators and Entrepreneurs   260
The Value of Increasing Returns   263
HYPER-DEMATERIALIZATION TIMELINE   265

Epilogue The Dawn of a New Era .268
    Terra Incognito   271

Glossary 275
Endnotes 284
Acknowledgments 299

Introduction

"The future is not something we enter.
The future is something we create."

—LEONARD I. SWEET

GIGATREND:
A phenomenon that has the potential to shape the
future of billions of people.

The future is a kaleidoscope of possibilities, filled with both promise and peril. As we write this book it seems that the pieces of the kaleidoscope are in a constant state of flux, revealing little more than a landscape of uncertainty.

As a species we consistently allow the peril of the present to eclipse the promise of the future, and by doing that we fail to comprehend just how much we can accomplish.

Imagine for a minute that we've just transported you back to 1960. There are barely a handful of computers in the world. These computers are enormous with glowing vacuum tubes and wires tangled about like an old-fashioned telephone switchboard.

Now, what if we had told you, in 1960, that by 2024 we would have more than ten billion computers—more than one for every person on the planet, and—wait for it—over seven billion of those computers would be small enough to fit in the palm of your hand?

What would your response to us have been? Or would you have been writhing on the floor, convulsing from laughter at our ridiculous view of the future?

And yet, here we are, at exactly that place!

So, what will the next seventy years look like?

You're standing at the precipice of a new era in human history—filled with unimagined opportunities and unforeseen challenges. Moving forward will require that you adopt a fundamentally different framework for how you'll think about the future, and how we all will create value for what will soon be its ten billion inhabitants.

We will need to shift from the relentless pursuit of scale to one of scope, in which issues such as sustainability take center stage.

We will need to build new healthcare system for an aging population that will overwhelm today's approach to healthcare.

We will need to adopt new technologies and economic models that understand, and can cope with, global business, economic, and political ecosystems that interact with each other in unpredictable ways.

We will need to find ways to provide an immutable digital identity, economic access, healthcare, food and shelter, to what we will call the other four billion, roughly half of the planet's inhabitants who today lack adequate access to these essentials.

The ambitious goal of this book is to help you understand and adapt to the Gigatrends that will drive these changes and build this bold future.

We are at a precarious and opportune moment in history, when we have the option to ignore the challenges ahead, keeping to a path that will increasingly lead to an ever more dysfunctional world, or we can acknowledge the Gigatrends that are shaping the world and build new social, economic, and organizational systems that will usher in the promise of a human-centered future.

So, what is a Gigatrend? Simply put, *a Gigatrend is a phenomenon that has the potential to shape the future of billions of people.*

Gigatrends are typically interconnected; they form a sort of latticework onto which we build the future. But they are not simply extensions or incremental improvements on the past. Instead, they represent radical departures from what we take for granted as the way the world is supposed to work. Ultimately, what makes a trend a Gigatrend is that it fundamentally changes how we think about what's possible, in ways that we could not have foreseen before it arrived. For example, while the Internet required digital computers, networks, and global communications, it didn't just repackage what was already there, but introduced entirely new industries, jobs, value, and of course, challenges. While many Gigatrends are the result of new technologies, some are contextual: they define a new landscape that presents new challenges. For instance, the first Gigatrend that we'll cover is Demographic Disruption caused by an aging population.

Gigatrends are also not inherently good or bad. They are simply change on the largest scale. Each Gigatrend we talk about, and the many that have preceded these, evolve in ways that can have severe negative consequences. For example, the Industrial Revolution vastly improved productivity and living standards, but it also led to unprecedented levels of pollution and environmental impacts that set the stage for future ecological challenges. Globalization connected markets and cultures, but it also facilitated the rapid spread of diseases, contributed to the homogenization of cultures, and created networks of interconnected financial and commercial systems that were highly susceptible to disruption from events thousands of miles away. The Digital Revolution—the rise of computers and the internet—radically enhanced communication and access to information, but also created deep digital divides, online echo chambers, cybercrime, and privacy concerns.

In each of these cases, the best way to understand the impact of a Gigatrend is to think of it as a commercial transaction that society conducts, with a resulting profit margin.

 In the same way that a healthy business has revenues and costs, a Gigatrend has negative and positive consequences.

In the same way that a healthy business has revenues and costs, a Gigatrend has negative and positive consequences. Our role, as shapers and builders of the future, is to do what we can to create a profit margin that sufficiently outweighs the costs of the disruption.

Gigatrends can also be hard to spot before they are right on top of us—and sometime behind us—because we cannot help but think of the future as an incremental extension of the present. By doing so, we diminish our ability to find new ways to meet the challenges of the future. Humans

3

are wired to be pattern-matching engines, to project and predict. As the economist Frank Knight said of the relationship between uncertainty and economics, "The role of consciousness is to give [an] organism 'knowledge' of the future"[1].

But we are shackled by the past. We desperately want to apply the patterns of what has been to what will be. Most times, that works. But in times of rapid change, when uncertainty rises, and the rules of the past no longer seem to work, we feel lost and confused. Our confidence wanes, and our trust in old habits erodes.

Gigatrends arise out of these moments of uncertainty and despair, forcing us to make sense of a changing world and new challenges, when our existing tools, technologies, and ways of thinking simply can't address them.

 Gigatrends arise out of these moments of uncertainty and despair, forcing us to make sense of a changing world and new challenges, when our existing tools, technologies, and ways of thinking simply can't address them.

When uncertainty increases rapidly, and the patterns of the past no longer work in projecting the future, sticking to business as usual can have devastating effects.

For example, the great dust bowl that decimated US agriculture in the 1930s was not just the result of a prolonged drought, but a series of unforeseeable events combined with a reliance on behaviors that were based on quickly outdated patterns.

Settlers who moved to the west from the much more humid climate of the eastern United States were used to weather patterns and soil conditions that weren't compatible with the dry soil of the heartland. At first nature treated them kindly, welcoming them with unusually wet weather which reinforced their old behaviors.

Wheat at the time was the single most in-demand crop, and the young country was growing rapidly, so naturally farmers attempted to plant as many acres of wheat as possible. The patterns of the past worked just fine and crops flourished, until farmers began to expand to sub-marginal lands for their crops. More crops drove crop prices down. Demand for machinery drove the cost of machinery up. More efficient machines, such as the John Deere plow and others like it, which by then were widely used, had the inadvertent effect of tilling soil in ways that made it more susceptible to wind and erosion.

In 1936, the US government, under what later became the Farm Security Administration, funded a documentary by Pare Lorenz, called "The Plow that Broke the Plains" to show how overfarming and greed had contributed to the drought and dust storms that laid to waste millions of acres of farm land on the heels of the Great Depression.

Perfectly sensible behaviors, a rational attempt at greater yields, new technology, and a burgeoning population, set the stage for unimagined uncertainty.

However, while machinery such as mechanized thatchers, tractors, and steel plows helped to increase yields and productivity, the Gigatrend was ultimately none of these. It was what has come to be called the Third Agricultural Revolution and it was started by a little-known agriculturalist and geneticist named Norman Borlaug, who saw the impact of the dust bowl and understood that while high-yield farming may have triggered the dust bowl, it was not the culprit, but the objective.

Borlaug realized that feeding the fast-growing population of the US— and the world—would need wheat that was more disease-resistant, could thrive with less irrigation, and produce far greater yields. Borlaug went on to develop a form of semi-dwarf wheat which was able to feed billions in countries such as Mexico, India, and Pakistan—countries which pundits had predicted would never be able to feed themselves. Borlaug's wheat ushered in the Gigatrend of the Third Agricultural Revolution which is credited with saving billions of people. Today the wheat he created represents 99 percent of all wheat grown globally[2].

History is littered with these sorts of episodes of Gigatrends, brought on by dramatic and unforeseen events.

Gigatrends are often driven by events and factors that are so outside of the scope of what we have experienced or what we can project, that we not only fail to recognize them and appreciate how they will change the way we live, work and play, but we also don't fully appreciate how they will create entirely new sources of value. As the economist Paul Romer once said, "We consistently fail to grasp how many ideas remain to be discovered. Possibilities do not add up. They multiply."[3]

Radio, an early twentieth century Gigatrend, was originally thought of as a device for one-to-one communication, rather than a broadcast medium. The telephone, on the other hand, was thought of as a device for broadcast rather than one-to-one communication. During the early twentieth century it was used to broadcast sports events and operas on what was effectively a large party line.

We can chuckle at the naivety of both of those anticipated uses, but there is little doubt that future generations will look back at us and find it no less humorous that we are similarly locked into ways of using many of today's nascent technologies—such as Artificial Intelligence (AI), Autonomous Vehicles (AVs), and quantum computing—that mimic the past and barely leverage their future potential.

If history has proven anything, it's that changes periodically come along that so disturb our field of vision, so dramatically depart from the trajectory of the past, that we are left unable to comprehend, much less predict, the tremendous change to come and the new value yet to be created.

If you doubt that, let's go back to how we started this introduction and take you on a quick journey into the past.

It's 1945 and you've just become aware of ENIAC, the world's first commercial computer, which takes up enough space to fill a large two-bedroom Manhattan apartment. It's powered by about 17000 vacuum tubes (the precursors to the transistor), and its limited purpose is to calculate complex math problems, such as the trajectory of a ballistic missile. About ten years later, IBM introduced its RAMAC 350 magnetic disk drive, roughly the size of an industrial freezer, with a storage capacity of about three megabytes. You could call it portable—if you had a large airplane.

Put yourself firmly in that frame of mind.

Now imagine that if we were to tell you, in 1960, that by 2020 there would be more than ten billion ENIACs and three quadrillion (300,000,000,000,000) IBM 350s. What would you have thought of us and our prediction?

We suspect a few questions would immediately have come to mind, such as: what would we use them for and what possible value would they

Source: U.S. Army Photo

ENIAC in Philadelphia, Pennsylvania. Glen Beck (background) and Betty Snyder (foreground) program the ENIAC in Building 328 at the Ballistic Research Laboratory.

create, or where will we find the natural resources and space to build and house all of those devices?

In both of those cases there would simply be no good answers. And yet, we've already well exceeded those projections with over ten billion computers in use globally and 175 zettabytes of global storage[4]. However, if you think that we have somehow improved on our ability to predict technology's trajectory, let's try another brain game.

What if we told you that by the year 2100 there would be one hundred times as many computing devices as there are grains of sand on all of the world's beaches, and more bits of data than there are atoms that make up the earth? What are you thinking now? Likely the same as you would have been thinking in 1960: there's no way we'd need or could produce that many computers. And yet, that's exactly where our current trajectory will take us by 2100.

In fact, if we project data growth and usage out to 2100, we end up with some astounding and very hard to believe amounts of data. At a 30 percent year over year growth rate, there will be more bits of data by 2100 than there are atoms that make up the earth. Raise that growth rate to 70 percent and we'll need all of the atoms in the universe. Bump it up once more to 100 percent yearly growth, and we've now used up all of the atoms in the visible universe (Figure i.1). It sounds absurd, yet there are already technologies that will provide the ability to store all of the world's current 175 zettabytes of data on diamond wafer media that can fit in the palm of your hand.[5]

By the way, before we move on, it's worth noting that the Eniac cost roughly $8 million in 2023 dollars to construct. A quantum computer, which uses the entirely new method of qubits rather than binary bits, today costs just about the same. And yet, despite the fact that we've seen how the trajectory of technology can change over the past seventy years, we still find it hard to grasp a similar rate of change for the next seventy— much less the exponentially accelerated rate which the next seventy years of technology evolution will follow.

But this conversation isn't just about technology.

We often try to foresee the future by predicting the trajectory of a technology's power curve: speed and storage. This is fairly easy to do—since 1965 and the advent of Moore's Law, which has predicted the increasing

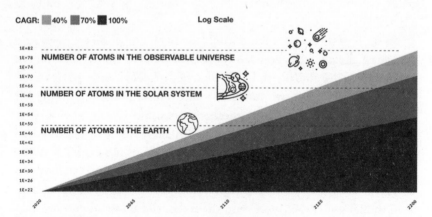

Figure i.1: Projected Growth of Bits of Data Over Time

The amount of data we have is growing at rates that are difficult to comprehend. At a 40 percent year-over-year growth rate we will have more bits of data than there are atoms that make up the earth. While we will clearly need to find ways to store this data—which do not yet exist today—a more useful question is: what will we do with all of this data and how will it create new sources of value?

density of transistors that can be etched onto a silicon wafer, we have been able to project the miniaturization of integrated circuits. But that doesn't help us better understand the ways we will use that technology.

What we cannot predict is the trajectory of society's behavior and the value that these new behaviors will create. Our imaginations are bounded by what we like to call the "cone of possibility." (Figure i.2) The cone's interior forms a sort of safe space within which we can easily project the future. But once we step outside of it, we are in the realm of science fiction. For example, the Starship Enterprise's warp-drive engines are still fantasy. If we gave you one million dollars and said you had to invest it in either Elon Musk's SpaceX or a new company that we just created which plans to create warp drives—even though there is no known technology to support that ambition—which would you choose? (And, no, you can't keep the one-million or invest it elsewhere.) Clearly, most people who place some value on one million dollars, would put it into SpaceX.

Now, roll the clock back twenty years. SpaceX has just been founded and your choice is between SpaceX and pretty much any well-performing public company. Would you have chosen SpaceX? Unlikely, unless you were already independently wealthy and could afford to place a huge

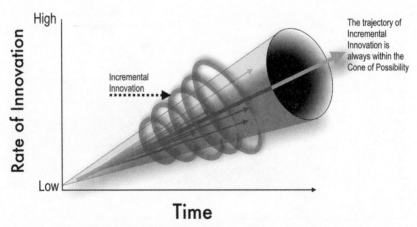

Figure i.2: The Cone of Possibility

Innovation typically happens incrementally within the confines of what we believe is possible. Over time our notion of what's possible increases, creating more diverse innovations within an expanding cone-shaped space. However, all of the innovations are measured against the same value axis.

hedge bet. In the first of those two scenarios SpaceX is inside the cone of possibility. In the second, it is on the outside.

However, what we don't expect, and what always takes us by surprise, is that periodically something will break out of the confines of the current cone and create an entirely new value axis that then spawns a new cone of possibility. This framework isn't just limited to Gigatrends. All innovation fits easily into the cone-of-possibility framework, but it's especially valuable to think of Gigatrends in this way because they always form their large cones of possibility within which we build entire industry, government, and societal ecosystems. Our business models, economic policy, and social values are all constructed to fit neatly inside of the cone. Try to step outside of the cones and you're a heretic—that is, until the new value axis develops, at which point you become a visionary.

So, how do we overcome the challenge of our narrow-mindedness in order to identify the ways in which we can break out of the confines of the cone and create new value?

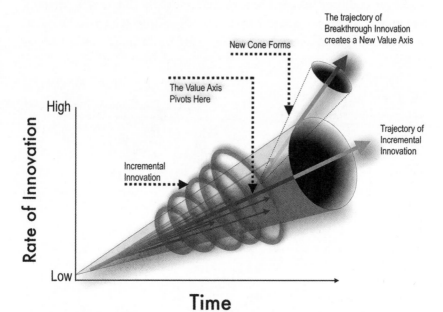

Figure i.3: Breaking Out of the Cone of Possibility

Eventually, a breakthrough innovation will exceed the boundary of the current Cone of Possibility, creating a new value axis and a new Cone of Possibility.

While the future can go in near infinite directions, there are always telltales that point the way.

While the future can go in near infinite directions, there are always telltales that point the way. Take the case we mentioned earlier of radio. Radio didn't suddenly change the world; there were numerous significant events that shaped its evolution. For example, the existing technology it replaced was that of the telegraph, which had some severe limitations in solving the emerging problems of global communication at the time.

During the early twentieth century, both commercial shipping and passenger transport were increasing. Wired telegraph was clearly impossible for ship-to-ship and ship-to-shore communication. Radio was a novel solution to an otherwise unsolvable problem. However, radio was still thought of as a point-to-point solution, initially just mimicking the telegraph by transmitting Morse code signals via radio waves rather than wires. We call that the Mimic: the initial introduction of a new technology Gigatrend that precisely mimics the way its predecessor was used (Figure i.3). A close cousin of the Mimic, but a much more precarious use of a radically new technology Gigatrend, is what we call the Panacea. In the case of the Panacea, a new technology is applied in a way that it's just not ready for. This creates issues that can lead to disastrous consequences, because our false expectations of what the technology can do at that stage far exceeds what the still-evolving technology can deliver. We'll look at examples of how today AI is moving through these phases of evolution. But there are many more scattered throughout history.

One of the most tragic examples of how the evolution of a Gigatrend plays out during the Panacea is the sinking of the *Titanic*, which was equipped with what was at the time thought to be leading-edge radio technology: Marconi's "spark-gap transmitter." This method of transmitting radio signals highjacked all available bandwidth, and created radio interference for all ships within its radius, by consuming much of the available radio frequency spectrum. That effectively jammed communications and caused great difficulty for communication between ships at sea. In addition, the content was the short and long taps of Morse code, unlike voice communication which could differentiate who was communicating with whom.

The spark-gap system also meant that the signals from *Titanic* had limited range—especially dangerous when it came to sending distress signals and receiving warnings from nearby ships. Even so, the *Titanic* was still able to communicate with nearby ships as well as receive warnings about icebergs ahead. The reality of what happened, as we know, was vastly different.

A mere fifteen minutes before the *Titanic* struck the iceberg, Cyril F. Evans, the wireless operator on the *Californian*—at that time only twenty miles away—radioed the *Titanic* to warn its officers of icebergs. According to testimony by Evans to the US Senate, "The captain said .... Better advise [*Titanic*] we are surrounded by ice and stopped. So I went to my cabin, and at 9:05 p.m. New York time I called [*Titanic*] up. I said, 'Say, old man, we are stopped and surrounded by ice.' He turned around and said [on radio] 'shut up, shut up, I am busy; I am working Cape Race' (Newfoundland) and at that I jammed him."[6]

Had the *Titanic* been using one of the alternative shortwave radio technologies which enabled communication over narrow frequencies, had regulators understood how to optimize the power of radio, and had Marconi not been able to so easily build a near monopoly based on false promises around his early and primitive deployment of radio—thereby limiting its evolution—1,514 passengers may well have been saved.

Marconi himself acknowledged as much. Fifteen years after the *Titanic* sank, Marconi spoke to an audience of radio engineers in New York City. Filled with a deep and powerful regret over his zeal to ignore alternatives to his radio technology, he told the audience, "Now I have realized my mistake." Later that day he laid a wreath at a memorial for Jack Phillips, *Titanic*'s radio officer, who had gone down with the *Titanic*, sending out distress calls that were never received.[7]

It wasn't until after the sinking of the *Titanic* that radio began to make its transition to what we call The Pivot. (Figure i.4). The Pivot is the stage at which a technology has the potential to turn into a Gigatrend, and to be used in an entirely unforeseen way to solve previously unsolvable problems.

Just two years after the sinking of the *Titanic*, radio started to play a crucial role in World War I as a means of coordinating troops across vast distances. However, here too, radio was used primarily to replace

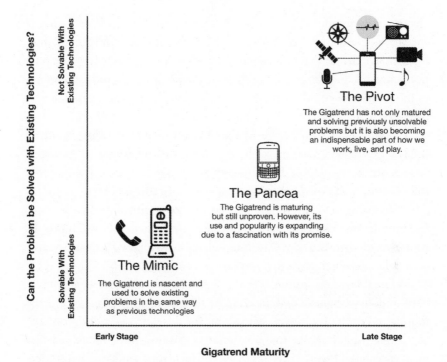

Figure i.4: The Three Stages of a Gigatrend's Evolution

Gigatrends begin by mimicking prior technologies. For example, cellphones were first only used as voice phones with minimal texting via SMS. They then progressed to a fast growth technology that includes new features which are considered to be revolutionary. For example, the rapid success of the Blackberry phone. Finally, the technology evolves in ways that were unanticipated to create new value, as well as a new set of opportunities and challenges. For example, the cellphone evolved to the smartphone to connect us with the myriad applications that we use to run our businesses and our lives.

buried cables and above-ground wired lines as a means of point-to-point communication.

However, something unexpected happened as soldiers returned at the end of the war. An entirely different use for radio emerged, which was the pivotal moment when radio went from just mimicking and replacing its predecessor technologies to creating an entirely new solution to a new problem.

It was one of those soldiers, Frank Conrad, who marked a pivotal point for radio. Conrad was an amateur radio operator and an employee of electrical equipment manufacturer Westinghouse. When Westinghouse Vice President Harry Davis saw an ad in a newspaper for consumer radios, the idea struck him that radio may well be more than a point-to-point phenomenon. His thinking was that by getting radio into the hands and homes of the masses he could create more demand for Westinghouse's radio set business, which until then was limited to amateur radio operators.

Working with Conrad, he was able to ultimately get a license from the US Secretary of Commerce to launch the first broadcast radio station KDKA, on November 2, 1920. Nearly every aspect of broadcasting that followed for next one hundred years started with that pivotal moment.

We're using radio as an example because it was one of the first modern Gigatrends, a technology that has impacted the lives of billions of people. Moreover, despite the rise of the internet, radio is still used by more people on a daily basis than any other method of communication.

While there are admittedly more Gigatrends than the six we will cover in this book, we believe that these six are the ones that will most shape the foundation of the future we will inhabit for the next two hundred years. The other thing they all have in common is that they have not yet reached what we call the Pivot. That means we still have time to shape their trajectory, and by doing that we can all be, in small or large ways, architects of the future.

Clearly, no Gigatrend exist in a vacuum. As our example of radio shows, they interact with unknown and unknowable circumstances which will change the way they are shaped, and in turn how they shape the future, and us.

 While we can't predict Titanic-level events that will create the Pivot, we can identify the Gigatrends that are likely to have the greatest impact on the future—whatever the circumstances to come—and, by doing that, provide the greatest likelihood that we can navigate the future in ways that will allow us to build resilience for ourselves, our organizations, our society, and our world.

While we can't predict Titanic-level events that will create the Pivot, we can identify the Gigatrends that are likely to have the greatest impact on the future—whatever the circumstances to come—and, by doing that, provide the greatest likelihood that we can navigate the future in ways that will allow us to build resilience for ourselves, our organizations, our society, and our world.

Before we embark on our journey it's important to acknowledge that we've left out one glaringly obvious item that would seem to qualify as a Gigatrend: climate change. We're hardly oblivious to the impact that climate change will have and already is having on our world. However, much of the trajectory for what is to come, in terms of global warming, sea-level rise, and more frequent severe weather events, has already been established. The task ahead of us is no longer to find evidence that all of these factors are real, but rather to identify the ways we can lessen their impact.

To that end, nearly everything we are going to talk about is intended to undo the legacy of the industrial age, which has created our current ecological quagmire. Central to this will be two themes that will come up repeatedly in the book.

The first is the shift from economies of scale to economies of scope. Economies of scale were needed to build an industrial machine to supply the goods and services needed for a world that was growing at an unprecedented rate for the past 200 years: from one billion to more than eight billion people. But they were also extraordinarily wasteful and toxic to the environment. Economies of scope are far more efficient and conservative in how they operate and in their ecological impact. Simply put, an economy of scope differs from the classic economy of scale model by enabling the many pieces of a supply chain to operate much more efficiently through the use of technology. In an economy of scale organizations had to acquire or build capabilities to do everything. That created large, bloated, and inefficient organizations. They had to do that because it was much easier to coordinate internal resources, inefficient as they might have been, rather than coordinate external resources that were experts but which they didn't own and control. In an economy of scope organizations run much leaner by using technology to partner with experts in nearly everything other than their core competency. One example, we will look closely at is that of healthcare where we'll see that economies of scale in the form of large hospital conglomerates drive up healthcare costs, increase administrative burden, and detract from the patient experience. Another path, that we explore in Chapter 3 on healthcare, is the use of smartsourcing in healthcare to help focus healthcare providers on their core competency while working with expert third parties on nearly every other aspect of running a hospital, eventually leading to what we'll call the hospital in the cloud.

The second, and perhaps the most critical theme that runs throughout the book, is the Herculean task of bringing into the economic mainstream the remaining 4.5 billion humans who today live a life of relative poverty and neglect. Many have no identity, little if any access to the global economy, less than adequate sanitation, virtually no access to healthcare, and unreliable energy sources. Trying to bring them into the socioeconomic future of the twenty-first century in the same way that we brought the previous 4.5 billion—the number who are today living in the developed world—into the nineteenth and twentieth centuries would doom our planet, ourselves, and our children.

 The Gigatrends we'll explore, and the ways in which we will suggest that we leverage them to meet both of these fundamental challenges, will ultimately determine how sustainable our future will be.

The Gigatrends we'll explore, and the ways in which we will suggest that we leverage them to meet both of these fundamental challenges, will ultimately determine how sustainable our future will be.

Our firm belief is that the journey paved by the six Gigatrends we cover will lead to unimagined opportunities as well as unanticipated challenges. Changes that restructure the fabric of society are daunting, disruptive, and often incredibly divisive as they force us to let go of the familiarity of the past. Yet, if we are able to persevere—if only for a brief moment in time—we may find ourselves entering an age of limitless abundance, in which every inhabitant of the planet will have the ability to participate in a truly global economy, benefiting from the fruits of their labor; where individuals take ownership over their lives, while secure in the knowledge that they have agency over their destiny; and most importantly, that we all inhabit a world in which the dignity and potential of each individual is protected.

CHAPTER 1

Why the Future Is So Hard to Predict

*"The fundamental difference [of] conscious life is that it can react
to a situation before that situation materializes; it can see things
coming... and the farther ahead the organism can "see,"
the more adequately it can adapt itself, the more fully
and competently it can live."*

—FRANK KNIGHT, *Risk Uncertainty and Profit*

It's the year 2100, and each of the six Gigatrends we explore in this book
have long since changed the world. Let's start with a bold premise of
what 2100 will look like:

- Your personal artificial intelligence powered digital assistant will
be your most valuable asset—so valuable that you'll include it in
your will.

- An overwhelming 90 percent of what we call knowledge work
today will end up being done by artificial intelligence (AI) and
non-human digital workers.

- The world's population has plateaued at just under eleven billion
people. Many developed nations have falling populations. Only the
African continent has a growing population under the age of fifty.

- If China continues at its current birth rate of 1.2 children per
couple, it will have half of its current population by the year 2100.

- Individuals no longer own automobiles. and there are 90 percent fewer cars on the road than there were in 2024.
- Vehicles will be more about leisure, entertainment, and socialization than as transportation from point A to B.
- Your identity will not require proof through any document, state agency, or centralized database, and every human will have an identity from birth that is digitally recorded and unalterable.
- Everyone will have a digital personal healthcare advocate that monitors and manages their health 24/7, owns their medical records and history, and communicates with their healthcare providers, creating cradle to grave continuity of care.
- The world's digital assets will exceed its physical assets in value.
- The notion of generational cohorts, such as Boomers, Gen Z, and Gen α will be meaningless.
- Retirement will be replaced by what we'll call a Third Act, in which you continue to somehow and leverage your knowledge and experience.
- There will be one hundred times as many computers as there are grains of sand on all the world's beaches, but you won't even be able to see 99.9999999999 percent of them.
- Digital ecosystems will allow autonomic innovation to occur without any human intervention. In the same way that your body does many things autonomically, without any conscious decisions on your part, digital ecosystems will innovate based on their ability to understand and respond to markets and socioeconomic context.
- Your therapist, doctor, lawyer, coach, and cheerleader will all be autonomous algorithms that have been specially tailored to understand your behaviors, preferences, likes, dislikes, circumstances, and situation.

Far-fetched? Of course, in today's context nearly all of that seems impossible to fathom. And yet, if there's one thing that is most consistent in humanity's collective behavior, it is our inability to fully appreciate how radically the world can change.

Let's say that you were a farmer in the 1800s and a similar set of predictions were made about what the world would look like in the year 2000, with one of them being that 95 percent of farm and agricultural labor would be replaced by machines that would feed an additional seven billion people.[1] No doubt, the way you would have felt then is exactly how you feel after reading the list of changes we're predicting above.

We can guess what you're thinking: "But that was different. After all, the bulk of civilization's advances in industrialization, machines, and automation in the last two hundred years were relatively easy to automate mechanically. But technology can't, and shouldn't, take the place of humans who use their intelligence, intuition, and judgement to do knowledge work." However, that depends on two things: how we define knowledge work and how humans will interact with new technologies (such as AI). And this is where we encounter a fundamental flaw in how we typically think about the future.

While much of the conversation around AI centers on replacing humans, that's an industrial-era way of thinking that we need to discard. The way we'll look at AI and technologies like non-human digital workers, is that they will work in collaboration with humans. Rather than this being a zero-sum proposition—human vs. AI—the approach we're proposing creates a multiplier effect which amplifies the value of human innovation and creativity.

Rather than this being a zero-sum proposition—human vs. AI—the approach we're proposing creates a multiplier effect which amplifies the value of human innovation and creativity.

Some of that collaboration is already starting to make its way into popular culture as well as knowledge work.

As this book is being written, a new wave of AI is quickly weaving its way into the fabric our lives. Companies such as OpenAI have started introducing the public to Generative AI using GPT (Generative Pre-trained Transformer)—a type of Artificial Intelligence that is able to understand human language and respond to prompts or questions from humans indistinguishable from a human's response. It can be used to create stories, poetry, prose, images, paintings, answer complex questions, or even write code in languages such as Python, JavaScript, C++, and Java.

What's amazing here isn't so much the technology behind AI, impressive as it is, but the degree to which we are readily embracing it. In its first two months OpenAI reached over 100 million users for apps such as ChatGPT, GPT-3, and Dall-E. According to a UBS study, that is the fastest ramp-up of any technology over the past twenty years.[2]

We could easily attribute all of this to the fact that we are drawn to the promise of AI, or—as Cade Metz said in a *New York Times* article on how AI apps such as ChatGPT have easily passed the Turing test (see sidebar):

Part of the problem is that when a bot mimics conversation, it can seem smarter than it really is. When we see a flash of humanlike behavior in a pet or a machine, we tend to assume it behaves like us in other ways, too— even when it does not. The Turing test does not consider that we humans are gullible by nature, that words can so easily mislead us into believing something that is not true.[3]

Beyond the Turing Test

The Turing test was developed by mathematician and World War II codebreaker, Alan Turing. He proposed a hypothetical test in which a machine would pass the test by convincing a human that they were speaking (by text at that time) to another human.

AI has left the Turing test in the rear-view mirror by simulating the voices, inflections, and attitudes of humans, rather than just their words in text (we'll talk more about deepfakes in Chapter 5). In November 2022, podcast.ai—a podcast generator powered completely by Artificial Intelligence—posted an invented interview by Joe Rogan of the ghost of Steve Jobs, as well as interviews using the voices of Alan Watts and Richard Feynman.[4] If you knew that these were generated by AI, you may be able to pick out the subtle nuances of language that are telltales of AI. However, without that knowledge you could easily be fooled into thinking that they are real.

Alan Turing is best-known for deciphering the German Enigma machines in WWII. He developed the Universal Turing Machine, the original model for the computer, and in 1950 the Turing test for artificial intelligence.

Because of AI's recent rapid advances, we'd like to suggest a modification of the Turing test. What if the test was whether AI could not just carry on a conversation in a manner indistinguishable from that of a human, but also add insight and innovative value to a conversation? We expect that we are less than a few years away from the point where AI is not just indistinguishable from a human, but just as insightful as a human in a conversational setting. While the immediate reaction may be to ask if AI can be considered sentient—able to experience self-awareness and feelings—the more radical implications will be of re-evaluating our own sense of self, what it means to be human, and how we find purpose in the value that we create. In many ways, when AI takes on some of what it means to be human, such as making various forms of art, we will be brought face to face with the most basic existential fear of all: that we are far less valuable than we want to believe we are. Or, perhaps, it will force us to find new ways to create value and define what it really means to be human.

In many ways, when AI takes on some of what it means to be human, such as making various forms of art, we will be brought face to face with the most basic existential fear of all: that we are far less valuable than we want to believe we are. Or, perhaps, it will force us to find new ways to create value and define what it really means to be human.

While the current state of AI may play to our gullible nature because of its novelty, we are clear that it will also play a critical role in the survival of our species. In the same way that we needed two hundred years of radical technological advances in agriculture to feed the addition of seven billion people to the planet's population, the Gigatrends we will talk about will require AI to build a sustainable future.

Still, predicting that future isn't easy; it never has been.

In 1993, AT&T ran a widely circulated mass-media campaign in a series of commercials on TV and in print advertising, called the "You Will" ads, which were intended to portray the distant future. They were incredibly well done; David Fincher, whose Hollywood directorial debut *Alien 3* had recently earned an Oscar nomination for visual effects, was chosen to direct them. As a backdrop video played—showing a car with GPS, touch screen laptops, tablet computing, electronic medical records, ebooks, web conferencing and on demand video—actor Tom Selleck's deep authoritative voice-over said, "Have you ever traveled the country... without a map? You will. And the one who will bring it to you? AT&T." The ads were frighteningly prescient. In fact, if you view them today, it seems that AT&T had a crystal ball to see into the future.[5]

However, although it predicted the technology of the future with uncanny accuracy, it turned out that AT&T wasn't the company that brought a single one of these technologies to you. AT&T was extraordinary at projecting the eventual destination of these technologies, but not so much at timing and capitalizing on their development. How is that possible? Shouldn't being able to predict the future of technology be synonymous with materializing that future? No, because the one thing that is nearly impossible to predict is the way that behavior will also change. It took another three decades for behavior to start supporting the widespread use of these technologies.

It's easy to say that the technology in 1993 just wasn't ready yet, but if AT&T or any other company had tried to push those same "You Will" technologies out into the market at that time, the products would have been met with the same sorry fate as Apple's Newton PDA—arguably the first tablet-based handheld computer—coincidentally also introduced in 1993 and flopped disastrously!

The problem is that, while technology is visible, tangible, mathematical, and predictable, behavior is influenced by far too many hidden and invisible variables. Technological progress can be predicted because the variables are known. For example, the last fifty years of technology have not been that hard to predict because they've followed the reliable trajectory of Moore's Law, which has proven to be an amazingly accurate predictor of the power, storage capacities, and costs of computing over any period of time.

But what if, as some scientists claim, Moore's Law suddenly reached its physical limits and we could no longer pack more nano-scale transistors onto a silicon wafer, or more ones and zeros onto a flash drive? Would computers start to plateau and would we, as a civilization, start to reach the limits of our own ability to solve the increasingly complex societal, economic, and ecological problems that face us?

Our answer is an emphatic no. We'll look at many ways in which technology will continue to accelerate. But Gigatrends are not just about the trajectory of technology, but rather the incredibly complex behaviors of the natural and man-made systems that make up the world. The better we understand the Gigatrends that will influence our collective behaviors and how they are shaped by both their context as well the tools and technologies available, the better we will be able to predict how those behaviors will evolve and manifest themselves in the future.

How Emergent Systems Are Redefining Our Future

Throughout history, we have experienced moments of profound insight that have helped us make significant shifts in the way we tackle increasingly complex problems. These breakthroughs, though they may not always be Gigatrends affecting over one billion people, have nonetheless revolutionized our understanding of the world, and the norms by which we form our society. These shifts are nothing new—there is an uncanny familiarity to them that makes it seem like we've been here before, and we've experienced these moments of cultural deja vu again and again.

From the Copernican model of the *heliocentric* solar system and Gutenberg's *printing press* in the 1500s, to the revolution in scientific thought that occurred when Newtonian physics reached its limits, giving way to Einstein's *relativity*, to John Vincent Atanasoff's first *digital computer* in 1937, to Tim Berners-Lee's World Wide Web in 1989, each of these Gigatrends created breakthroughs in the way we thought about and understood how the world works. They gave us more accurate insights into otherwise unknowable forces and the ability to stand on the metaphorical shoulders of these Gigatrends and see a little further into the future.

You might ask, "Yes, but what have they done for me?" Consider that were it not for Copernicus, Einstein, and Atanasoff, you would not have the benefit of something as basic and essential as the GPS on your smartphone. The movement of the planets, time dilation, and digital technology are all critical to the operation of a satellite.

In fact, every one of the technologies in AT&T's "You Will" ads would have been impossible to develop without these fundamental advances in understanding the forces involved in how the world operates. That is the power of Gigatrends: they act as the foundation for myriad changes in technological possibilities and how we create new sources of value.

Simply put, Gigatrends give us greater visibility into how and why our world will change.

 Gigatrends also always seem to come along at a time when the complexity of the world is approaching the limits of current understanding.

Gigatrends also always seem to come along at a time when the complexity of the world is approaching the limits of current understanding—the point at which we have been comfortable with a framework of the world that's convenient, but no longer working. At these times the accepted and comfortable ways of navigating the past are no longer adequate for building the future.

We've long since started reaching the end of the useful life of industrial era models that were built for scale and not scope. Scale helps to deliver products and services to an increasingly larger population. As the world begins to experience an overall slowdown in population growth, with a peak carrying capacity anticipated to be around ten-billion people, we need to switch to "economies of scope" that remove the inherent friction, waste, and inefficiencies that have come from the rampant growth of the past two-hundred years. By the way, you'll see us use the word friction a fair amount. In our use it refers to anything that creates unnecessary impediments or inefficiencies to how something works. Just as in a mechanical engine, friction is almost never a good thing. It wears things down and requires maintenance. The same is true in organizations or even social systems where things like drawn out processes or bureaucracy can slow, add costs, and frustrate users of the systems.

We'll talk more about economies of scope in Chapter Four, when we look at digital ecosystems. For now it's important to note that an "economy of scope" differs from an "economy of scale" in one very important way. In an economy of scale the focus is on achieving efficiency through size—for example, greater purchasing power results in lower costs. Economies of scale work well in a context of relative certainty when change is predictable. That's because trying to constantly orchestrate and manage partnerships in times of uncertainty or frequent change is difficult and can slow time to production or innovation. That's why in an economy of scale companies will try to own as much of the production process as possible.

However, economies of scale are enormously inefficient and wasteful when compared to economies of scope. The reasons are many, but there are two primary ones. First, behemoth economies of scale can't adapt quickly enough to address emergent markets that change rapidly and without warning. Second, the waste produced by economies of scale create an unsustainable economic and environmental business model. In an economy of scope the friction of working with partners is eliminated through the use of technology. This means that every function is performed by an organization which has a core competency in that specific function. The result is far greater overall efficiency, lower overall costs, faster time to innovation, and less waste.

One of the best ways to understand how technology enables economies of scope is to look at all of the services that a business would have had to do on its own just twenty years ago but which today are all enabled by technology that allows a third party with deep expertise in each to provide these.

Accounting and Bookkeeping: With software like QuickBooks, Xero, and FreshBooks, businesses can automate their financial tasks instead of having to do them manually. They can also outsource these tasks to virtual accounting firms.

Payroll Processing: Tools like ADP, Paychex, and Gusto have simplified payroll, tax filings, and compliance. These can also be outsourced to dedicated payroll service providers.

Marketing and Advertising: Platforms like Google Ads, Facebook Ads Manager, and Mailchimp allow businesses to create and manage their own marketing campaigns. Businesses can also hire digital marketing agencies to handle this for them.

IT Infrastructure and Services: Cloud platforms such as AWS, Google Cloud, and Azure allow businesses to outsource their IT infrastructure needs. They also provide a wide range of IT services, negating the need for an in-house IT department.

Website Design and Management: Platforms like WordPress, Wix, and Squarespace enable businesses to create and manage their own websites. They can also hire freelance web designers or agencies.

Customer Support: Customer service can be outsourced to third-party companies, or automated with tools like chatbots, AI-powered helpdesk software like Zendesk or Freshdesk, and community forums.

Data Storage and Management: Cloud storage services like Dropbox, Google Drive, and OneDrive make it easy for businesses to store, access, and manage their data. These replace the need for in-house servers and dedicated IT staff.

Human Resources Management: Software like Workday, BambooHR, or Zenefits help businesses manage their HR tasks including benefits, onboarding, and employee data management. These can also be outsourced to HR service providers.

Project Management: Project management tools like Asana, Trello, and Basecamp allow teams to collaborate and manage projects without the need for in-house project management.

Inventory Management: Software like Zoho Inventory, TradeGecko, and Stitch Labs help businesses manage their stock levels, orders, and sales. They can also use third-party logistics providers (3PLs) to handle their warehousing and fulfillment needs.

Not only do these services reduce costs for business but, more importantly, they allow a business to focus on developing and innovating what's aligned with its core competency without having to worry about keeping up with all of the changes in each of these other areas.

The shift to economies of scope sounds simple, but it can be extraordinarily difficult for organizations that have invested heavily in large integrated functions such as the ones outlined above. Nonetheless this shift will be critical if an organization is to survive the next fifty years. Making a quantum leap of that sort will require a radically different framework for understanding how individuals, businesses, organizations, social institutions, governments, and even ecosystems will need to operate, so that we can better predict how they will shape our future.

In order to do that, we need to look in new ways at how we solve many of the world's current and future problems. Part of that will be the fundamental shift from solving problems for engineered systems to solving the problems presented by emergent systems. Emergent systems are those that arise unexpectedly in ways that often surprise us. Much of what we will talk about in this book represent emergent systems that demand a new way of thinking and problem solving.

Much of the thinking around the differences between engineered and emergent systems was crystalized by Sir Karl Popper, one of the twentieth century's most highly regarded philosophers of science. Popper provided an analogy that simplified the difference between engineered and emergent systems by making the observation that all complex problems are either clocks (engineered) or clouds (emergent).

Of Clocks and Clouds

Anyone who's ever taken even a rudimentary physics course has at one time or another been presented with the notion of reverse engineering a system. For example, throw a clock against the wall and you can still pick up all of the pieces and somehow, with enough time, reverse engineer them into a clock. You can do that because the clock had been engineered to begin with—the design adheres to known and well-understood principles of mechanics and physics which were used to make it work in the first place. That's precisely what we've been doing with science and engineering for the past two centuries; for example, we literally use the Large Hadron Collider at CERN to smash atoms against each other to see the elementary particles that make up the universe.[6] We're like children smashing our Lego creations into each to see what pieces they're made of.

The challenge is that this same approach can only take you so far when you're dealing with complex systems that are not engineered, such as ecosystems (natural or manmade), biological organisms, economies, marketplaces, and weather, all of which exhibit behaviors driven by complex and often chaotic forces. These "emergent systems" are constantly in flux and behave in unpredictable ways. Just knowing how they have behaved in the past provides no guarantee of being able to accurately predict how they will behave in the future.

Engineered systems, such as our clock, can be complex, but they still follow predictable rules. Emergent systems don't, or if they do, the rules are either unknown or just too difficult to tease out with our current technologies.

 All of the Gigatrends we will talk about represent this fundamental shift to emergent systems, because they involve not only complexity but high degrees of uncertainty.

All of the Gigatrends we will talk about represent this fundamental shift to emergent systems, because they involve not only complexity but high degrees of uncertainty.

Here's how Popper's simple idea can help us to reframe how we think about today's challenges and the Gigatrends we'll be talking about.

The World's Largest Clock Problem

Popper observed that in a clock-like system, parts and their interactions with one another are "regular, orderly, and highly predictable in their behavior." This way of thinking is the ultimate example of what's referred to as reductionist thinking, an ideal approach for understanding how to solve even the most complex clock-like problems. From the great pyramid of Giza to the Burj Kalifa, it's how we've solved problems and built solutions for thousands of years.

Perhaps the greatest example of solving one of the most complex clock-like problems occurred just a few years after Karl Popper's 1966 book *Of Clocks and Clouds* was published, when Apollo XI delivered two men to the surface of the moon and returned them safely back to Earth. The sheer number of individual problems that had to be solved in order to make those incredibly complex Apollo missions successful truly boggles the mind.

Twentieth-century philosopher, Sir Karl Popper categorized all problems as either clocks or clouds.

However, once each aspect of that complex whole was broken down into its component parts, more than 400,000 engineers and technicians began to design and manufacture each of the clock-like components that were needed to do the job. These individual components were then assembled into ever more sophisticated subsystems. Eventually, each subsystem was successfully integrated with others into the whole system that brought us to the moon.

The race to the moon is still an amazing story of ambition, perseverance, and genius, but there's a part of the story that's seldom told, because it's simply taken for granted. Getting to the moon and back to earth was only partly about building magnificent vehicles that could escape the Earth's gravity and travel in outer space. The other part was being able to create highly predictable models that would be used to guide and navigate the precise route these vehicles would take. Keep in mind that the Apollo astronauts were navigating in a spaceship traveling at 3,400 km/hour to meet up with a moon that was moving at 3,700 km/hour—two objects flying four times as fast as a .38 caliber bullet with a rendezvous 250,000 miles away.

To precisely predict the position, velocity, acceleration, and other variables involved in -flight maneuvers was an incredible achievement at the time, especially with a computer that had 64 Kbytes of memory and ran at a speed of 0.043 MHz. An iPhone 13 is 80,000 times faster with 15 million times as much memory[7].

It was with that paltry computer, probably less powerful than the one in your microwave, and an abundance of slide rules, that humanity solved one of the world's most complex clock problems.

It was with that same approach, and infinitely more powerful computers, that we've continued to try and solve all of our problems. It's worked to get us this far. But it doesn't work for cloud problems, which couldn't be more different.

Unsolvable

While you can use the same reductionist thinking that works so well for dissecting clock problems to "take apart" a cloud, all that accomplishes is getting down to individual water molecules, and does very little to help you understand the ever-changing behavior of an emergent system like a cloud. Keep in mind, as we go through Popper's cloud example, that we understand in theory that we could build a large enough classical, or digital, computer to model how every single water molecule would interact with every other water molecule in a cloud. But from a practical standpoint that's not possible, due to the exponential scaling of the number of quantum states of every atom in every molecule. Here too, we need to shift from classical digital computers to quantum computers in order to solve emergent problems. We'll come back to that in Chapters 5 and 6.

In physical clouds, water molecules are suspended in a constant tug-of-war, always in flux yet also always working together. The clouds we see floating above us are formed of tenuous relationships between separate but temporarily aligned "partners." As anyone who has flown through fluffy cumulus clouds can attest, they are filled with air currents that are rapid and unpredictable; in their ultimate form, cumulonimbus clouds, which form violent thunderstorms, are among the most powerful and destructive forces in nature.

Tiny water droplets with near zero potential for harm on their own can become nature's most ferocious phenomena when combined, especially when combined *quickly*!

That unpredictable nature of countless small, seemingly inconsequential particles, joining in unpredictable ways, creates the same sort of uncertainty that we see in all emergent systems. We can see the parts of the system and still not understand the behavior of the entire system. To make sense of them, we must look at the whole and identify patterns. This means understanding all the individual factors that contribute to a phenomenon, as well as how those factors interact with each other.

To understand any single cloud, you need to understand the way millions of other clouds behave. And you have to then add to that understanding the knowledge of countless equally complex interactions, like temperature, barometric pressure, wind, sunlight, even the terrain over which they form. And still there are variables influencing the cloud that can't be fully understood. Clouds, by their very nature, are inherently irregular, disorderly, and highly unpredictable in their behavior.

As with all emergent systems, we just don't fully understand why they behave as they do. If we could fully understand clouds, the way we do clocks, we wouldn't need to compare and contrast weather forecasts, because every forecast would provide the same precise and guaranteed outcome.

Emergent systems come with no such guarantees; they frustrate us because they involve not only unknown variables but unknowable variables. The rules that govern the behavior of an emergent system can only be understood after they have been experienced.

What often trips us up is that we confuse the presence of some known subset of rules about how an emergent system works, with the conclusion that the entire system is engineered—it's not. A simple example of this is comparing board games such as tic-tac-toe, checkers, chess, and Go.

Tic-tac-toe is a simple clock problem. You can hardwire a basic circuit with just a few semiconductors and without the use of a computer, to create an automated opponent that will be just as successful as any human. One of us (the older one) did that at the age of sixteen, long before personal computers were available. The rules are clear and there are a finite and limited number of moves. In fact, there are only 255,168 potential game variations.

Checkers gets a bit more complicated. There are 500 quintillion (500 followed by eighteen zeros) possible games in checkers, which makes it far more interesting as a clock problem, but it is still a clock problem because it has a finite number of moves and each one follows a simple set of rules that can be programmed on a computer.

With chess, however, things get interesting and change dramatically. You can calculate the number of possible games at 10^120, a number larger than the number of atoms in the known universe. In other words, the number of games might as well be infinite, since we could never find enough storage to keep all of those games in a computer's memory (at least not with any technology we know of today). Suddenly we have a problem that can be only partially solved mechanically, but which ultimately ends up being an emergent problem since we cannot use a formula to determine every possible outcome.

At this point you might be thinking, "Wait, a computer has won chess games against the best human players." Yes, IBM's Deep Blue, a high-performance computer built specifically to play chess, won against Gary Kasparov, the world's best chess player in 1997. But Deep Blue—even according to its creators at IBM—solves clock problems, just faster than less powerful computers. While Kasparov could only evaluate three moves per second, Deep Blue could evaluate 200,000,000 moves per second—literally using millions of times more brute force than a human opponent. This is what we mean by being able to partially solve an emergent problem mechanically. And yet, the degree of superiority of the computer over a human opponent is still marginal. Although Deep Blue won, it did so by a rather slim margin, winning three games to Kasparov's two (one game of the six was a draw). This implies that humans are uniquely wired to solve emergent problems in a way that doesn't require brute force processing power. It's what we call intuition, and it's something we consider uniquely human.

Since Atanasoff's first digital computer in 1937, this has been the trajectory of computing—to increase speed, bandwidth, and storage capacity, the idea being that when you eventually have enough power, brute force will solve the problem. Not so with problems involving emergent systems; the scale of the problems is just too great.

Take the game of Go. While seemingly a very simple game played with only white and black stones, Go is considered to be one of the most complex, intricate, and challenging of all board games, requiring a level of intuition and creativity that is considered to be uniquely human. Go is

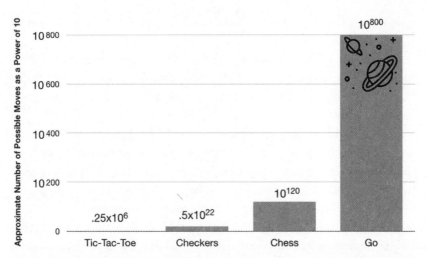

Figure 1.1 Total Number of Legal Moves for Four Board Games (Log Scale)

The number of possible moves, as a power of 10, increases dramatically from the simple game of Tic-Tac-Toe to that of Go. Since the illustration above uses a log scale it does not do justice to the actual scale of that change. For example, if we were to draw this same chart to scale, leaving the bar for checkers at approximately 1 mm in height, the bar for the game Go would extend outside of the bounds of the visible universe at 10^34 kilometers in height.

not a solvable game. The number of possible games that can be played on a board of nineteen by nineteen squares borders on the absurd. A conservative estimated is 10^170 (assuming that the moves being made are legal and not random), more than the 10^80 atoms in the observable universe! Other estimates put the number of games as high as 10^800. If all moves are legal, the number of games could be as large as 10^10^100—a googolplex!. So, you could say that Go is as close to emergent as a board game with rules could possibly be. However, the world's best Go player, Lee Sodol, was overtaken in three games out of four by the Google DeepMind AlphaGo AI player on March 15, 2016.

The victory speaks volumes about both the complexity of emergent systems and the ability that computers now have to deal with them. Even with all its processing power, AlphaGo was only able to win because it incorporated machine-learning technology, allowing it to play against itself millions of times in order to develop an intuition for the game, something human players do as well, but on a much smaller scale. The difference is that AlphaGo can learn much more quickly than any human ever could.

While we still have much to learn about emergent systems and how they can be harnessed with technology, AlphaGo's victory over Lee Sodol made clear that computers are becoming ever more adept at taking on tasks that were once thought of as uniquely human.

The match between Deep Blue and Garry Kasparov in 1997 is often seen as the point at which computers surpassed human intelligence at chess. However, the advantage that machines like Deep Blue have over a human opponent is still marginal. While Deep Blue won by three games to Kasparov's two, the games were much closer than many people may had expected. AlphaGo's victory over Lee Sodol is different—it showcased a level of understanding and creativity that was thought to be reserved only for humans. Relying on brute force is like asking a carpenter to build a skyscraper with just a hammer.

What Makes AlphaGo So Much Better at Dealing with Emergent Problems than Deep Blue?

First, AlphaGo uses a considerable amount of computing power: 1,920 standard processors and 280 beefed-up processors called GPUs, which are customized for the much more demanding task of gaming. But AlphaGo's real power is not measured in MIPS (millions of instructions per second) or gigabytes of memory, but rather in its ability to develop a form of intuition through what's called Deep Learning. Simply put, Deep Learning gathers patterns from experience with millions of games of Go, which it then uses to determine the best moves.

In the case of AlphaGo, its developers seeded the AI with 30 million possible Go positions that were available from online gatherings where humans play against each other. To then reinforce this learning, AlphaGo played against itself—over and over and over, millions of times.

Keep in mind that AlphaGo was not trained by programmers. Instead, it trained itself. We'll come back to this, because it's one of the most important and least well understood aspects of how AI is changing the way we look at computing. But for now, let's just say that a human looking under the hood of AlphaGo, or any other AI, may not necessarily understand why a particular decision was made, or why it's behaving the way it is.

Unlike computers that are programmed by people, the way AI learns is not unlike the way humans learn. Nobody really taught you how to walk by talking you through it, since most of us mastered walking long before we mastered language. You learned by watching and mimicking, and the reward of having trial and error result in positive outcomes.

The ability to "learn how to learn" is one of the most significant advances in AI. Generative AI technologies, such as GPT, have revolutionized AI by learning how to reason and understand, by being trained on a massive amount of text data from sources such as books, articles, and websites. By doing this, Generative AI learns the structure of language, grammar, facts about the world, and even some reasoning abilities. During the training it tries to predict the next word in a sentence based on the words that came before it. By doing this repeatedly, Generative AI becomes proficient at understanding the context and relationships between words. Generative AI is then fine-tuned on a smaller, more specific dataset to learn the nuances of a particular task or domain. This could be anything from answering questions to generating content in a particular style. Fine-tuning helps Generative AI become more accurate and relevant in generating responses for specific use cases.

When you ask Generative AI a question or give it a prompt, such as the beginning of a sentence, it uses its understanding of language and context to generate a response or to finish the prompt. It does this by assigning probabilities to different words, based on the likelihood that they will appear next in the given context, and then selecting the most probable word. To get a sense for the accelerated rate at which Generative AI technology is evolving, consider how many parameters each version uses. A parameter is the number of values a learning algorithm can change as it learns. While it's not a precise analogy, think of this in terms of the connections that are created between neurons in the human brain. As we learn our brains wire these neural connections. The original GP-1 had 0.12 billion parameters, GPT-2 had 1.5 billion, GPT-3 had 175 billion, and GPT-4 has 1.8 trillion parameters. That's an order of magnitude increase in under three years. GPT-5 will likely increase that by at least another order of magnitude. We should note that OpenAI is notoriously opaque about the actual number of parameters used. None the less, while parameters in a neural network do not precisely correspond to human neurons and connective synapses, it is interesting to consider that with this sort of trajectory we are within two to three years of having as many parameters in GPT as there are neural synaptic connections in the human brain.

 We are within two to three years of having as many parameters in GPT as there are neural synaptic connections in the human brain.

Generative AI is also accelerating faster than most thought possible. On February 1, 2023, Cathy Woods and ARK Investments projected that a 70 percent yearly drop in costs to train GPT-3 level generative AI. By those estimates it would take until 2028 for training at the GPT-3 level to drop below $1000. The projections were off by five years and nine months. By March, the cost to train GPT-3-level AI had fallen to $600. By the end of March 2023, 1300 prominent AI experts, tech executives, and scientists had signed a letter calling for a pause on the development of AI more powerful than GPT-4. In part the letter read, "AI research and development should be refocused on making todays powerful, state-of-the-art systems more accurate, safe, interpretable, transparent, robust, aligned, trustworthy, and loyal.[8]"

Although OpenAI's CEO Sam Altman has consistently under-played GPT's capabilities—saying at a StrictlyVC conference that people looking forward to GPT-4 were "begging to be disappointed," as well as having called many of the rumors around GPT, such as the number of parameters, "complete bullshit,"—in that same interview he was clear that AGI (Artificial General Intelligence) is OpenAI's goal.

One thing we can be certain of is that when AGI is achieved, it will likely be as difficult to understand the inner workings of an AI and its "thought" process as it is to fully understand that of a fellow human.

We'll come back to some of this in Chapters 4 and 6 when we talk about autonomous vehicles and hyper-dematerialization. For now, let's assume that emergent systems cannot be fully understood or predicted with any single and static set of pre-defined rules.

Emergence also isn't a concept limited to physical and mechanical devices. It's a fundamental part of economics as well. The economist Frank Knight, whose quote we started this chapter with, wrote extensively about uncertainty in his book *Risk Uncertainty and Profit* Knight's approach to economics was unorthodox, but his premise was profoundly simple: uncertainty is the absence of future knowledge. He even went so far as to state that "the very role of consciousness is to give living beings 'knowledge' of the future."

Knight constructed a complex matrix of the ways in which uncertainty is factored into our lives. His economics describe situations where no amount of information can create greater certainty about an event. This is perhaps the most counterintuitive aspect of Knight's work. After all, if the uncertainty of an emergent system is because of the absence of knowledge about the future, shouldn't there be some amount of information that would rectify the situation? In a Knightian scenario, such knowledge can only be gained by experiencing the event, not beforehand. In fact, more information in these situations only leads to delayed decision-making and lost opportunity.

 When you're faced with uncertainty, your instinctive reaction is to slow down and think through the situation. Yet, it is in these cases when you most need to act quickly in order to respond within a shorter window of opportunity.

Think of this in practical terms. When you're faced with uncertainty, your instinctive reaction is to slow down and think through the situation. Yet, it is in these cases when you most need to act quickly in order to respond within a shorter window of opportunity. This is what's we're calling "the Uncertainty Principle"[9] (not to be confused with Heisenberg's principle of physics). As uncertainty increases the time to react decreases. The reason is that increased uncertainty typically increases the rapidity of change. That means that the rules and the context of a decision are constantly changing quickly. If you don't make a decision quickly the variables that go into that decision have likely changed, making the decision obsolete.

We are surrounded by the uncertainty of emergent systems: the weather, the stock market, the economy, marketplaces, political campaigns, the biosphere, traffic patterns, human behaviors, pandemics, wars, some diseases, healthcare systems, or digital ecosystems—all have a level of complexity impossible to fully understand.

More powerful computers with greater connectivity cannot solve the challenges of cloud problems. They can make an incrementally larger dent in the problem, but we are reaching the limits of how far we can move the needle of progress through brute force alone.

These are physical limits. Not only is Moore's law reaching its upper bounds, but we have some rather ridiculous scenarios ahead if we continue to just store data at current rates of acceleration. It's been projected that the world's data centers (which store all of the data used in the cloud) already have a carbon footprint greater than that of the entire aviation industry.[10] If we continue on our current trajectory, we will simply run out of space to store all of the data needed to solve clock problems. In 2020 the world already had an estimated 64 zettabytes (that's a 10 followed by 21 zeros) of stored data. By 2025 that will have exploded to 175 zettabytes per year. That means the amount of data we produce is doubling every two years and accelerating. At that rate, by 2100, even if we have the ability to store one bit of data on every atom in the solar system, we will not have enough capacity.

We simply can't continue to try and solve every problem as though it was an engineered system with a finite set of solvable rules. That doesn't mean that we will discard the way we address clock problems—we will have more of them than ever. But it does mean that we need to recognize the difference between technology problems—which are clock problems to be solved by linear, reductionist reasoning—and emergent problems, which require solutions that can keep pace with the changes of emergent problems.

We are at a watershed moment for civilization where we can either continue to muddle along using the same industrial era tools we've used to build the past, or we can add a new set of tools that more adeptly handle the challenges of the future.

We are at a watershed moment for civilization where we can either continue to muddle along using the same industrial era tools we've used to build the past, or we can add a new set of tools that more adeptly handle the challenges of the future.

The Gigatrends that we are describing in this book, from the evolution of autonomous vehicles to the emergence of frictionless digital ecosystems and digital workers, to hyper-dematerialization, are all the result of this fundamental shift in how we approach problem-solving, from dealing with the known and familiar patterns of the past to the emergent and unknown pattern of the future. And nowhere is that shift more striking than the dramatic change we are undergoing in the demographics of the world.

CHAPTER 2

The Future of Population: Demographic Disruption

"An aging population will bring many changes to our world, from economic and health-related issues to how we interact and communicate with each other. We must be prepared to adapt and adjust as needed to ensure a strong and vibrant society for future generations."

—JANE GOODALL

GIGATREND—DEMOGRAPHIC DISRUPTION:
The global shift from a youthful fast-growing population to an aging stable population.

If we had to pick one Gigatrend that will most stress, change, and challenge every segment of the world we have become accustomed to, from healthcare and education to economics and commerce, it would have to be the changing nature of age demographics around the globe. In many ways demographic disruption challenges nearly every aspect of how we think about aging as individuals and as a society.

In many ways demographic disruption challenges nearly every aspect of how we think about aging as individuals and as a society.

This Gigatrend also forms the foundation for socioeconomic changes more disruptive than anything we've experienced during the past 200 years, because it upends nearly every institution—economic, social, education, medical, political, or otherwise—that has been built for a specific demographic. To understand that, let's fast forward to the year 2080, which will mark the first time in recorded history that every five-year age band, from newborns to sixty-five-year-olds, will account for almost exactly the same percentage of the world's population: six percent.

This nearly perfect symmetrical demographic distribution is without precedent, and will exist in stark contrast to the pyramid-shaped global population distribution that has been pervasive for the majority of recorded human history. Yet the underlying shift in global demographics is on a trajectory leading to just that, whether we are prepared for it or not.

The End of Population Pyramids

Throughout history, population age distribution has generally been shaped with a larger base of youth, steadily tapering as we progress through older age bands. However, the pyramid shape that we have become familiar with is an artifact of the last two hundred years—it began to emerge in the mid 1800s and was firmly in place by 1900[1] (Figure 2.1) Though there have been fluctuations in the pyramid shape due to events such as natural disasters, famines, pandemics, and wars, these have been temporary, and the distribution of population has, until recently, reverted back to a pyramid shape.[2]

A population pyramid is shaped by three primary components: birth rate, mortality rate, and life expectancy. Birth rate refers to the number of live births per thousand. In order for the pyramid to have a broad base, the birth rate has to exceed the death rate.

Mortality rate refers to the number of deaths in a particular population age band for every 1000 members. It dictates how many individuals are removed from each layer of the pyramid.

Life expectancy is another factor impacting population pyramids. As life expectancy increases the pyramid gets taller. As we'll see, this can have interesting implications for the shape of the pyramid.

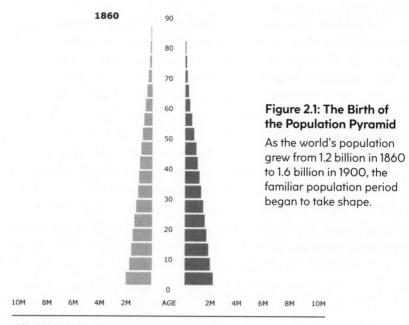

Figure 2.1: The Birth of the Population Pyramid

As the world's population grew from 1.2 billion in 1860 to 1.6 billion in 1900, the familiar population period began to take shape.

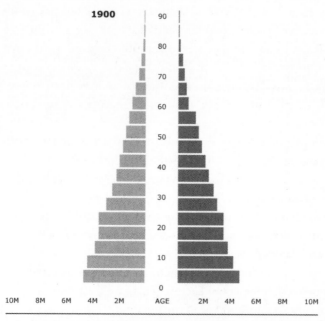

Over the past two centuries, mortality rates across the globe have decreased in all age groups due to improved health care, sanitation, hygiene, access to clean water, a reliable food supply, and successful disease prevention. This decrease in mortality has led to a longer lifespan for individuals, resulting in a more even spread of deaths across all age groups compared to two hundred years ago.

It is important to note that while mortality rates in each age band have decreased over the past two hundred years—and will continue to do so as long as health care, sanitation and disease prevention initiatives are implemented around the world—the overall mortality rate is still 100 percent. We will all exit this life eventually, but there are more age bands in the pyramid as it grows taller, which creates a decrease in the mortality rate for each age band.

Throughout the course of human history, population growth at the bottom of the pyramid has been steadily increasing. This is largely due to birth rates regularly surpassing death rates, resulting in a larger base for the pyramid as the total population rises. Consider that it took 300,000 years for the world's population to reach one billion. From 1804 to 1950, population more than tripled to 3.5 billion people, and then more than doubled from that point to the present-day population of over 8 billion people. Think about that for a moment. It took about twelve thousand years for world population to grow from a few million to 1 billion, 150 years for it to triple, and another sixty for it to double again.[3]

It took about twelve thousand years for world population to grow from a few million to 1 billion, 150 years for it to triple, and another sixty for it to double again.

Over the past sixty years we've experienced a global population perfect storm that includes a dramatic drop in infant mortality, increasing life expectancy, and greater participation in the benefits of a global economy. Global life expectancy during that time frame has increased significantly, with low- and middle-income countries experiencing a 60 percent rise from an average of forty to sixty-five years. Since 1960 there has also been a more than 50 percent drop in the number of children dying before their fifth birthday—from 20 million to 9.2 million annually (a decrease from 180 deaths to 72 per 1,000 live births).[4] This reduction can largely be attributed to improved healthcare and nutrition, greater access to education and better living conditions. While all of these improvements started to take root in developed countries, they are increasingly reflected

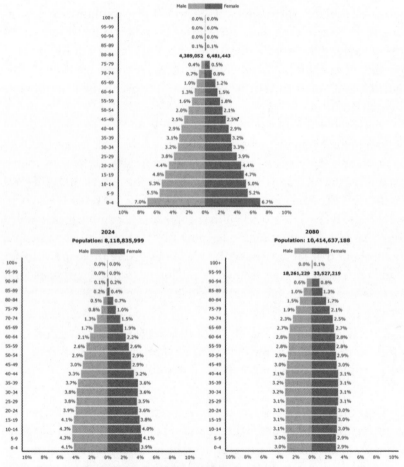

Figure 2.2: The Shift from Pyramid to Skyscraper

From 1950, the pyramid shape has given way to today's dome shaped demographic. By 2080, the dome will transition to a skyscraper with nearly identical population distribution in each five-year age bands from birth through sixty-four years old.

in nearly every major global geography. The result is a global population pyramid that, although still growing in terms of overall population, has been growing more slowly at the base and expanding toward the top.

Now do a simple thought experiment and picture what the population pyramid will look like over time as we move toward 2050. What do you envision?

The increasing number of educated individuals who are able to connect through the Internet in order to amplify their ideas will bring about significant changes in how we interact with the world around us. With ten billion people connected through technology, there will be an enormous potential for innovation, knowledge sharing, and collaboration. It will lead to the emergence of new industries and disruptions in existing ones. In order to make sure we have a successful transition into the future, it's essential to understand both the opportunities and challenges that come with such a drastic global population shift.

If you stop to consider the long-term implications of this phenomenon, it's cause for serious concern. For example, how does the well–established principle of welfare for the most elderly third of the pyramid continue to survive when it's growing relatively faster than the rest of the pyramid? The flawed assumption many social welfare systems have made is that a growing middle class will always support an increasing but radically smaller group of elderly and retired workers. The simple economic consequence of that flaw in our pyramid-based system of welfare is ensconced in myriad other social implications of a redistributed global population that will look more like a skyscraper than a pyramid.

Scaling the Skyscraper

By the year 2080, global population is projected to reach a staggering ten billion. This will result in approximately 600 million people in each five-year age band between zero and sixty years old. In the United States this phenomenon has already occurred with between 5.5 percent and 6.2 percent of the population in each of those five-year age bands.

With an ever-growing aging population, there are demands on healthcare systems, retirement savings schemes and support services that must be met. With fewer people of traditional working age, people will be

working longer and governments will have to embrace innovative strategies to ensure those jobs are filled, such as lax policies for immigrant labor
as well as incentives to draw in workers of all ages.

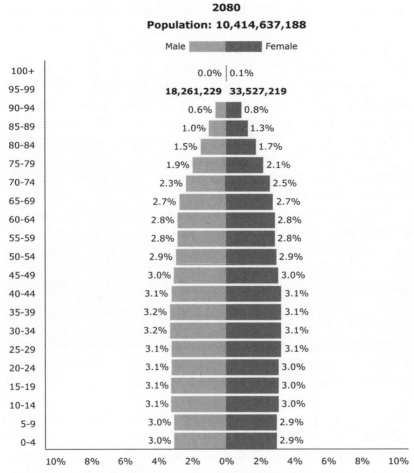

Figure 2.3: The Skyscraper—Global Population Distribution by Age in 2080

The Skyscraper represents a nearly equal distribution of population in every
5-year age band from birth to sixty-four years old. Compare the shape of 2080
global population with that of Figure 2.2, which shows the global distribution
of ages in 1950—about five years into the Baby Boomer generation—when age
distribution formed a neat pyramid, with a range from 14 percent of world
population at its base to 2 percent at sixty-five years of age, and with nearly
50 percent of the population under the age of twenty.

Stop. Did you just shudder at that last sentence? Did the phrases "working longer," "encouraging immigration," and "draw in workers of all ages" cause some discomfort? They should, because each of these represent solutions to these demographic challenges that are rooted in industrial-era strategies. To be clear, these are not the solutions we see to the challenges of demographic change which will become clear in the coming chapters.

It's important to keep in mind that this shift is not a globally isolated phenomenon. This same dramatic trend in demographics is mirrored in virtually every developed economy. Even currently lagging and under-developed economic regions such as the African continent and the Indian subcontinent will catch up to this distribution within the next fifty years. The long-term impact is undeniable. By 2100, the population distribution across the globe will look more like a skyscraper than like a broad-based pyramid. In some case, such as China, the pyramid begins to invert as the number of births is insufficient to replace the number of deaths (Figure 2.4).

 If China continues at its current birth rate of 1.2 children per couple it will have 100,000,000 fewer people by 2050 and half of its current population by the year 2100.

China has had to reverse its one-child per family policy in an attempt to spur more births. According to some estimates, if China continues at its current birth rate of 1.2 children per couple it will have 100,000,000 fewer people by 2050 and half of its current population by the year 2100. Imagine the global impact that will have on labor shortages and labor costs for a country that exports over 3.5 trillion USD of goods each year.

When looking at the root of this aging problem, it's clear that cultural expectations have played a major role in its development. In many Asian countries such as Japan, women face intense pressure from their families and cultural norms to be perfect mothers, while also having success-ful careers. This leaves them with little time or energy to have children, leading them to postpone childbirth or decide against it altogether.

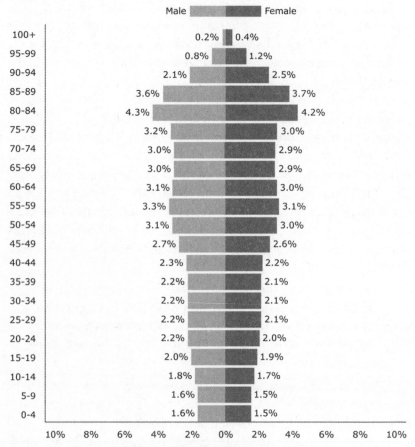

Figure 2.4 China's Top Heavy 2100 Population

China will find itself in an especially difficult situation due to the tremendous burden that its top heavy aging demographic presents to its economy, social welfare, and shrinking industrial workforce.

Additionally, life expectancy within these countries is longer than average, which could be seen as a positive thing on the surface—as happy centenarians are celebrated on islands like Okinawa—but there is a darker side that needs to be taken into account. With so many elderly citizens requiring care, and not enough workers available for the traditional economy's need for labor, these societies are in for a world of hurt during the coming decades. In this new reality, demographics become a significant determinant of a nation's global stature and economic clout.

In Tokyo specifically, where older citizens continue working manual jobs despite their age, there are many signs that point to just how much of an impact this trend is having on society: little nooks where canes can hang next to cash registers at banks; extra seating arranged specifically for seniors at train stations; delivery personnel arriving with grey hair rather than youthful vigor; reading glasses left out by employees at post offices; and movers appearing much too old for such strenuous labor yet adamant about getting their job done regardless.

One the other side of the world, Italy's rate of aging is among the fastest in Western Europe. And if you may think the US is somehow exempt from this equation, US population growth remains extremely low at 1.64 births per woman, down to less than half of what it was in 1980.

The one most notable exception to the shift from a population pyramid to a skyscraper is Africa. With roughly 25 percent of the world's population by 2050, Africa will be the only global region with a demographic that still looks like a pyramid (figure 2.5) . We'll come back to the implications of this in Chapter 7 on hyper-dematerialization; however, for now consider the impact on sourcing of factory labor, which is now primarily done in Asia, or the impact on the investment that will be needed in Africa's infrastructure. Ultimately, what will a global shift in economic power mean for a continent that has been mostly absent from mainstream conversation about its contribution to the global economy? We see Africa as playing one of the most critical roles in long-term global prosperity and in providing a new order to the balance of global economic power. It's no surprise that China is the largest investor in Africa—50 percent more than the second largest—the US.[5]

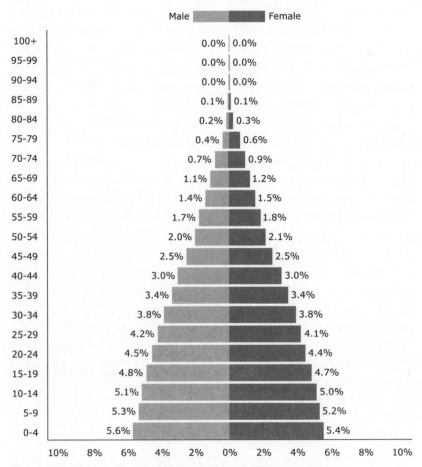

Africa 2050
Population: 2,485,135,538

Figure 2.5: Africa's Population Pyramid in 2050

By 2050, the African continent will be the world's only geographic region to maintain a demographic distribution shaped like a pyramid.

The Power of Influence

When talking about the population pyramid, it's important to understand the incredible disparity among the global population that makes up the pyramid. Oxfam reports that the eighty wealthiest people in the world possess wealth equal to that of the 3.6 billion poorest individuals[6]. What that means is astounding: the wealth of the bottom half of the pyramid is equivalent to the wealth of the top one-millionth of 1 percent. To put this in perspective, if the global population were represented by the Great Pyramid of Giza, the world's eight richest people would fit into a child's tiny plastic sand shovel. and their wealth would amount to 44 million cubic feet, or an acre of land one hundred stories high.

This glaring disparity underscores the urgent need for increased equality and fairer resource allocation. However, this common narrative about wealth inequality often overlooks the fact that the 3.6 billion people at the pyramid's base collectively possess significant wealth, but they lack the

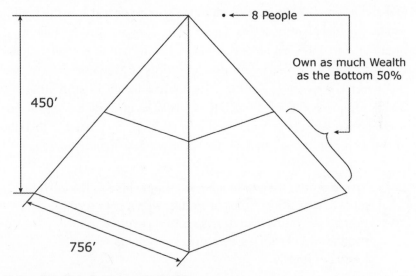

Figure 2.6: Population and Wealth

Picture the world's population represented by the Great Pyramid of Giza: the dot, near the capstone of the pyramid in this illustration, represents the world's eight wealthiest people—less than a sand pail's shovel full of the pyramid's volume. Yet they have as much wealth as the 3.6 billion poorest people—represented by the 44,000,000 cubic feet that make up the bottom half of the pyramid.

collective or individual agency to exert influence beyond their immediate village or community.

This situation is undergoing a significant transformation for two primary reasons. First, the dynamic of a silent and unseen population of 3.6 billion is poised for change, as Gen Z (born after 1995) and Gen Alpha (born after 2010) emerge as influential forces. With adeptness in leveraging social media, they possess the power to make their voices heard unlike any prior generation. While Gen Z and Gen Alpha do not all share one political or social agenda, they wield significant influence that has the potential to disrupt the balance of power in society, businesses, and government. Influence is clearly not unique to these generations, in fact we'll argue later in this chapter that these generational differences are quickly dissolving as all generations develop an understanding and adeptness in the use of social media.

This disruption will not be solely driven by a digital divide, but also by the chasm of economic inequality between those with access to the global economy and those without it. We'll delve deeper into the significance of digital identity in Chapter 5 and how we onboard the billions of disenfranchised in Chapter 6. For now, it's important to note that digital disconnection means economic disconnection. (By the way, the last time the world saw anything close to the current level of disparity in global wealth was just before the French Revolution, an uprising that resulted in forty thousand of France's men and women losing their heads—literally. Disparity breeds despair, and despair results in desperate actions.)

 The last time the world saw anything close to the current level of disparity in global wealth was just before the French Revolution, an uprising that resulted in forty thousand of France's men and women losing their heads—literally.

We find ourselves at a precarious and perilous crossroad for the global economy. However, the distinction for Gen Z and Gen Alpha is that the power to instigate change is increasingly determined by access and influence rather than wealth alone. This ability to exert influence beyond local geography, combined with individual identity, will likely create an entirely different social dynamic—one that not only fosters greater transparency in society, but also empowers those who would otherwise be silenced and increasingly frustrated by their inability to shape society's agenda and their future.

The Last Generation

As we move toward the skyscraper demographic, one of the most significant challenges we'll face is the seemingly immutable, but increasingly outdated, social construct: generational categories, or what's often called the generation gap. The very idea of a generation gap is a myth that breeds division among generations and their behaviors, rather than celebrating the advantages of age-based diversity and inclusion.

 The very idea of a generation gap is a myth that breeds division among generations and their behaviors, rather than celebrating the advantages of age-based diversity and inclusion.

A common misconception is the belief that a generation gap is inevitable and will perpetually fuel discord and friction among age groups. The emergence of a generation gap is often seen as a natural result of defying authority and establishing individual identities within groups of like-minded peers.

Interestingly, while the term "generation gap" has become ingrained in our cultural lexicon, it represents another outdated phenomenon. Cultural anthropologist Margaret Mead popularized the term, but even she questioned its validity. As explained in *Margaret Mead: A Biography* by Mary Bowman-Kruhm, Mead eventually felt that "era gap" was a more accurate term for the conflicts arising during rapid cultural changes, but by then, the term "generation gap" had already taken root in the public consciousness. According to Bowman-Kruhm:

> Mead may not have coined the term "generation gap, "but she popularized its use to refer to the difference in sense of history between

those who were born and reared before World War II and those born after it. She later felt the term was a poor one and that "era gap" better represented the conflict that occurs when a culture is in a state of rapid flux, but by that time the catchy term generation gap was embedded in public consciousness[7].

We argue that the primary reason behind the societal concept of a generation gap is not the difference between young and old minds. Rather, the existence of a gap enables the younger generation to establish a recognizable community where they can find validation and support for their ideas. Labels such as hippie, boomer, Gen Xer, Millennial, Gen Z, or Gen Alpha connect individuals with a collective ideology, values, and beliefs, similar to belonging to a political party.

However, there's an inherent flaw in this approach. Not all conservatives support the right to bear arms, and not all liberals advocate for its removal. While community can be convenient, it becomes problematic when used for identification purposes if it relies on overly broad generalizations. That's especially true when we think of the role that social media has to facilitate crossing generational cohorts and becoming part of whatever group we want, based on interests, beliefs, values, and behaviors.

We have to acknowledge that we currently work, live, and play simultaneously across five generations and that our ability to share experiences and events across all boundaries will increasingly blur generational distinctions over time. While we were once limited to reading about or watching footage of concluded events, shared experiences are now accessible through social media, streaming, and virtual reality on a continuous basis. And with virtual and augmented reality, as well as Apple's new special computing category of technology, the experience of watching an event is becoming increasingly indistinguishable from the experience itself. Experience is also no longer bound by time or location; it can be captured, shared instantly, and perpetuated. Although an age-based gap may always persist, the use of generations as a means of categorizing our identity and lifestyle will gradually be replaced by a societal blend of shared experiences, with individual behaviors being the primary differentiators—a topic we will revisit in Chapter 5.

The Third Act

Another aspect of the generational framework that we've all become accustomed to is that of retirement. Retirement meant that not only were you no longer part of the workforce, but that you also had to make way for a younger generation to take your place. That too is changing. Increasingly, people in their fifties and sixties are entering their "Third Act," a time following traditional education (the first act) and a traditional career (the second act). The Third Act is more than just a catchy term we're slapping on a small number of workaholic octogenarians. According to our research, 29 percent of the overall population do not expect to *ever* retire. That increases to 37 percent for twenty-two- to thirty-two-year-olds. Don't mistake this for simply a trend born of economic necessity. While many in the workforce have suffered because of multiple recessions in the 2000s, there is another factor at play that we've already talked about: locality and age do not stand in the way of our ability to work.[8]

 We want to challenge the very nature of "retirement," and feel strongly that this too is a term and concept that is stuck in the industrial era, and which has outlived its usefulness.

In fact, we want to challenge the very nature of "retirement," and feel strongly that this too is a term and concept that is stuck in the industrial era, and which has outlived its usefulness. Since 1950, a definitive trend line has emerged, pointing to a narrowing gap between life expectancy and work-life expectancy. Both are increasing, but work-life expectancy is increasing at a slightly faster rate that life expectancy. While that does not mean we will at some point be working after we're dead—at least that's not a claim we're making in this book—it does illustrate how underlying trends are challenging some of the most basic generational and societal beliefs, such as retirement.

If you're thinking, "But wait, I want to retire! I'm looking forward to it!"—don't miss the point. Going forward, retirement is not a chronologic watershed that marks the end of work and the beginning of leisure. Most knowledge workers do not expect to, and will not have to, disengage from work that is financially or personally fulfilling. Instead, they will simply move into a new stage of life where the balance between, or the purpose behind, work and play may shift. That's why we prefer the term Third Act as a way to describe a period of life when the venue and the rules of how you work may change, allowing you to integrate and balance work as a meaningful part of your life.

The End of Retirement

Traditional Retirement is being replaced by what we're calling your Third Act; and it could be the best chapter of your life, but only if you plan for it. Here's how.

Because the nature of knowledge work involves a lifetime's worth of intellectual creativity you may get to the point where you no longer need to work for the money, but it's unlikely that you'll get to the point where you no longer want to share what you've learned and generate value for what you know.

Yes, you may have enough money to live the rest of your life on a tropical island watching the waves roll in, gently lapping against the shoreline. It will be a soothing, tranquil scene for about thirty minutes, or until you notice the small cove next to you with five hundred yards of abandoned sandy beach and ask yourself, "Hey, wait a minute...why hasn't anyone developed that yet?"

So, what do you do to fuel that passion, after you've sold your business, cashed in, or just reached the point where you no longer need the mantle of a corporate title, ten direct reports, and sixteen-hour days? Your Third Act—it's what we used to call retirement.

What will your Third Act look like? Have you thought about it? Most people haven't. And yet, fewer and fewer knowledge workers want to *fully* retire—completely unplug and bury their toes—and head—in the sand.

In fact, knowledge workers are especially terrified by the thought of retirement. It's not that they fear the loss of income, but rather the loss of the intellectual, creative, and social engagement that has fueled their passion for so long.

There are at least three pillars that you need to have in place to support a Third Act. First, start with a simple question. What's my brand? Your brand needs to reflect a unique point of view and the value that you bring to the world. Make it specific, concise, and relevant. Second, create content that reinforces your brand and gives you visibility: books, social media posts, videos, articles, and speeches all help to reinforce your value. Third, start planning now; don't let your third act take you by surprise. In the same way that traditional retirement didn't afford you the luxury of waiting until you retired to invest in a retirement portfolio, you can't wait until your second act is over to start investing in your third act!

Hopefully your Third Act is going to last a very long time and provide you with the deep intellectual and emotional satisfaction that we all crave, along with the flexibility for those tropical island getaways. We never said there was anything wrong with regular visits to paradise, just don't get marooned there!

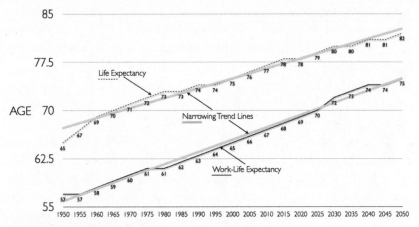

Figure 2.7: The Coming Intersection of Life Expectancy and Work-Life Expectancy

Both life expectancy and work-life expectancy are increasing, although work-life expectancy is increasing at a slightly faster rate. The narrowing trend lines indicate a long-term trend toward the merging of life expectancy and work-life expectancy within the next one hundred years.

The High Cost of Aging

The implication of these changes in global demographics—on so many of the institutions that have been built on the premise of a bottom-heavy population pyramid—are far reaching, impacting each of the other five Gigatrends we will discuss. However, nowhere will the impact be more pronounced than in healthcare.

An aging demographic is already having significant implications for healthcare. According to the Population Reference Bureau, the percentage of Americans aged sixty-five and older is projected to grow from 16 percent in 2018 to 23 percent by 2060.[9] This rapid increase in an older population will put tremendous strain on healthcare systems.

One stark example of how an aging population can impact healthcare is the historical trajectory of heart disease during the 1900s. During the first half of the century there was a remarkable increase in life expectancy from 46.3 to 69.7 years, due to advances in sanitation, the introduction of vaccines and antibiotics, and declines in infectious disease. However, a longer life meant that heart disease and stroke replaced infectious diseases as the predominant illness, because many more people were living to an age when they were more likely to encounter heart disease from factors such as atherosclerosis. But then something even more perplexing happened[10].

Coronary heart disease (CHD) mortality rates began to decline, and continued to decline in the US and the rest of the industrialized world. Since 1950 the age-adjusted annual heart disease mortality per 100,000 has fallen by 56 percent. (Figure 2.8) The reasons for this decline include social factors such as the effort to reduce smoking, greater emphasis on a healthy diet, and improved clinical management of hypertension and high cholesterol. However, all of that has come at a cost which is anticipated to skyrocket over the next ten years. The cost of coronary disease is expected to double to $1 trillion in 2035, from $555 billion in 2016[11]. While an increased prevalence of obesity and Type 2 Diabetes is partly to account for this, the greater variable is the growing percent of the population which will be in older age bands and thus most likely to suffer from cardiovascular disease.

According to one study, in 2019 people over sixty-five account for 35 percent of all healthcare costs, yet they represent just 17 percent of the

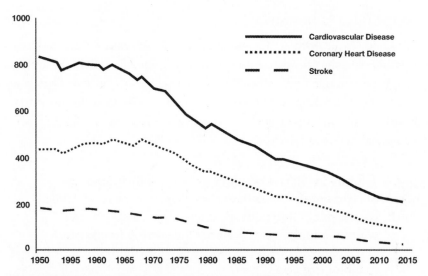

Figure 2.8: Drop in Cardiovascular Disease 1950–2015

During the past seventy years the rate of cardiovascular disease, coronary heart disease, and stroke have all fallen precipitously. However, that trend is stalling as the demographics of the U.S. and the globe shift to an aging demographic.

population.[12] Older individuals are also particularly vulnerable to acute and chronic illnesses such as stroke, heart disease, cancer, diabetes and arthritis—all of which require significant medical attention and costly treatments. To create even more complexity, these conditions rarely occur alone, but create what are referred to as co-morbidities: multiple chronic conditions that require simultaneous coordinated ongoing care[13]. According to the CDC, "More than half (51.8 percent) of adults had at least one of ten selected diagnosed chronic conditions (arthritis, cancer, chronic obstructive pulmonary disease, coronary heart disease, current asthma, diabetes, hepatitis, hypertension, stroke, and weak or failing kidneys), and 27.2 percent of US adults had multiple chronic conditions.[14]" The elderly are also disproportionately affected by medication errors, due to deteriorating cognitive abilities and complex drug regimes. Medication errors account for 25 percent of hospitalizations for adverse drug events in people age sixty-five and older.[15] All of this is happening at a time when the promise of living longer has never had more science behind it.

At the Edge of Immortality

We stand on the brink of unlocking incredible potential for dramatically extending our health span. A future in which one hundred is the anticipated age of retirement, rather than sixty-five, isn't as far-fetched as you might think. Imagine what you could achieve with an additional forty healthy years—a future when chronological age becomes irrelevant when compared to biological age.

 A future in which one hundred is the anticipated age of retirement, rather than sixty-five, isn't as far-fetched as you might think. Imagine what you could achieve with an additional forty healthy years—a future when chronological age becomes irrelevant when compared to biological age.

The longevity and anti-senescence therapies market is expected to exceed $44 billion globally by 2030, according to Allied Market Research. Anti-senescence therapies work to moderate or shut off senescent cells, which secrete harmful molecules that cause chronic inflammation, leading to damage to the surrounding tissue and negatively impacting the behavior of nearby healthy cells. Over time, without proper cellular health management, this can significantly affect an individual's overall quality of life.

Recently, Saudi Arabia announced plans to spend $1 billion a year on anti-aging research, while longevity-focused private equity funds have raised several hundred million dollars in just the last few years alone. The goal is to bring together and enhance independent factors aimed at increasing the human lifespan and ultimately achieving immortality. We realize that there is a rich philosophical debate around the idea of immortality, but while the arc of technology may be influenced by that debate, its trajectory rarely is.

Francis Fukuyama, Senior Fellow of the Freeman Spogli Institute at Stanford University, describes this quest for immortality, and what has also been called the evolution to Transhumanism, as "the world's most dangerous idea," citing concerns ranging from equity in access to these technologies and therapies—where only the ultra-rich become immortal—to the inevitable slippery slope of unintended consequences. Without diving into the philosophical debate, few of us would disagree with the benefits of maintaining our health and well-being over merely living an extended life of pain and suffering.

Advancements in bionics (the merging of AI and artificial limbs) are creating prosthetics that increasingly resemble natural limbs. Artificial organs are being developed using 3D printing technology, making it possible to replace worn-out organs with biocompatible alternatives. Brain-computer interfaces like Elon Musk's Neuralink aim to enable humans to control computers using only their thoughts, opening up countless possibilities for improving quality of life for people with spinal cord injuries, or diseases such as Parkinson's or ALS.

In the emerging field of regenerative medicine, there are treatments designed to regenerate damaged cells or tissues in the body, using stem cell therapies such as bilogics which utilize the body's natural healing capacities. Companies such as Eyestem, Spiderwort, Hy2Care, Mesentech, and Toregem BioPharma are at the forefront of research and development in these regenerative treatments.

One of the most promising recent developments in treating life-threatening diseases is the ability to provide unprecedented control and accuracy over the manipulation and editing of our genome through technologies such as CRISPR (Clustered Regularly Interspaced Short Palindromic Repeats). In 2015, scientists made headlines by using CRISPR to perform genetic modifications on human embryo cells, something that had long been a dream for researchers. It was a turning point for genetic engineering.

In a more controversial development, researcher He Jiankui announced the birth of two genetically engineered female twins in 2018. While this advancement sparked a flurry of ethical debates, it also demonstrated the vast potential of CRISPR.

In 2020, the first CRISPR-based therapy, CTX001, entered clinical trials for the treatment of two blood disorders: sickle cell disease and beta-thalassemia. CTX001 is an ex vivo gene-editing therapy, meaning that it involves editing patients' stem cells outside of their bodies. The edited stem cells are then infused back into the patient, where they repopulate the bone marrow and produce red blood cells containing higher levels of fetal hemoglobin, reducing the severity of these diseases. CRISPR technology is also being researched and developed for a variety of applications, including cancer therapies, HIV treatment, and the development of disease-resistant crops.

As if all of this isn't enough to consider, immortality is not just a matter of extending our physical forms. Researchers at Project Blue Brain, at the École Polytechnique Fédérale de Lausanne (EPFL), believe that we are closer than ever to understanding and replicating all of our physical, mental, and emotional traits in a digital form. Futurist Ray Kurtzweil, who is also Google's director of engineering, has long proposed that the ultimate form of immortality will be the merging of humans and machines.

Clearly, the next several decades will see all of these approaches to longevity advance rapidly, creating possibilities and challenges that are nearly impossible to imagine from our vantage point today. While we can't turn back the clock on the changing demographics, or alter the trajectory of the technologies which will only amplify these changes, we can use the power of the Gigatrends we are about to discuss to help better manage the needs of an aging world, and to create a context within which aging is transformed from a burden on society to a valuable contributor. We'll start that journey by looking at the changing face of healthcare in the next chapter.

DEMOGRAPHIC DISRUPTION TIMELINE

2021–2030: Aging Populations & Global Challenges

Global population grows to 8.5 billion, and the median age of the world's population rises from twenty-five years old to thirty-two years old in 2021. In developed countries, aging populations will face increasingly complex health challenges with more co-morbidities. We will start to experience the early stages of stress on social welfare and senior care for this new demographic. It's likely we will see countries attempt to raise the retirement age, something that will not be easily accepted. The over-sixty-five demographic will make up 17 percent of global population, as opposed to 10 percent in 2000. In the US there will be just over one percent difference in the percentage of the population in each of the five-year age bands through seventy-five years old. In countries such as China, Japan, and Italy, a top-heavy population demographic will become especially pronounced, creating crisis-level stress on their economies and social welfare systems. Japan will have reverted to population levels it hasn't seen since 1980, creating severe labor force shortages.

2031–2040: Declining Fertility & Labor Shifts

The global fertility rate is expected to decline to 2.29 live births for each woman, less than half of what it was in 1950. In the US it will be at 1.75, meaning that population will be declining steadily. Fewer births will lead to a refocus of medicine for those who are living longer. The over-sixty-five population is projected to become more concentrated in developed countries such as the US, China, and Japan, as well as in EU countries, while developing nations will lag behind with a younger demographic profile overall. This will cause a shift in labor away from traditional Asian outsourcing to regions such as Africa, which will still have a pyramidal age distribution through 2050. Retirement ages will have been increased by at least five years in developed countries, despite intense protests from workers, creating a heated political climate.

2041–2050: Population Skyscrapers & Technological Advancements

Global population growth will continue to slow with the global median age of thirty-six years old, rising to forty-six years old in high-income

63

countries. The population skyscraper will now be typical for almost all developed nations. One notable exception will be China, which will have a bulging older demographic and a nearly inverted population pyramid with three times as many people in the thirty-one to eighty age group as in the zero to thirty age group. Africa will be in an enviable position with continued population growth and a solid base of younger workers. Technological advancements in healthcare such as Digital Advocates (see Chapter 3), Artificial Intelligence, and robotics are likely to help seniors stay healthier and independent longer. Age-related cognitive conditions such as Alzheimer's, Parkinson's, and many forms of dementia will be diagnosed, treatable, and reversible, leading to longer life and work-life expectancy. Retirement will have changed dramatically across the globe, both in terms of the age at which it is considered to be socially acceptable and the age at which it is funded by government programs, although it's also likely that by this time incentive-based approaches, such as tax incentives to promote delaying or putting off retirement, will be implemented, rather than simply continuing to raise the age of eligibility.

2051–2060: Below Replacement Fertility & Economic Adaptation

The global fertility rate will finally drop below replacement level and the median age of the world's population will have risen significantly to forty-seven years old. China will have lost 15 percent off of its peak population by 2025 and will have already adopted policies to encourage fertility. However, this will not lessen the already dire impact on its economy, causing it to consider more drastic measures in order to maintain its global economic standing. High-income countries will have adjusted to this new normal by refocusing on knowledge work and offshoring even greater amounts of labor to regions such as Africa, in which they will have made significant investment for manufacturing and industrial infrastructure. The elderly population will become more concentrated in wealthy countries and many nations will have to adapt their social safety nets accordingly.

2061–2070: Stabilized Population & Africa's Global Impact

By this decade, global population is expected to stabilize at just over ten-billion people. There will be approximately two percentage points difference in five-year age bands through age seventy-five. Advances in medical technology will give seniors an unprecedented level of independence, as will autonomous vehicles and robotic devices, while personalized precision medicine and AI will help treat age-related conditions better than ever before. Lifespan will be approaching one hundred years with a nearly equivalent ninety-year work-life span, although the nature of work will have changed dramatically due to digital workers (see Chapter 4). Africa will now be the only global region with continued population growth and will have transitioned to being the world's largest employer and an economic force on the world stage for manufacturing.

CHAPTER 3

The Future of Healthcare: Ambient Care

"The future of healthcare is a future of possibility."

—ATUL GAWANDE

GIGATREND—AMBIENT CARE:
Care based on a continuous and comprehensive understanding of each individual's healthcare needs, independent of location, provider, or the patient's self-advocacy abilities.

Healthcare Tomorrow: A New Standard of Care

Jake didn't need confirmation of the fact that he'd been feeling unwell for several days, but he was relieved to see a doctor's appointment in his calendar. At eighty-five, he was still going at full throttle and planning a long overdue holiday in the Himalayas. He really didn't want to take the time to visit his doctor, but he knew better than to question Deehpah's advice; she knew him better than he knew himself.

Deepah was Jake's digital personal healthcare advocate. Like assist dogs who could sense a change in their owner's heart rhythm, Deepah was always aware of Jake's health, scanning his vitals, diet, biomarkers, medications, and behaviors to check for anything out of the ordinary. If Deepah said he needed to go see a doc, he wasn't going to second guess her.

Jake also didn't have to worry about the cost of his healthcare and how it might cut into his vacation budget. With the end of population growth, the economics of healthcare had also changed. Long gone were the throngs of administrators dealing with things like denied insurance claims. Now nearly all medical diagnostics and treatments were targeted to match an individual's specific genomic markers, making moot any debate about whether or not a procedure or pharmaceutical was necessary. While private insurance was still very much alive and well, everyone in the developed countries of the world also had a guaranteed fail-safe national healthcare plan that filled in any gaps not covered by private payers. That would have been unthinkable with the waste, inefficiency, and lack of precision medicine in twentieth century healthcare.

When Jake arrived at his doctor's office there was no check-in process or paperwork to fill out. His healthcare records followed him wherever he went. Deepah already had permission to share Jake's healthcare data with the doctor's office, and had done so well in advance of Jake's visit. Jake sat and waited until his doctor came out to greet him.

Despite all of the advances in medicine there was nothing like a caring physician to reach out a hand and take the time to listen. In many ways the role of the physician had only become more important as the result of technical advances in the past seventy years. Since Deepah had already done her job, the physician had more time to spend with her patients. What used to be a short ten-to-fifteen-minute visit was now a comforting and unrushed conversation between patient and doctor.

"So, Jake, I've chatted with Deepah about your health. Everything looks great. Deepah has been adjusting your meds and supplements based on diet and activity. No significant changes there. There's just one thing that she alerted me to that I wanted to talk with you about. There's a slight arrhythmia in your cardiogram which by all indications appears to be benign. It's not alarming and it's typical for someone of your age. But when we ran stress simulations on your digital twin the arrhythmia became a bit more pronounced. The good news is that we can treat this condition easily with precision medicine which uses a pharmaceutical targeted specifically to your DNA. However, we'll want to monitor your progress closely."

As would be the case with any patient being given a complex diagnosis, it was a lot to process, but one of the benefits of having Deepah was that Jake could always get a thorough recap of the conversation and get more details and background information later. "What about travel," he asked. "I was planning to take a trip overseas next month and it was going to include hiking and biking in the Himalayas. Should I rethink that?"

"I saw that in what Deepah shared with me. It looks like, based on your itinerary, you'll be staying under 10,000 feet above sea level. Just to be safe I put in a script for Deepah to connect to our cardio team about that, and to notify you if you stray to higher altitudes. I don't see an issue, but we can have one of our own biobots monitoring you 24/7. If cardio sees anything they can have Deepah alert you and we can take it from there." The doctor looked at Jake and with a caring but confident look, she said, "I can reassure you that in looking at the data our digital docs collected from several thousand people with the same genetic markers for this that I'm not worried. We're well ahead of it."

Jake felt relieved. With Deepah keeping an eye on him he knew he was in good hands.

Healthcare Today: Nobody Is at Fault, Yet Everybody Is to Blame

Marissett and Francisco Tolentino and their six-year-old daughter Isabella had traveled to the Dominican Republic for what was to be a relaxing vacation and an opportunity to build lasting memories; instead, they returned early to mourn the unfortunate and untimely death of Isabella.[1]

Before they left the US, Marissett did what many travelers fail to do: carefully review her health insurance plan with Blue Cross Blue Shield to make sure that they could get medical care in the Dominican Republic, as well as emergency evacuation, on the off chance that it was ever needed. Not only did she discover that there was a nearby hospital, but reassuringly, the Blue Cross Blue Shield plan even covered emergency air evacuation by private medical jet in the event of a life-threatening situation.

Shortly after arriving, Isabella developed a fever and started to experience stomach pains. The Tolentinos consulted the resort physician who urged them to go to the local clinic to have Isabella evaluated. There was some relief in at least knowing that they did not have to worry about coverage. That relief quickly gave way to a much deeper concern when doctors at the clinic diagnosed Isabelle with appendicitis, which required immediate surgery.

The Tolentinos first reaction was to return to the US, where they felt much better about the quality of care Isabella would receive. After all, Florida was only a short one-hour plane ride away, and they had already confirmed that BCBS provided medical evacuation in the case of an emergency of this sort. However, both the Dominican doctors and Isabella's pediatrician in the US cautioned against a commercial flight. Unfortunately, Blue Cross Blue Shield denied the Tolentinos' request, stating that it didn't consider Isabella's appendicitis a life-threatening emergency.

The Tolentinos only remaining option was to proceed with the surgery at the Punta Cana clinic.

When Isabelle came out of surgery she was intubated and still sedated. Doctors assured the Tolentinos that everything had gone well and that Isabelle would soon wake. However, hours passed and Isabelle did not wake up. Marissett, a nurse, also noticed that Isabella's oxygen levels were low. She was told by the staff not to worry, yet Isabella's condition worsened, and the Tolentinos were notified that she would be transferred to intensive care. This did not happen until midnight of the day after Isabella's surgery.

The Tolentinos continued pleading with BCBS to arrange Isabella's medical air transfer, but BCBS refused to consider the request until they received a full written report from the DR clinic. Another day passed.

On the third day, BCBS finally agreed to set up a medical jet transfer. But it was now the clinic's turn to further delay the process, by demanding that the Tolentinos pay their bill, something that BCBS should have handled, given that the clinic was already confirmed to be in-network. What the Tolentinos did not know at the time was that BCBS had been in constant contact and receiving updates from the clinic. Yet another day passed.

After a full four days of what can only be described as a tragedy of miscommunication and a procedural nightmare, a medical team and a private plane arrived to transport Isabella back home. Immediately, upon attempting to stabilize Isabella, the plane's medics determined that her vomit and blood had clogged her intubation tube—a narrow one that was meant for an infant rather than a six-year-old. Worse yet, it had likely been blocked for the four days since her surgery.

Upon arrival in the US Isabella was declared brain-dead from lack of oxygen.

It's easy to look at the tragic story of Isabella's death and point fingers at virtually everyone responsible for Isabella's medical care. But what most conspired against Isabella was a process that in total took far too long to resolve because each player was following procedures and protocols that made sense to them, without any coordinated effort to resolve the urgent decisions necessary to provide quality care.

It's a situation where nobody is at fault, and yet everybody is to blame. A process that is inherently disconnected and places priority on process over patient, is subject to miscommunication, poor management of risk, and delayed resolutions that compound the severity of what is—in many cases—a scenario requiring coordinated, complex, and timely decision-making.

Teetering on the Edge

So, why start this chapter with the fictional account of Jake and the very real and heartbreaking story of Isabella? Because they illustrate a stark anachronism: despite the proliferation of technologies that connect us 24/7, healthcare is still struggling to keep up with the increasing complexity of disconnected systems and processes.

In many ways healthcare is the canary in the coal mine, sounding an alarm for what has become a technology landscape littered with disconnected systems, processes, and people.

In many ways healthcare is the canary in the coal mine, sounding an alarm for what has become a technology landscape littered with disconnected systems, processes, and people. Although we are connected through a mind-boggling array of devices and networks, the intelligence—what we're calling "Ambient Care" and will define more specifically and discuss in Chapter 3—with which to coordinate all of this information seems to be sorely lacking across so many industries. While there are undercurrents of that in all of our Gigatrends, the severity of healthcare's impact on the global economy is why it is our second Gigatrend, following closely on the impact of changing global demographics.

Even without the implication of an aging population, healthcare is already on the precipice of enormous transformation brought on by the proliferation and increasing sophistication of diagnostic tools, therapies, and pharmaceuticals, as well as the exponential rate at which digital healthcare technology is advancing, while the means with which to coordinate care appears to be going in an entirely different direction, mired in administrative overhead and horribly disconnected.

These changes are creating unprecedented challenges but also the opportunity to build a future for healthcare that will put the patient at the center of a rich ecosystem with the power to positively impact the quality of life for each of us in dramatic ways. The idea behind "Ambient Care" is a simple one: as we build out the network of devices and sensors that will be able to monitor our health—from wearables to autonomous vehicles to digital advocates—we will experience a dramatic shift in how we view healthcare: from an acute and periodic service, meant to deal with injuries and illnesses, to an ongoing service that constantly monitors and maintains our well-being—a simple but profound transition from "periodic sick care" to "ongoing health care."

With the ability to capture and store data for every healthcare interaction, our digital genomes, our behaviors, and health patterns across vast populations, we will be able to predict disease and illness more accurately than we can currently predict tomorrow's weather forecast. It could be an amazing future in which healthcare becomes not only a fundamental human right, but one that is accessible and affordable to everyone.

Note, however, that we said, "could be." That's because healthcare is also at another precipice—one that threatens to send it, and all of this promise, plummeting out of control into the same economic abyss that Isabella so tragically fell into.

If we don't do something dramatic, courageous, and deliberate within the next decade, healthcare will simply become economically unsustainable and unable to provide quality care to an aging population with ever-increasing and ever more complex healthcare needs. What we think of as a crisis in healthcare today will pale in comparison to what lies ahead.

 What we think of as a crisis in healthcare today will pale in comparison to what lies ahead.

A World Health Organization policy brief[2] framed the situation in simple terms:

> According to the WHO, "it is apparent that life expectancy is increasing, is this due to people living longer in poor health (a prolongation of the process of dying)? Or are they benefiting from healthier lifestyles and effective treatments, so that they enjoy longer periods of good health, with postponement of a now shortened final period of disability?

Life expectancy as a measure does not mean an inherently positive outcome. As life spans increase, there are two possible scenarios for the impact that longer life expectancy will have on society, healthcare, and us as individuals.

Lifespan may increase, but with a longer period of disability, creating a greater need for long-term care. In terms that demographers use, this is called the "period of morbidity": the time during which the level of care people need to stay alive precludes their ability to enjoy that period of their life and to participate as an active member of society. Few of us would opt for that scenario if we had a choice in the matter. What we'd hope for is the second scenario: a longer lifespan with the shortest possible period of disability. The United States has the longest and most expensive average number of years of disability, at just over eleven years, and an average health care expenditure per capita of $9,775 per year.

Twentieth-century medicine has extended lifespans considerably, from forty-eight years in 1900 to seventy-eight years in 2020. However, a study at the University of Cambridge claims that medicine's focus has been on extending the quantity of life over the quality. According to the study, "ten times as much is spent on cancer as on dementia research in the UK, although dementia contributes five times as much morbidity as cancer."[3]

This is an especially critical challenge for countries with nationalized healthcare systems. For example, public expenditure for the retired population is about 25 percent of GDP in the EU.[4] When you consider that the over-sixty-five population is expected to increase by nearly 50 percent in the US and EU by 2050, and 120 percent[5] worldwide, you start to realize the magnitude of the strain this will put on the global economy. And all of this doesn't factor the additional burden that will come from providing healthcare to the half of the world's population that, according to the United Nations, does not have access to essential healthcare services.[6]

Few things in recent history have been a better illustration of just how fragile the global healthcare system is than the COVID-19 pandemic, which resulted in the loss of well over one million lives globally, and cost the global economy in excess of $24 trillion in added debt alone. This does not include all the other factors such as lost productivity and potential contribution of over one million lives lost in the U.S. alone. While it has been, and continues to be, argued that the response to the pandemic by the WHO and global governments was a significant contributor to its economic impact, the bottom line is that we were unprepared to deal with the toll that a global epidemic had on healthcare. If we tally up all of these contributing factors, then the cost to the U.S. alone could be $22 trillion.[7] The high price of the pandemic is a harbinger of what the state of healthcare may well look like in a few decades time, if we do not undertake some significant changes in how we approach healthcare today.

While our objective is not to solve all of the challenges that face healthcare in a single chapter, we do want to look at some of the foundational changes that will need to occur in order to begin setting a trajectory for healthcare that will not only serve those who already have access to healthcare, but the half of the world's population which does not.[8] These are changes that need to happen on a global scale. While there are clearly issues that set US healthcare apart from nations where healthcare is funded entirely through public means, the implications of the demographic changes we described in Chapter 2 will create a burden that will bring every healthcare system to its knees within the next two decades.

Ambient Care is the ability to diagnose and deliver coordinated care based on an ongoing and continuous view of each individual's healthcare needs, history, and real time medical condition regardless of location, provider, or the patient's capacity to advocate for themselves.

Our focus in this chapter will be on the Gigatrend that we call "Ambient Care." Ambient Care is the ability to diagnose and deliver coordinated care based on an ongoing and continuous view of each individual's healthcare needs, history, and real time medical condition regardless of location, provider, or the patient's capacity to advocate for themselves. The objective of Ambient Care is to create continuity of care, reduce the cost of care, increase access to care, and improve the immediacy of care.

Before we deconstruct the current state of healthcare, it's helpful to make what we're discussing a bit more tangible by considering what healthcare could look like if we take the steps we're about to outline. Let's take a quick jump into the future and imagine a healthcare system where each of the following is the norm.

What if…

- …the patient experience and journey are streamlined so that administrative friction, paperwork, documentation, and the burden on the patient of denied claims and erroneous and surprise billing was removed?

- …physicians were able to spend their time focusing exclusively on delivering care and healing, rather than spending over half of their time documenting and justifying procedures?

- …everyone had a personal digital advocate who followed them from birth through their lifetime, which not only had access to their entire medical history and could interface with any healthcare provider, but also was able to communicate with clinicians when the patient was unable to?

- …healthcare's contribution to GDP accelerates GDP growth, and changes the cost of healthcare from an ever-increasing percentage of GDP to an ever decreasing percentage of GDP?

- …healthcare costs were reduced through the use of analytics and predictive models that leveraged large pools of data to better understand the short- and long-term costs of different outcomes on patient populations and individual patients?

- …medicine, therapies, and pharmaceuticals were tailored to the specific genome of each patient rather than simply looking at what works for a majority the population suffering from a particular illness or disease?

- …healthcare could be delivered in the cloud as a service, in much the same way that nearly all businesses now access nearly all of their services?

- …almost no healthcare requires in-clinic visits, diagnostics, or therapies. Instead, it can be delivered directly in a home setting.

No doubt, it's a stretch to imagine that sort of healthcare system in the next few decades. However, the unabashedly bold claim we're making in this chapter is that all of this is possible. The changes we're suggesting will not only increase the quality of healthcare, while decreasing its costs, but also improve access to healthcare, within both developed and developing economies. Granted, that's a tall order, but it is not only achievable, but achievable in the near term without a wholesale restructuring of health-care systems—all the while preserving the option of choice for the patient and the benefit of significantly improved outcomes.

It's important to keep in mind that this is a global crisis. While the means by which individual healthcare is paid—through public, private, or a combination of both sources—can differ dramatically from country to country, the underlying Gigatrend of an aging global population and the top-heavy demographic described in Chapter 2, which are driving higher costs and more complex healthcare, apply to every healthcare system across the globe.

The other aspect of changing healthcare, which often gets woven into the narrative about why healthcare cannot be easily fixed, is that we cannot treat healthcare the same way that we do other efforts to achieve efficiency in business and industry. Healthcare doesn't follow the same unyielding rules that govern the production of airplanes and automobiles, nor is it subject to the callousness of single-minded profit-driven motives.

However, the economics of healthcare are not so unique that it is unable to take advantage of tried and tested approaches to applying technology and process-improvement methods in other industries. For example, viewing patients in the same light we view consumers, for whom customer satisfaction and consumer experience is an essential metric, is a hotly debated topic among healthcare professionals, who often feel that equating the two somehow detracts from the integrity and value of the relationship between the patient and the physician. By saying that healthcare is *different*, we sideline the conversation rather than addressing the cultural issues that are holding healthcare back because they are harder to change.

The idea of "fixing" healthcare is a misconception. There is no single static solution, policy, or business model that will "fix" healthcare, since both the science of medicine and the needs of the populations it serves are constantly changing and increasing in their complexity. As we said in Chapter 1, this is the very nature of the sort of emergent systems that we will need to contend with in the future. The objective of healthcare should be to meet these changing needs by improving the rate of innovation, and then making these innovations available to the broadest possible population. That has been and always will be a process of evolution.

The issue of cost is also one that typically ends up being mischaracterized. As medicine extends our lifespan, we need to also extend the quality of those added years. That will cost more—it's the price we will need to pay for the benefit of living longer, more productive, and more enjoyable lives. But that doesn't mean that the price has to include all of the inefficiencies and constraints of the industrial-era model of healthcare that we are saddled with today. The assumptions that we have built the healthcare system around over the past one hundred years have changed dramatically, as have the tools and technologies available for the practice of medicine. Consider that only 54 percent of men in 1935 could expect to live to the age of sixty-five. Today that number is 80 percent.[9] If you lived till sixty-five in 1940 (the first year Social Security benefits were paid out), you could expect to collect for thirteen years. Today you would collect for twenty years.[10]

As life expectancy increases, so will the numerous coexisting conditions (or co-morbidities) that an older population has to deal with. As our ability to diagnose and treat disease increases, so will the cost associated with treating many of these illnesses. For example, a gene therapy for cystic fibrosis, which promises to benefit 90 percent of patients with the disease, can cost $300,000 a year.[11] New treatments for Alzheimer's, such as Leqembi and Aduhelm, can cost nearly $30,000 per year.[12]

As demographics change, new technologies will continue to drive up the cost of healthcare. On the one hand, we could say that such is the responsibility of a civilized society. However, what needs to be factored into that conversation is that today's healthcare system is simply not built to deal with a future in which today's older minority becomes tomorrow's older majority.

According to a 2017 report by the National Academy of Medicine, over 50 percent of US healthcare spending is for only 5 percent of all patients, and 20 percent is for the sickest 1 percent of patients.[14] (See Figure 3.1) Defined as "high-needs" patients, they are increasing rapidly

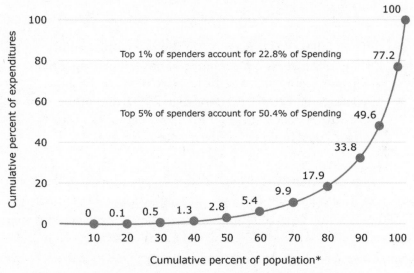

Source: https://meps.ahrq.gov/data_files/publications/st506/stat506.shtml
*Cumulative percent of non-institutionalized civilian population

Figure 3.1: Cumulative Healthcare Expenditure by Percentage of Population

Healthcare costs are dramatically skewed toward the sickest of the patient population, with 1 percent of patients accounting for 22.8 percent of all healthcare spending and the top 5 percent accounting for 50.4 percent of spending on healthcare.[13]

as the over-sixty-five cohort also increases. Today, 55 percent of those over sixty-five are considered high-needs patients (with three or more chronic diseases and functional limitations). If that trend continues (as we first said in Chapter 2) and the sixty-five-and-older cohort doubles to become half of the US population by 2060, we will have as many patients in the high-needs category as we have total patients today.

Based on that trend, the US healthcare system will grow to the point where it constitutes nearly 40 percent of US GDP by 2040 (Figure 3.2). Keep in mind that this does not take into account all of the money spent on US healthcare, just the portion spent by the government. In fact, if you follow this trajectory, for the rest of this century US healthcare as a percentage of government spending will be roughly equal to the last two digits of the year: 40 percent in 2040, 50 percent in 2050, and 60 percent in 2060. It doesn't take a PhD in mathematics to see the absurd destination of that trajectory.

 If you follow this trajectory, for the rest of this century US healthcare as a percentage of government spending will be roughly equal to the last two digits of the year: 40 percent in 2040, 50 percent in 2050, and 60 percent in 2060. It doesn't take a PhD in mathematics to see the absurd destination of that trajectory.

It all points to the unyielding fact that's repeated often in this book: the industrial-era model is simply no longer sustainable. Tomorrow's healthcare, hospitals, and doctors will have the same mission that they have always had, to keep us healthy and to heal us when we're not. But tomorrow's healthcare, hospitals, and doctors will not look like what we have today—to survive, they can't.

A New Narrative

This is where we'd like to offer a different narrative with which to look at and talk about the cost of healthcare. Let's say that you're self-employed with no source of income other than what you can generate yourself. If

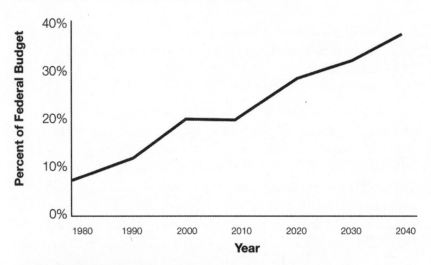

Figure 3.2: Federal Healthcare Spending as a Percentage of the Federal Budget

Under the federal government's current policies, the Congressional Budget Office projects that the share of the federal budget spent on mandatory healthcare programs will increase from less than 10 percent in 1980 to just under 40 percent in 2040.

you were facing a medical procedure that provided you with two options: the first a low-cost procedure that would mean a twelve-month recovery, during which you could not work, and the second a more expensive procedure that would guarantee you'd be able to get back to work within just a few days, which would you choose?

You would probably first determine exactly how much you'd pay for each procedure, and then weigh that against lost income. In other words, you wouldn't base your decision on the cost of the procedure alone, but on the overall cost. While that makes perfect sense when presented in that way, it's not the way we typically talk about the cost of healthcare. By focusing our social and political conversation strictly on the element of cost and increasing costs, we isolate the cost of healthcare from the value it has to society.

The simple truth is that the health of a population has a direct impact on the productivity and prosperity of a society, which we can reduce to a quantifiable problem.

What if we made a simple and rational assumption that better healthcare equates to greater economic prosperity?

What if we made a simple and rational assumption that better healthcare equates to greater economic prosperity? A McKinsey study projected that the economic contribution of improved healthcare could add $12 trillion to global GDP in 2040—that's an 8 percent boost to GDP[15]. The result is that healthcare costs could continue to increase in absolute terms, but would decrease as a percentage of GDP, since they are contributing to accelerated GDP. In the same study, McKinsey analyzed the health difficulties faced by nearly two hundred countries and uncovered that successful interventions—which include adopting healthy habits, increasing access to primary care services, and ensuring proper adherence of medications—could drastically reduce the global disease burden by a whopping 40 percent in two decades. This is an incredible opportunity for many nations whose healthcare systems are struggling due to poverty and lack of resources.

The challenge with including contributions to GDP in the healthcare conversation is that it's not the way most legislative processes—which focus primarily on costs to the taxpayer—prioritize healthcare legislation. In the US, for example, Congress "scores" healthcare bills based on costs provided by the Congressional Budget Office (CBO), an independent, nonpartisan agency responsible for providing cost estimates and projections for proposed legislation. These scores prioritize a bill and its likelihood of passing. That makes sense on the surface; we should weigh costs against benefits. Here's the catch: while the CBO scrutinizes direct costs and direct savings, it steers clear of putting a dollar value on healthcare benefits and outcomes and how a bill might impact GDP. Why?

First, it keeps its analysis firmly anchored in the federal budget's realm, which is its primary responsibility. Second, it tries to be non-partisan, and subjective claims of the potential value of healthcare tend to be politically divisive. Third, and most relevant to how we will change the process, objective assessments about the value of healthcare require significant indisputable data. For example, in the United States, the first Surgeon

General's report on smoking and health wasn't published until 1964. It wasn't until the 1980s and 1990s that more comprehensive studies began to emerge, attempting to quantify the economic costs of smoking-related illness and disease, such as lost productivity, and premature deaths. What has changed since that time is our ability to capture data. However, in healthcare that data is often siloed and not easily accessible. Trying to create a single continuous history of a patient's illnesses, treatments, pharmaceuticals, therapies, and outcomes over a lifetime is nearly impossible. That hinders efforts to compare the true cost of healthcare in any meaningful way.

However, as the population ages the economic value of a longer health span will become apparent, which will force us to rethink how we value healthcare. The evolution of what we call "healthcare disruptors" will improve our ability, and amplify the imperative, to understand the economic value of healthcare in the future and our ability to capture and analyze health data in ways that have not been available in the past.

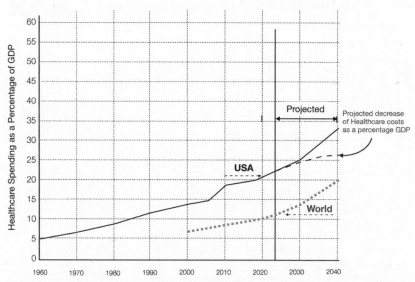

Figure 3.3: Decreasing the Cost of Healthcare as a Percentage of GDP

Rather than continue increasing as its percentage of U.S. GDP, Healthcare could contribute to greater GDP and thereby become a smaller share of GDP over time. Also shown is World Healthcare expenditure as a percent of global GDP.[16]

The Healthcare Disruptors

There are four forces that we believe will most define the landscape for change to Ambient Care over the coming decades: The Existentialists, Home Care, Personal Digital Advocates, and The Hospital in the Cloud.

Although these four forces do not represent a comprehensive review of all the technologies and innovations that will shape the future of healthcare, they are key to aligning it with the changing needs of patients and the necessary transformation of hospitals and the role they will play in healthcare. Most importantly, they will give us the ability to capture and leverage healthcare data across the entirety of a patient's lifespan regardless of their location. This is the ultimate value of Ambient Care.

One thing to keep in mind as we delve into some of these disruptors is that while technology increasingly gives us ways to engage with healthcare providers from anywhere, we continue to think of a hospital, doctor's office, or clinic as the place we go to be healed. Ambient Care doesn't completely obviate the need for in-person care in a doctor's office, clinic, or hospital setting. Technology cannot yet make obsolete the simple fact that we are humans made of flesh and blood, who still periodically need the physical presence of medicine, diagnostics, and surgical centers. And perhaps most importantly, we still want to feel the physical presence and emotional connection of a therapist, physician, or nurse as we have difficult and complex discussions about our health and well-being.

Of course, we could easily speculate how technology will make this physicality moot with the advent of therapies that cure diseases at the level of our genomes, making surgery unnecessary, or how virtual reality, including holographic images, will replace the physical presence of a physician or a therapist, or how autonomous clinical robots will arrive in autonomous vehicles to perform home visits for the elderly. We're as tantalized by these futures as anyone else, and we have little doubt that many of us will live to see much of that, and that it will be far stranger than anything we could predict here. But the task at hand, and the focus of this chapter, as with all the Gigatrends we explore, is to look at the practical application of technologies and methods that would put healthcare on the right track within the next few decades.

The Existential Threat

 The greatest threat of disruption for any industry typically comes from outsiders who are unencumbered by the legacy of the past and have no sacred turf to defend. Few industries are as ripe for this sort of disruption as healthcare.

The greatest threat of disruption for any industry typically comes from outsiders who are unencumbered by the legacy of the past and have no sacred turf to defend. Few industries are as ripe for this sort of disruption as healthcare. It's a $12 trillion global industry, one of the largest line items on most people's personal budgets, a source of continuous frustration for patient-customers, an industry that's constantly criticized in the media for its inefficiency, an increasing burden on the bottom line of nearly every business, and desperately in need of innovation. So, it's hardly a surprise that many of the largest tech companies have strategies in place to play in the healthcare space. The typical response to these existential threats to the current healthcare enterprise is that they just don't get the "business of healthcare." While that may be true at first, tech companies such as Amazon are demonstrating that they are more than willing to fail as they learn it. It would be folly to discount the impact these hyper-scale tech players will have on healthcare, just because they have a learning curve ahead.

The bookselling and publishing business was not disrupted from within its ranks. The music industry wasn't upended by a large record label. It wasn't a major telecommunications firm that replaced cellphones with smartphones. The movie and cable entertainment industries weren't disrupted by a major Hollywood studio. The taxi wasn't decimated by a larger transportation company. Amazon, Apple, Netflix, and Uber were all outsiders that were barely taken seriously by incumbents in each of these industries, and yet they were able to not only change the business models in each case, but also create customer experiences that were unimaginable before they came along.

In the case of healthcare, a very similar scenario is starting to play out. Over the next five years, tech giants such as Google, Apple, Amazon, and even Meta will step in and attempt to use their scale, technologies, and most importantly, their access to behavioral data, to create new approaches to how the patient-customer engages with the healthcare system.

The scale of that opportunity eclipses anything we can today imagine. Just consider that medical data doubles every seventy-three days, and will increase by orders of magnitude with the advent of genomic medicine. With 30 percent of worldwide data estimated to be healthcare-related, that equates to roughly fifty zettabytes—the entirety of the global datasphere in 2020.[17]

One of the more notable examples of alternatives being delivered by these tech companies is the Amazon Care program, a novel healthcare service that Amazon piloted in 2019 for its employees. Amazon Care promised to upend the healthcare industry by creating a comprehensive managed healthcare alternative for large enterprise customers. It included virtual and in-person medical services, partnerships with nurse practitioners and doctors from local healthcare providers, and access to clinical advice, diagnosis, prescriptions, and treatments.

The model Amazon intended to use was not unlike what it had done with its AWS cloud computing and data storage business, which provides virtualized computing power to customers on demand. Amazon would leverage its internal economies of scale to build a healthcare system that it would initially use for its own employees, and then offer to customers as a managed service. It's a form of what we will call a "Hospital in the Cloud" later in this chapter.

However, building a healthcare ecosystem ended up being much more difficult than building AWS. Despite expansion across all fifty states—including major metropolitan areas like San Francisco, Miami and New York City—Amazon Care ultimately failed to gain a foothold with employer clients. Amazon shuttered Amazon Care in December of 2022.

However, in July of 2020, Amazon also announced plans to acquire concierge primary care provider One Medical in a deal worth approximately $3.9 billion. The deal would significantly accelerate Amazon's presence in the $4 trillion healthcare market, by giving it rapid access to the same market it had targeted with Amazon Care, through One Medical's 8,000 company partners.

The lesson here is an important one: healthcare requires trusted relationships that take time to develop and are nearly impossible to dislodge once in place. The three areas where these companies, and many others that are currently lesser known, will have the greatest impact are likely to be Ambient Care wearables, the monitoring of behavioral and lifestyle data and risk, and data storage and analytics.

Ambient Care: Wearables and Monitoring

One in four adults in the US has a wearable health-tracking device.[18] Unlike their early counterparts—which simply stored data about distance walked, stairs climbed, hours of sleep, or calories burned—today's devices are able to monitor vital signs, blood sugar, potassium, oxygen levels, blood pressure,[19] and even take ECGs and detect certain cancers.

While all of that is very impressive, what's missing is a clear connection from the device to the patient's record, and ultimately to the healthcare provider's systems. If you tell your doctor during your annual physical that your Apple Watch shows an arrhythmia, his response, and more importantly his diagnosis, is not going to be "let me take a look at your Apple Watch," but "let's do an EKG in the office." However, that's going to change over the next few years as the value of that real-time data becomes apparent. Apple is already working with providers such as Stanford University School of Medicine to study the accuracy and impact of an Apple Watch wearable ECG monitor, on 419,000 participants.[20]

What we are creating with these devices is the initial form of a digital twin medical record, or what *Wired* magazine writers Kevin Kelly and Gary Wolf in 2007 called the Quantified Self.[21] Over time, the volume and value of this data has increased dramatically. According to Statista, global monthly data traffic from wearables increased from eleven exabytes per month in 2017 to seventy-seven exabytes per month in 2020. How will the value of that data be realized and who will benefit from it? Providers certainly aren't oblivious to its value. At Atrium Health (formerly Carolinas HealthCare System), data from up to seventy different health-tracking devices can be stored by patients as part of their medical record.[22]

As wearables become more sophisticated in their diagnostic applications and the data they produce more comprehensive and reliable, consumers will have more data about their healthcare than their healthcare providers do.

As wearables become more sophisticated in their diagnostic applications and the data they produce more comprehensive and reliable, consumers will have more data about their healthcare than their healthcare providers do. One study by the AMA on digital health found that although 85 percent of doctors saw the potential benefit of wearable technology, less than 30 percent were using it with their patients.[23]

It's inevitable, however, that over time data from wearables will prove much too valuable to ignore, at least for the patient, if not the provider. In 2020, 1.3 million lives were saved by wearables, and of those, 600,000 were non-medical devices used outside of a hospital or clinical setting.[24] In other words, they were purchased and used solely by consumers to track their personal health. If providers are reluctant to embrace wearables and collaborate with the technology vendors who develop these devices, it will only accelerate the move to patient-owned electronic healthcare records (something we talk about later in this chapter). Given the propensity of millennials and Gen Z to shun primary care physicians (PCPs) we expect that the power to use this data in a self-service approach to medicine will end up accelerating the move to alternative healthcare providers, for example, those being put in place by tech providers such as Amazon's One Medical.

Behavioral Data, Lifestyle, and Noncompliance

The prevalence of patient-owned data from wearables will result in more available data from which to identify patterns of behavior that affect lifestyles and habits. This has always been one of the hardest areas of patient engagement for doctors to manage. Many clinicians see even offering advice on lifestyle to be outside of their scope of responsibility, or believe that it will not be followed. Only a slight majority of physicians (61 percent) and nurses (53 percent) say they always offer such advice.[25] As we'll see in Chapter 6, these behavioral clues provide some of the most reliable and invaluable insights into ourselves or our habits that go well beyond our own ability to describe them.

 According to the CDC, only one out of four patients who are prescribed drugs for high blood pressure actually take them, and 20 to 30 percent never even have their prescription filled.

According to the CDC, only one out of four patients who are prescribed drugs for high blood pressure actually take them, and 20 to 30 percent never even have their prescription filled. The American College of Preventive Medicine[26] and Johns Hopkins peg the cost of patient noncompliance in the US at $300 billion a year.[27] This also results in direct costs of $500 billion for hospitals that are penalized by Medicare for readmissions.

Clearly, there's more to this problem than wearables can fully address. Much of it comes down to a basic distrust of pharmaceutical companies and an inherent unwillingness to change lifestyle. A stark testimonial to that is the divisiveness caused by vaccines for COVID-19.

However, wearables shift the relationship from the patient, the provider, and/or the pharmaceutical company, to a relationship between the consumer and the device. Anyone who's ever owned a wearable that tracks even their most basic activity—steps taken, miles walked, or calories burned—has experienced the slight effects of behavioral modification resulting from their wearable's regular reminders about their progress toward goals. The other, and perhaps more powerful, behavioral modification technique is that of peer groups. Many users of wearables join informal groups that compete for the most activity in a day, week, or month.

This, too, is part of how the notion of healthcare is changing from a relationship purely between provider and patient, to one that is diffused into many aspects of our lives that help to improve outcomes, but have little to do with the traditional understanding of healthcare. This transformation is in part something that will need to change from within, but much of that change will come from the disruptors that are completely outside of the healthcare industry and thus are initially perceived as threats by some in the healthcare space.

Another novel way wearables could be used is as a means of aligning patient-doctor incentives, by increasing what's termed "healthcare literacy"—the ability of patients to better understand their medical conditions and available options. One way to do that is through the use of wearables and predictive models that help put the doctor and patient on the same page.

For example, one model that's been proposed and researched notifies the patient and the doctor of a health condition, after an event is recognized by a wearable, after an office visit involving a diagnosis or treatment plan, or whenever a claim is submitted. An algorithm that has access to the patient's digital health record uses information about the patient, their history, current condition, and the doctor's diagnosis, to identify current evidence-based medicine or health articles related to the patient's condition. The doctor then forwards this information to the patient who, in turn, needs to review the information and then demonstrate adequate knowledge of it. Think of this as a sort of online training program that has a short quiz at the end. Part of the incentive for both doctor and patient to do this is a financial incentive of some nominal but reasonable amount. For example, the patient may have the office visit deductible waived and the doctor may receive some equal amount of compensation.

Although the approach of using a quiz-like mechanism may sound trite, research has shown that forms of it do work in populations that have been studied in controlled tests. In one peer-reviewed study published in the Journal of Medical Internet Research, over 1500 patients and 100 physicians were tracked over a five-year period from 2013 through 2017. During that time, hospitalizations and emergency room visit rates (per 1000 patients) decreased 32 percent and 14 percent respectively.[28] To put that in perspective, with the average cost of a three-day hospital stay at $30,000[29] and an ER visit at $2200,[30] the savings in just this one very limited study would be $14,862,000. If we expand that to the entire US healthcare system, the impact on the 145,000,000 yearly hospital admission alone would total potential savings of $388,441,920,320.[31]

Public Health and Prelytics

In the short term, much of the value and benefit of wearables will come from the two areas we've already talked about. However, there is a longer-term benefit that will eclipse much of what we've already described and influence many of the ways in which the healthcare system provides value in what's termed public health, a topic that has received much attention in the wake of the COVID-19 pandemic of 2020.

According to the American Public Health Association, public health "promotes and protects the health of people and the communities where they live, learn, work and play."[32] This includes a variety of activities from promoting vaccinations, to tracking disease outbreaks, educating people on health risks, safety, and nutrition, to raising awareness about the use of tobacco products.

Until recently, the tools used to identify public health issues were primarily manual means of data collection through surveys, pools, point-of-care data capture in a clinical setting, pharmaceutical-use data, and self-reported data from patients. All of this made public health an analytical discipline that relied on data from past experiences rather than real-time data. This is broadly called data analytics in healthcare (and most industries that rely on historical data analysis). With the advent of not only wearables and mobile devices, but the proliferation of behavioral tracking through internet-based interactions with social media, GPS, and web search, a new discipline is emerging, which we call prelytics or predictive analytics.

For example, during a 2014 West African outbreak of Ebola in Senegal, mobile data from the French wireless carrier Orange used anonymized and aggregated data from 150,000 customers to identify patterns that emerged, which could be used to identify the pandemic's progress and spread.[33] (An interactive version of this data shows an up-to-date animation of how the pandemic has spread around the globe and can be found in this footnote.[34]) While this data was still retrospective, rather than in real time, the same approach is being used in real time to track the spread of flu epidemics.[35]

Prelytics is one of the most powerful tools available to the public and the healthcare industry to overcome one of the greatest sources of friction for most providers: predicting staffing levels, pharmaceuticals, and resources needed to handle what can be significant fluctuations in the capacity needed to address public health issues. The implications of having this sort of real-time data are far-reaching. One project at MIT used autonomous robotic devices that crawled through the Boston and Cambridge sewer systems to sample sewage and determine the health habits, pathogens, and other fluctuations in these samples that could provide real-time data about health issues down to the street level of a neighborhood.

MIT's invention is reminiscent of the 1854 outbreak of cholera in London, which took the lives of more than ten thousand people. A local London physician, Dr. John Snow, is ultimately credited with stopping the epidemic by using data to identify that the predominant cases centered on a water pump located just outside of a home on London's Broad Street, where it was likely that the first case of cholera (the index case) was that of an infected infant girl whose mother had used the cistern outside of her front door on Broad Street to rinse the baby's diarrhea-soaked diapers. The cistern, it appears, was seeping into an adjacent pump used by the community for fresh water. Dr. Snow's recommendation was to simply remove the handle from the pump, something that was at first met with less than enthusiasm by the local board of guardians of St. James Parish, in which Broad Street was based.[36]

Just as interesting is that the only way to determine if shutting down the pump was effective was to wait and see, which prompted talk about how the outbreak had probably run its course anyway, and therefore the pump's handle being removed was not a factor in slowing and ultimately stopping it.

Data analytics hasn't changed much in principle since that time. Sure, we are analyzing huge amounts of data with computers that dwarf, almost comically, the data available to a nineteenth-century physician, but the processes has always been retrospective. And the delta in time between identifying a possible cause of a health issue, and taking action to correct it, has always made the relationship between cause and effect more difficult to determine. The ability we now have to observe an act in real time is a line of demarcation that, once crossed, opens up entirely new ways to think about the challenges of public health. We can better correlate causes to their effects and treatments to their outcomes.

The ability we now have to observe an act in real time is a line of demarcation that, once crossed, opens up entirely new ways to think about the challenges of public health.

However, we'll once again bring you back to the question: who will own this data and how will they extract value from it? (We talk about this in much more detail in Chapter 6 on Digital Identity.)

Large companies such as Apple, Google, Amazon, JPMorgan, and Berkshire Hathaway all have efforts underway to evaluate the option of building their own healthcare networks for their employees, including taking on the role of payer, and, in some cases, owners of the provider. The impetus here is that the cost of healthcare has become so steep for large corporations that it is in their best economic interests to build their own solutions. Will these become role models for the rest of the health-care industry? Will they become competitive weapons for talent in the same way that post-WWII employers used health insurance as a benefit to attract employees? We're not convinced that they will. Amazon tried this approach (as we discuss in Chapter 3) and then shifted gears to pur-chase its own provider. While these captive networks may make sense as an interim measure, they are falling back on centralized economy of scale models with closed ecosystems, which inevitably involve a lot of admin-istration and perpetuate the difficulty in easily sharing healthcare data outside their ecosystem.

One thing is certain: the current state of using technology to identify health risks and predict health outcomes is falling behind the increas-ingly complex needs we've discussed of an aging population. When that happens, free markets have a way of rectifying the situation by building new solutions that take the incumbents completely by surprise. Call it the Uber-ization of industry. Uber didn't just refine the taxi experience; it decimated it by reimagining what a frictionless experience that removed much of the tedium of booking a taxi ride would look like.

While all of this existential change threatens to upend healthcare, there is also a great deal of internal change that will be reshaping health-care. One of these is the shift to home-based healthcare.

The Patient Will See You Now

One of the most important and widespread shifts in Ambient Care—which will be enabled by new advances in the technology of remote monitoring, diagnostics, and treatments—is the move away from inpatient hospital care to outpatient and home care. This alters the trajectory of healthcare by switching from a strictly location-based set of services to which the patient has to travel, to a set of services that go to where the patient is.

Few things will define the line of demarcation from the past into the future of healthcare as profoundly as this fundamental shift in the way healthcare is delivered and consumed. Consider that from 1995 to 2016, the average length of stay at a community hospital dropped by 15 percent, from 6.5 days to 5.5 days.[37] Across all community hospitals, the number of inpatient days per 1000 people dropped by 18.75 percent from nearly 800 to approximately 550 (Figure 3.4).

At the same time, hospital revenues have been steadily shifting from inpatient to outpatient services. Much of this is enabled by new technologies that allow remote patient monitoring through wearables, sensors, and mobile devices (often called the Internet of Things, or IoT). Information from IoT-enabled devices and sensors provides not only real-time monitoring capability, but also data which can be used to predict health issues and risks.

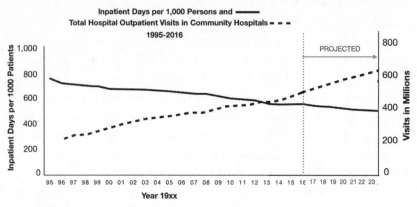

Figure 3.4: As inpatient days per thousand persons have decreased, outpatient visits have increased in almost direct proportion.[38]

One of the simplest, yet one of the most dramatic, examples of how easily Ambient Care can impact healthcare, is the case of falls among the elderly, which—according to the CDC—medical cost related to fall injuries in those over 65 amount to over $50,000,000,000 yearly.[39] Keep in mind that this number does not include the subsequent long-term costs of healthcare, nursing homes, and time lost for family members who must take time to care for an elderly parent or loved one, nor the loss of those individuals in what could continue to be a relatively productive life and their ongoing contribution to society and the economy.

David Park, the founder and CEO at VirtuSense, which has developed sensor-based systems to help predict and prevent falls, describes how sensors can have an enormous impact on healthcare for an aging population:

> "In the US alone, one in three seniors reported falling each year. Our mission, simply put, is to reduce falls so seniors can age well. We're doing that by deploying predictive and preventive solutions for homes and senior living facilities. We're also planning to deploy these fall prediction and prevention solutions for hospitals. We do it using machine vision, artificial intelligence, and data analytics. The big goal is trying to provide successful aging through innovative technologies and data analytics. This has tremendous implications for the health industry because the mega trend that we're all riding is the aging of our population globally; it's going to impact our society, healthcare, and government for decades to come. The advent of these sorts of remote sensor-based applications enable new pathways for the delivery of healthcare outside of a traditional clinical setting."

These are not just futuristic scenarios. Home healthcare is already an area of intense growth as the population ages. According to the CMS Office of the Actuary, the US Medicare system spent approximately $108.8 billion on home healthcare in 2019. By 2027, that's expected to reach nearly $190 billion, making home healthcare the fastest-growing segment of Medicare spending.[40] However, what that masks, and the greater problem, is the enormous economic burden that it already creates for informal caregivers.

A comprehensive 2015 study by the National Alliance for Caregiving and AARP[41] found that there were 43.5 million adults who had been caregivers to an adult or child in the twelve months prior to the study. What's even more startling is that a 2015 AARP report, "Valuing the Invaluable,"[42] estimated the economic value of home caregivers' unpaid contributions at approximately $470 billion in 2017—up from an estimated $375 billion in 2007. To put that into perspective, it's approximately the same as Walmart's total yearly revenues, or about 10 percent of all federal spending.

The strain put on the lives, work routines, and the health of these caregivers creates a ripple effect that is much larger than even the direct economic value of their time. Caregivers over the age of fifty experience on average lost wages and benefits of $303,880 during their lifetime, as well as the additional reduction in their Social Security benefits as a result of lower wages.[43] They suffer from increased risk of cardiovascular events due to higher cortisol levels and report higher levels of depressions and psychological illness, and one often-quoted study[44] went so far as to conclude that caregivers had a 63 percent higher chance of mortality than non-caregivers. The label used to describe this is "Caregiver Syndrome," a term first coined by Dr. C. Jean Posner, a neuropsychiatrist in Baltimore, Maryland, who defined it as "a debilitating condition brought on by unrelieved, constant caring for a person with a chronic illness or dementia."[45] The graying of the population will only amplify the home healthcare burden on the entire healthcare system, as well as the added socioeconomic toll it takes.

Ambient Care, by its very nature, is highly distributed, both geographically and in terms of the many processes involved, which necessitate a much larger and richer ecosystem of facilities, resources, personnel, touch points, and devices. According to Definitive Healthcare, there are currently 9,280 ambulatory surgical centers (ASCs)—1.5 times as many as there are hospitals—and they already perform 56 percent[46] of all surgeries. But even this is barely a glimpse of the magnitude of the change to come in Ambient Care, as both hospitals and physicians are charged with moving their services closer to the patient. We'll talk more about this virtualization of healthcare later when we look at the "hospital in the cloud." But for now, consider what healthcare might look like when consultations, diagnostics, and even many procedures which now require a clinical setting, take place in the patient's home or an assisted living facility. While it may seem we are far from that sort of reality, that is the direction healthcare is moving in, and the next two innovations will bring us closer to that future.

Digital Healthcare Advocates

One of the most serious flaws in the current healthcare system, which leads to higher costs, redundancy, errors, and episodic care, is the lack of continuity of care and coordinated care for a patient who does not have an advocate who can provide critical information to medical personnel when the patient is physically, emotionally, or cognitively impaired. And this will be dramatically amplified based on the demographic shifts we outline in Chapter 2.

As population ages, the prevalence of dementia and related neurological and cognitive diseases will also increase. This creates a mandate to look at patient advocacy as an essential component of the healthcare system without which no change to healthcare can adequately future proof its ability to deliver care.

 This creates a mandate to look at patient advocacy as an essential component of the healthcare system without which no change to healthcare can adequately future proof its ability to deliver care.

While electronic health records (EHRs) were meant to address this, they only do so within very narrow cases where the patient is already part of a healthcare system and every diagnostic record, treatment, and medication is available within that same healthcare system, which is often not the case.

First, people change PCPs frequently and the transfer of records might not happen during each of those handoffs. Even when a PCP refers a patient to a specialist, over 70 percent of specialists rank the quality of the health records they receive during a transfer as fair or poor.[47] Consider that patients over sixty-five years of age have seen an average of 28.4 individual doctors during their lifetime, including PCPs, specialists, hospital physicians, and urgent care providers.[48]

Second, despite the fact that most providers who have an EHR use one of the two leading systems (Epic or Cerner), even within a single

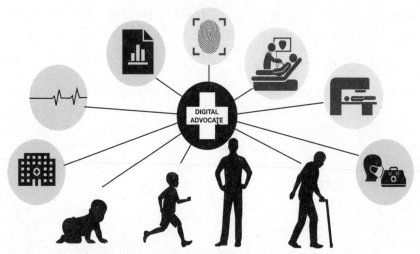

Figure 3.5: Digital advocates will create continuity of care throughout a patient's lifetime. Not only will they have access to all of the patient's medical history and records but they will also be in constant communication with healthcare providers in order to predict and identify illness, adherence to pharmaceuticals and therapies, and even psychological risks.

hospital system, there are often differing and incompatible implementations of the same EHR. A typical hospital averages sixteen separate EHRs across its network.[49]

Third, insurers who may have access to the procedures and treatments during their coverage of that patient sometimes don't share that data with other insurers or care providers. (CMS has recently proposed changes to MyHealthEData[50] that are intended to improve patient access and sharing of patient data.)[51]

Not surprisingly, many companies that develop the EHR systems in use by most hospitals have pushed back on the idea of interoperability between EHRs. Judy Faulkner, Founder and CEO of EPIC—one of the two largest providers of EHRs—has urged hospital executives to oppose regulations that would make it easier to share medical information.[52] while CMS Administrator Seema Verma was quoted at a healthcare industry event as saying:

> It's important to understand that the disingenuous efforts by certain private actors to use privacy, vital as it is, as a pretext for holding

patient data hostage is an embarrassment to the industry. Access to one's data can be a matter of life and death, and this Administration will not waver in ensuring that patients enjoy full ownership of it when they need it.

This sort of disconnected healthcare causes episodic care for patients, since every encounter with a healthcare provider lacks the context and continuity of care that ultimately drives patient outcomes.

The Steep Price of Episodic Care

Stanford University physician Dr. Ilana Yurkiewicz shares the story of her patient, Michael Champion, who arrived at the hospital via ambulance after his wife noticed his 102.4-degree fever and growing lethargy over the weekend. Michael, a veteran with a history of diabetes and a previous stroke, required a feeding tube and daily catheters. His communication abilities were limited, making his wife Leah his advocate—acting as his "living, breathing medical record."

After treating Michael, Dr. Yurkiewicz carefully prepared his discharge to a rehab facility, carefully detailing his medical issues, antibiotic plan, and new insulin regimen. She was well aware that her discharge summary might be the only guidance the rehab facility would receive, and even then she was dubious of how well it would be followed. Despite her thoroughness, Michael returned to the emergency room days later with blood sugar levels four times higher than normal, due to the prescribed insulin not being correctly administered at the nursing facility.

Dr. Yurkiewicz likens treating a patient with a complex medical history like Michael's to starting a book on page 200, with missing, shuffled, and unrelated pages. This sort of fragmented care hinders the continuity needed for effective treatment, leading to episodic rather than continuous care that is informed by a patient's specific context and history. The solution is Ambient Care, designed to provide care based on a continuous and comprehensive understanding of each individual's healthcare needs, independent of location, provider, or the patient's self-advocacy abilities.

The role of a digital healthcare advocate in this capacity would be three-fold: to provide continuity of care through access to all of the patient's historical and current healthcare information, coordinating care with clinical staff, specialists, and the patient's PCP; to provide early warnings of potential health problems based on changes in behavior and habits that could be indicative of an underlying undiagnosed condition; and, through the use of wearables, integrated pharmaceutical dispensers, cameras and AI that monitor the patient, ensure compliance with prescribed pharmaceuticals, therapies, and other treatments. We do realize that these sorts of descriptions of digital healthcare advocates may raise concerns about privacy. However, it's important to keep in mind that the component technologies that we're describing—cameras, integrated pharmaceutical dispensers, wearables—are already widely used and the data they gather is being stored digitally. The digital healthcare advocate simply orchestrates and leverages all of that data in a more meaningful way. As with any digital technology the risk of privacy and cyberthreat is critical to how these solutions are deployed. However, we believe that the benefits will far outweigh these risks.

The patient also often needs advocacy to help navigate insurance companies and claims. This can be hard enough to do when you are healthy and have the mental, emotional, and physical capacity to do the work involved, but it's typically the last thing someone battling an illness can manage. The irony is that the worse the illness, the greater the costs and complexity that need to be managed, and the less able the patient is to manage them.

While there are already many companies and individuals providing advocacy as a service, an alliance of professional health advocates with over six hundred members, and even advocacy certification, what's much more interesting is envisioning the role of advocate being filled, at least in part, by AI and what we'll call a "digital worker" in Chapter 4.

In the next section of this chapter, we'll also introduce the idea of a hospital in the cloud as being a portfolio of services that can be disaggregated and then reconstituted as needed. It's not much of a stretch to go from that to an app that plugs into the hospital in the cloud, is integrated with data analytics that can use public health data, access a patient's healthcare and insurance records, monitor the patient's health, and communicates with the patient, designated family and friends of the patient, and medical personnel. Again, this brings us closer to the notion of an Ambient Care system that becomes an intimate part of each patient's digital self.

To take that even one step further (albeit a large step), the digital healthcare advocate could use pharmacogenomics[53] (identifying the specific drugs that are best suited to the patient's unique genome) to become the ultimate form of hyperpersonalization: analyzing the patient's genetic predisposition to specific pharmaceuticals, and creating individualized therapies aligned with the patient's behaviors.

Again, all of this can be done today; for example, companies such as Geneticure offer genetic testing to identify specific hypertension drugs that work best to reduce blood pressure, based on an a simple pinprick blood test that can be done by individuals in their home without the need for a prescription.[54] However, the burden of coordinating these treatments falls on the care provider of the patient.

Driven by the astounding drop in the cost of gene sequencing, the ability to explore how various therapies and treatments affect an individual based on their personal genome promises to create a sea change in the future of medicine from the "standard of care" approach—which used a one-size-fits-all model of medicine—to a hyperpersonalized model where the unique genetic profile defines the treatment with the best outcomes for that patient.

Cancer treatments have been among some of the most promising that are following this approach, using genetic markers to indicate the type of pharmaceuticals and therapies that particular cancers in specific patients respond to. To date, there are over 1,800 genes that have been identified as markers of specific diseases, 2,000 genetic tests, and more than 350 clinical trials for genome-specific biotechnology therapies.[57]

Given the rate of population changes we've described, the continuously increasing complexity of care, the lack of adequate PCP coverage, and the personalization of healthcare, having a digital advocate isn't just a nice-to-have—it's imperative in creating a sustainable healthcare system. But there's another piece of this intricate puzzle that we're still missing. For at least the foreseeable future there will be a need to use traditional hospital setting for the many situations where home care is simply not enough.

 Having a digital advocate isn't just a nice-to-have—it's imperative in creating a sustainable healthcare system.

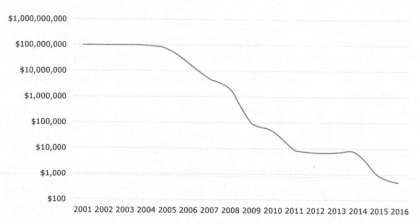

Figure 3.6: Decreasing Cost of Sequencing the Human Genome
The amazing drop in the cost of sequencing the human genome, which has plummeted from $300 million in 2000 (the cost of the original genome sequencing) to under $10 million in 2007. to $1 million in 2008, to under $1,000 today.[55] The expectation is that the cost will have dropped to under $100 within the next five to ten years. The rate of decrease in the cost exceeds even that which is predicted by Moore's law when projecting the exponential advances of semiconductor technology.[56]

The Hospital in the Cloud

The last disruptor we'll look at is what we call the "hospital in the cloud," and it comes from a much larger trend in technology and business over the past decade: the advent of cloud-based models for the use of software, computing, and data storage. Most often, the idea of cloud computing is presented as a way to purchase and use technology services—such as software applications, computer power, or data storage—as needed, in the volume needed, and where needed. Think of this in the same way that you might an electric utility where you only pay for the electricity you use. This creates a much more cost-effective way to consume the resources required for an organization's information technology systems, but it also allows organizations to outsource noncore activities such as IT, and to focus on their core goals and expertise. In many ways the cloudification of healthcare may be the ultimate example of Ambient Care.

In our use, a "hospital in the cloud" refers to a much more important and significant aspect of the cloud. By disaggregating the various services

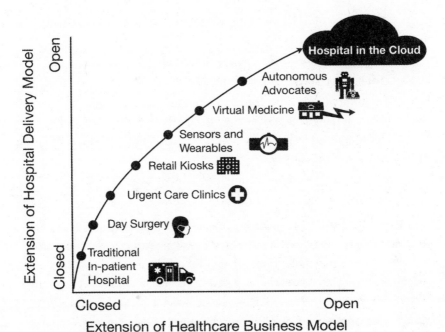

Figure 3.7: The Evolution Towards a Hospital in the Cloud

The evolution toward a hospital in the cloud includes new business models for healthcare as well as new methods of delivering patient healthcare services. Over time, the various services that make up a traditional hospital are disaggregated into individual services. These can be delivered to the patient as a customized and hyperpersonalized healthcare system that understands the patient's needs and the context of their lifestyle. Many of these services ccan be integrated in a localized way that maximize convenience and optimal outcomes.

that a traditional hospital delivers and adding new ambient offerings such as virtual medicine, these services can be re-aggregated as needed and delivered to the patient in a variety of settings. Think of this as a personalized set of healthcare services that are built to suit each patient: the ultimate form of Ambient Care that follows patients wherever they go—a portable hospital for one.

In its simplest form, a hospital in the cloud provides:

- A set of managed virtualized administrative and clinical services.
- Ongoing integration and communication with a patient's digital advocate.

- Integration of EHRs, and documentation and analytics across disparate EHRs.
- Data analytics for care management and public health.
- Protection against cyberthreats.
- The ability to use advanced technologies such as AI and NLP (Natural Language Processing) to eliminate the friction and high-overhead tasks such as clinical notes, medical coding, and claims submissions.
- Collaborative AI to help clinicians identify health markers and provide predictive diagnostics.

The obstacle to deploying a hospital in the cloud isn't nearly as much that of the technology, as it is the reluctance of providers to give up control of vertically integrated functions. That's especially true of provider systems which are trying to create very large self-contained healthcare ecosystems.

The obstacle to deploying a hospital in the cloud isn't nearly as much that of the technology, as it is the reluctance of providers to give up control of vertically integrated functions. That's especially true of provider systems which are trying to create very large self-contained healthcare ecosystems.

During the past two decades there have been, on average, fifty hospital mergers per year.[58, 59] At the same time, hospitals have been closing at the rate of thirty per year.[60] And two-thirds of all community hospitals are already part of a hospital system.[61, 62] This consolidation is also expected to reduce the number of hospital beds by as much as 50 percent over the next ten years.[63] With only those four dynamics at play, it's hard to see how the current notion of a freestanding local hospital will survive beyond the next decade.

The irony to this is that consolidation doesn't reduce costs or improve outcomes. So, why is it being done? The reason is found in the perverse way that healthcare economics work. Economies of scale enable providers to exact higher reimbursements from insurance companies. These higher reimbursements provide greater capital to large providers for further consolidation, and the cycle continues. This is like the mythical Ouroboros serpent who bites its own tail to devour itself.

Smaller mergers and consolidations that bring together a handful of smaller providers are not the issue; they help in creating better patient access to specialists, managing complex care, and operational efficiencies from shared systems. The concern is at the high end, where mega-hospital systems drive up healthcare costs (without evidence of better outcomes), shift the priorities from the patient experience to efficiency, and focus on operational excellence over innovation.

While efficiency and operational excellence are indeed crucial to healthcare providers, prioritizing these aspects at the expense of patient experience has detrimental effects on healthcare outcomes.

Patient satisfaction is tightly interwoven with health outcomes. When patients feel heard and respected, they are more likely to trust their healthcare provider. That translates into all sorts of behaviors that contribute to the patient's wellbeing. For example, adherence to prescribed pharmaceuticals, a higher likelihood of engaging in preventive measures and follow-up care, and better communication with clinicians and physicians.

Healthcare is also not just about diagnosing a condition or prescribing a medication. It's a holistic process that encompasses the physical, psychological, and emotional aspects of a person's wellbeing. A patient might be dealing with chronic stress or depression alongside a physical ailment. In a healthcare setting obsessed with operational efficiency, these interconnected factors might not be adequately addressed, resulting in less-than-optimal outcomes.

While there may be limited cases—such as the Mayo Clinic—where a single integrated provider requires scale in order to be able to handle highly complicated cases involving many specialists and availability of extensive in-house labs and diagnostic capabilities, this is only a fraction of healthcare.

And it's not just consolidation through acquisitions that's concerning. While there is no lack of controversy over this next point, we want to be clear that other options for consolidation, such as single-provider national healthcare systems, can have equally detrimental effects on innovation.

While there is currently precedent for the single-payer model in the way the VA (Department of Veteran's Affairs) provides healthcare, any attempt to nationalize that same approach has so far been met with enor-mous pushback from Americans, who place a high premium on choice. This model is also the least likely to provide the sort of healthcare innova-tions that result from a competitive free market.

Another popular option is the single-payer model fashioned after Medicare, or a variation of it, as a private-public model in which there is both the option of national healthcare for anyone who wants it, with added private healthcare for those prefer to augment their safety net with private insurance. Again, these both limit choice for the overwhelming majority of people, while the latter also creates social bifurcation and elitism—two more things that do not play well to the American psyche.

It's easy at this point to say that's a problem for the US healthcare system due to US culture, but we'd suggest a note of caution here. Choice in any industry is synonymous with innovation and competition. Driving both of these out of healthcare does not help to address the issues we will face as the result of the new challenges we've already discussed.

Perhaps, the least politically-loaded way to think about what we're describing is by keeping two things in mind. First, an aging demographics will bring every form of healthcare that we currently have to the brink, and second, none of the mechanisms we've described is in any way exclusive to how healthcare is funded and paid for by individuals.

What all of these models of consolidation have in common is that they shift the focus of healthcare towards a more consolidated industry at a time when just the opposite is true of nearly every other industry. While most industries are forming economies of scope where partnerships are held together by strategy to deliver a service personalized to the customer, all of the options that we just described are pushing healthcare back into the industrial-era model of economies of scale. The greatest risk to health-care is that we stifle its evolution into a post-industrial-era model that takes advantage of the economies of scope.

Instead of consolidation, imagine a healthcare system in which the basic building blocks of today's hospital are virtualized and available in the cloud.

Instead of consolidation, imagine a healthcare system in which the basic building blocks of today's hospital are virtualized and available in the cloud. These building blocks include: revenue cycle (insurance claims and payment processing), IT, analytics, public health, remote diagnostics and sensor-based technologies, and even the patient-owned EHR. Also in the cloud is the patient's personal digital advocate, which is able to coordinate all of these technologies. In this future, everything that today causes friction and distraction from the core competency of the provider is available as a service. Hospitals can now focus on their core expertise and mission—taking care of the patient—while being assured of the best possible efficiency for their operations and their business.

In the absence of this sort of hospital in the cloud, the healthcare industry will continue to create larger walled-garden ecosystems that wield greater power over insurers, while limiting patient choice and innovation. You may notice that we're being careful in our word choice by saying "limit" rather than "eliminate." That's because the insidious nature of walled gardens is that they provide just enough innovation to keep customers—in this case patients—within their walls as long as possible.

This is precisely the case with many users of technology who are locked into a particular technology platform such as Apple, Google, or even Meta; they end up being held hostage by the fear of losing their content and the highly integrated nature of the many apps that exist within the confines of their technology platform's walled garden.

It's not coincidental that this approach has also resulted in devices whose value commands much higher price tags. Apple, with the most restrictive walled garden, commands a steep premium from its users who are accustomed to happily paying two to three times as much for mobile phones, laptops, and tablets than for non-Apple alternatives. That may be a point of some irritation when it comes to our mobile devices, but it's an extraordinarily dangerous path to go down for healthcare.

Ultimately, moving the administration and operations of a hospital into the cloud as a series of best-of-class services, hosted and managed by a third party, will allow healthcare to become fully integrated with all of the advances that we've been discussing—from wearables and behavioral tracking to public health and prelytics—while alleviating the burden of administration.

It's naive to expect that the sort of transformation we're describing will be anything but enormously disruptive to the many providers already pursuing a strategy predicated on massive consolidation, as well as those organizations which feed off the inefficiency of the current system.

Like patients who stubbornly refuses to accept their illness despite the many obvious symptoms, many in the healthcare industry will likely continue to ignore the signs for change which line the road into the future, until the crisis is just too large to ignore. By then it will be too late to change organically. It seems inevitable that in the absence of the changes we've discussed, a large scale global government bailout of healthcare is somewhere on the horizon in the next twenty years.

Still, we're hopeful. In the aftermath of the COVID-19 pandemic we are all more fully aware of the connection between the health of a nation—or for that matter the world—and prosperity. Moving healthcare in the right direction by focusing more on the value of healthcare than just its cost will require a difficult social and political dialog. But the inevitability of the demographic changes that we've talked about will demand looking carefully at the alternatives we've described in order to live not just longer, but better lives.

This is where our story takes an interesting turn. If we are indeed at the precipice of extending our life in ways that will allow us to remain healthy and engaged for a longer portion of life then we also need to consider how we will live, work, and play during these added decades. If we are to stay engaged in a longer work-life, then what will the future of work look like and what kind of work will we want to be doing? That's where we'll go next.

AMBIENT CARE TIMELINE

2021–2030: Digital Disruption & Healthcare Transformation

During this decade the healthcare system will continue to suffer from accelerating inefficiencies and high costs. Healthcare will still be in the early stages of a major shift, with hospitals moving more and more of their operations to cloud-based services. Consumer demand for digital healthcare options will increase, and technology companies—which are outside of the traditional healthcare ecosystem—will develop products to meet this need. Wearable devices, behavioral tracking technology, and prelytics will gain greater popularity as people become more aware of their health data. Pressure will mount from consumers for traditional healthcare providers to integrate with these services, although mainstream healthcare will still see these advances as an existential threat. Insurance companies will incentivize healthy behaviors through wearable monitoring. These opportunities will begin to reduce operating costs and open up new avenues of care delivery. For example, remote monitoring technology will be used to determine the need for home health services while reducing the cost and risk associated with in-person care. In addition, data collected from wearable devices will be used to track patient health in real time and alert medical professionals immediately if an issue arises.

2031–2040: Value-Driven Care & Global Health Challenges

This decade will witness a shift in focus towards the value of healthcare rather than its cost, due to a greater awareness of the connection between health and prosperity brought about by multiple global pandemics during the preceding two decades. Hospitals will continue to embrace cloud-based services that allow them to streamline their operations, while continuing to focus on patient care. The pressure from consumer experience in the last decade will now be joined by pressure from insurers to better integrate behavioral tracking. Improvements in public health and the increased availability of digital healthcare options have made it easier for people to access quality care wherever they are. Prelytics is gaining greater acceptance among providers, payers, and patients as a way to better understand and manage chronic conditions. Technology will have to play a much greater role in diagnostics and care management, since the ranks of clinicians will have suffered significant fallout and attrition as they age out of healthcare and suffer the increasing stress of the profession. The traditional healthcare system will have waited too long to reengineer many of its processes. This will be especially true of smaller community hospitals who will have suffered most. Unable to deal with the aging demographics of patients and the lack of clinical staffing there will be increasing demands for global government bailouts. These will initially impact the US but, as the decade winds down, they will have worldwide implications. Simultaneously, reliance on the developing world for better access to healthcare will create mounting pressure on developed countries to subsidize their healthcare infrastructure. With a new level of global funding the healthcare industry will finally begin to make a whole-scale transition to the digital age.

2041–2050: Technological Integration & Personalized Medicine
By now the healthcare industry will have become much more reliant on a host of technologies to eliminate administrative friction. Improvements will take place within traditional hospital settings, with rising demand for automated processes that enable staff to focus on providing better quality care instead of spending their time on mundane administrative tasks. Data-driven diagnostics and decisions, personalized care, and precision medicine will have become commonplace. Wearable devices and implants are used by nearly all patients, not only providing people with convenience but also giving them access to better health information than ever before. Healthcare providers will use AI and machine learning to automate many of their clinical processes, freeing up time for more quality patient interactions.

Healthcare will become more efficient due to advances in technology that promote integration and collaboration among medical practitioners and other stakeholders. Universal patient records will be the norm. With improvements in medical treatments resulting in increased lifespans there will also be an increased focus on staying healthy during our extended years as well as providing personalized healthcare services tailored specifically for individual patient's needs. Digital advocates will begin to make their way into the healthcare industry as aging consumers experience the benefits of having continuity of care and fully interoperable healthcare systems. However, these advocates will most likely be offered and managed by technology players rather than healthcare providers or insurers

2051–2060: Ambient Healthcare & Home-based Services

This decade will see drastic changes within the healthcare system thanks to the convergence of many of the technologies introduced during the past three decades. Autonomous medical technologies aided by robotics will revolutionize diagnostic speed, as well as most basic surgical procedures. Almost all of the non-surgical procedures and therapies that required outpatient services at a healthcare facility will be delivered in a home setting. The foundation of sensors put in place will by now form a truly ambient healthcare system. Technology will have made it possible to provide personalized care to each patient. Digital advocates will be in constant communication with doctors who are able to predict potential health issues before they arise. Behavioral tracking, ingestible sensors that ensure patient compliance, real-time monitoring by AI-driven digital medical assistants will diagnose and predict illness before they require more costly and aggressive interventions. Healthcare services are also fully integrated, allowing for instant and ongoing collaboration between providers and creating a streamlined experience from diagnosis to treatment.

2061–2070: AI-Driven Healthcare & Universal Access

The healthcare industry has been fully transformed by digital technology with artificial intelligence and machine learning playing a primary role in patient care. Digital advocates will manage every aspect of a patient's healthcare journey, from the administrative tasks and processes to identifying conditions that need medical attention. Patients will have complete ownership over their healthcare records from birth and will be able to instantly grant access to a healthcare provider (as will their digital advocate). Prelytics will drastically reduce the cost of healthcare by predicting potential issues before they arise. While there may still be options for those who want it, the need for private insurance will have all but disappeared with the ability to identify with high precision each person's risk factors. With a static, and in many cases falling, population all governments will underwrite their healthcare systems, without the inefficiencies and long wait times for treatments typical during the early part of the century.

CHAPTER 4

The Future of Work:
Digital Workers and Digital Ecosystems

*"Technology has the capacity to liberate us from the drudgery
of everyday life and open up alternative possibilities."*

—MICHEL FOUCAULT

**GIGATREND—DIGITAL WORKERS AND DIGITAL
ECOSYSTEMS:**
The transition to autonomously staffed and managed
organizations.

During the twentieth century the US experienced a 1400 percent increase in productivity[1] over the nineteenth century. An *MIT Sloan Management Review* article, "The Mysterious Art and Science of Knowledge Worker Productivity," went even further to claim that there was a 5000 percent increase in productivity in manual labor alone. Consider how much the world has changed during the past two hundred years, and then think about what a similar increase in productivity might mean for the twenty-first century.

Most of the increase in productivity during the past century was due to improvements in the automation of manual work. In this chapter we'll focus on knowledge work. The term "knowledge worker" was first used by

Peter Drucker in his 1959 book, *The Landmarks of Tomorrow*. According to Drucker, knowledge workers apply theoretical and analytical knowledge to create products and services. Drucker felt strongly that knowledge workers will be the most valuable assets of the twenty-first century.

In his 2013 book, *The Glass Cage: How Our Computers Are Changing Us*, Nicholas Carr argues that computers and the Internet haven't increased productivity. While they automate mundane tasks and increase efficiency, computers also have negative consequences such as "numbing of cognitive abilities," as workers become overly reliant on technology, losing their ability to think creatively. According to Carr, this problem is exacerbated by automation which can result in job losses and a decrease in quality due to lack of human oversight.[2]

Carr's argument—that businesses should use technology judiciously as a tool, rather than relying too heavily on it for decisions requiring critical thinking skills—wasn't without merit, at the time. Much of the technology that promised to eliminate the drudgery and the cost of repetitive tasks has instead only added to the burden of the knowledge worker. It seems that we need more knowledge workers than ever, because there is more technology to manage than ever.

 Despite enormous increases in the power of computers and the volumes of data we have created, the promise of knowledge worker productivity is still a topic of much debate.

Few topics are as relevant to leaders trying to navigate uncertain economic challenges as that of the future of work and the role that new technologies will play in shaping the workforce of the future. So far, however, despite enormous increases in the power of computers and the volumes of data we have created, the promise of knowledge worker productivity is still a topic of much debate. At best it seems that we are continuing a trajectory of two-percent annual increase in productivity across all categories of workers. However, a great deal is about to change in how we will be using technology to run organizations and assist knowledge workers.

But before we look at what that future of work will look like, it might help to understand how we created the way we work today.

The Legacy of Detroit's Whiz Kids

One of the most basic problems in today's highly specialized workforce is that of process visibility—the understanding of the larger process that a worker is part of. Simply put, increasing task specialization in complex organizations tends to isolate workers from one another, and one's knowledge of what others in the organization do is scant, or even non-existent. Much of that philosophy of segmenting work originates with Henry Ford, who designed a system in which each worker on the assembly line was concerned only with his or her highly specific, highly routinized task.[3]

For the better part of the last century, most large organizations discouraged process visibility. The theories of Ford and Fredrick Taylor (who was obsessed with time motion studies that broke work down to its most granular elements) held that a worker need know very little about the production process as a whole. Guidance of the organization and decision-making on all matters—even the most minute—was left to management, which was invariably composed of people who had very little idea of what workers actually did in the performance of their jobs. Strict lines of authority and bureaucracy kept the average employee confined within the boundaries of a strict job description or grade. Management and labor were separated not only by class and educational attainment, but by philosophy as well. The theory was that workers worked better by focusing only on the most minute aspects of their job. Like a plow horse with blinders, anything other than what was immediately in front of the worker was considered a distraction.

The highwater mark of this approach was the Ford Motor Company of the 1950s, when Robert McNamara was head of the Ford division, and later, president of the company. McNamara had come to Ford shortly after the end of the Second World War as part of a group known as the "Whiz Kids." These men, with mathematical and scientific backgrounds, had invented Systems Analysis for the Army Air Corps, and were eager to test their theories in a business setting. Led by Charles "Tex" Thornton (who later went on to found defense contractor Litton Industries), the group offered its services, en masse, to the ailing Ford Motor Company, which was then on the brink of collapse. As the writer David Halberstam notes in *The Reckoning*—his study of the postwar American and Japanese automobile industries—this would have profound consequences for Ford, as well as other American car makers, when they later were forced to compete with the Asian automobile juggernaut.[4]

Empiricists to the core, the Whiz Kids believed that an organization—any organization, from the military to the smallest local business—could be managed efficiently through the application of statistical control, centralized accounting procedures, and strict adherence to metrics. Soft variables—such employee-management relations, morale, job satisfaction, and reflecting on the organization's mission—were largely, if not totally, ignored, for the simple reason that human emotions cannot be reduced to numbers. Productivity was still very much a matter of speeding up the assembly line to increase output, which was easy to measure: it was simply a matter of knowing the cost of inputs to a process and the value of outputs from that process.

Most of the Whiz Kids eventually left Ford for other pursuits, but McNamara stayed, rising through the ranks. He was named president in November 1960. Several months later, he was summoned to Washington by President John F. Kennedy to become Secretary of Defense, which, as we'll see, had dire consequences for the country. Through all of his years at Ford and as Secretary of Defense, McNamara was obsessed with numbers over people. As Halberstam notes, "He was at once a man who soon knew everything quantifiable about the business and who had absolutely no feel for it."[5] He had grown up in California, not Detroit. After coming to Ford, McNamara did not mix with his industry peers in Grosse Pointe; he pointedly chose to live in the college town of Ann Arbor, sixty miles and a whole other world away.

In the Detroit of the 1950s, Halberstam notes, you were either a "car guy"—with a feel for design, engineering, and the buying public—or you were not. If you were not, you could never understand the emotionally complex and often ineffable aspect of the business. Cars were more than a simple tool for transportation; they were embodiments of freedom, adventure, sophistication, and sexuality—an attitude which has defined the culture of the automobile since that time. At General Motors in the 1950s, it was Harley Earl, the chief stylist, who was the most powerful executive, not its president, Harlow Curtice. Alfred Sloan, GM's chairman of the board, imbued Earl with the concept of the dream car and then gave him organizational carte blanche to achieve it.[6]

 Cars were more than a simple tool for transportation; they were embodiments of freedom, adventure, sophistication, and sexuality—an attitude which has defined the culture of the automobile since that time.

McNamara, on the other hand—with his fetish for choreographed meetings featuring charts and graphs—cared little about Ford Motor Company's automobiles, how they were made, and whether they had an ounce of sex appeal. He was interested only in whether "the numbers added up." The chasm between the manufacturing divisions and the enormous management structure was immense. Ford's plant managers took to devising their own procedures for meeting the Accounting Department's daunting cost criteria while still producing a solid automobile. Ford's products suffered for the simple reason that people from different departments were discouraged from talking to one another. To use terminology that we'll come back to later in this chapter, Alfred Sloan focused on the numerator, or value, while McNamara focused on the denominator or cost—two very different ways to think about growth and success. The latter is driven strictly by productivity measured by outputs, while the former is obsessed with productivity as measured by outcomes. That apparently trivial distinction is something that we'll see has enormous implications for how we view and measure knowledge worker productivity.

McNamara's failure to appreciate the nature of the product was highlighted during a meeting to investigate production bottlenecks. The paint ovens in Ford's plants were old, outdated, and too small to accommodate larger cars. At a meeting convened to examine the problem, an executive from the manufacturing division explained to McNamara that there was no way to expedite the painting process.

According to Halberstam, McNamara then suggested that a car chassis be built in two parts, painted, and then welded together into one piece. The executive told McNamara that such a plan wouldn't work; the welding could not come after painting, and even if it could, the chassis would be

114

greatly weakened. Yet McNamara insisted that the manufacturing division find a way to speed up the painting. At this point, the executive shouted at McNamara, "The problem with you is that you don't know a goddamn thing about how our cars are actually made!" After the meeting broke up, McNamara turned to the executive's superior and said, "I don't want that man at any more meetings."[7]

McNamara's "by-the-numbers" approach, which left little room to assimilate the actual state of a problem, would have tragic consequences a decade later during the war in Vietnam. Field commanders had to ignore, or at least transmogrify, the truth in their combat reports in order to satisfy "body counts," the Pentagon's (and McNamara's) metric for measuring military success.

As Detroit went, so went American manufacturing. The steel mills of the Midwest began to lose market share to upstart competitors from South Korea and Japan. In the consumer market, people began to realize that the quality of goods was usually sacrificed to cost control. With planned obsolescence and advertising imagery so firmly embedded in the national culture, we came to expect that the things we bought would fall apart, wear out, or quickly become unfashionable.

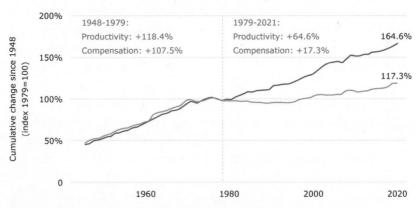

Figure 4.1: Productivity Growth vs Compensation
Measuring knowledge worker productivity has historically been difficult to do. However if we look at the increase in non-farm productivity over the past seventy years, we find that after 1980, productivity has continued to increase while workers' wages have stagnated. One interpretation of this is that technology has had a significant impact on productivity. Source: World Economic Forum[8]

Clearly, a crisis was at hand. People complained that the United States was no longer a country that "made things," and those things that were made were not worth buying.

The failure to appreciate the importance of product quality, innovation, and value in manufacturing was a symptom of a much larger problem that had been growing for decades. As companies shifted their focus from creating products with lasting quality to making goods quickly and cheaply, it became clear that American industry was facing an existential crisis. This had far-reaching effects across many industries, leading to job losses, economic hardship, and a deep sense of dissatisfaction among consumers and workers.

However, a new wave of entrepreneurs began to emerge in the late 1970s and early 1980s. These visionaries had a different approach to manufacturing than their predecessors: they focused on quality over quantity, outcomes over outputs, investing in research and development to produce goods with longevity and dependability. Through their efforts, companies such as Apple, Microsoft, Intel, and Dell revolutionized the tech industry by introducing products that were not only more reliable and better suited for customers' needs, but which also promised to do for knowledge work what factory automation had done for the factory. That last point is something that is often lost in the narrative of twenty-first century progress. These companies focused on technologies whose ultimate purpose was specifically to free up knowledge workers so that they could be more creative and innovative.

In all the debate around white collar productivity one thing is apparent: knowledge workers are the only class of workers who have experienced a collective increase in real wages over the past forty years.

The importance of that cannot be understated. In all the debate around white collar productivity one thing is apparent: knowledge workers are the only class of workers who have experienced a collective increase in real wages over the past forty years.[9] (Figure 4.2) While productive metrics for knowledge workers are not readily available (see the sidebar discussion later in this chapter about output vs. outcomes), what's clear is that since

1980 there has been a steadily widening gap between the increase in wages and productivity.[10] (Figure 4.1)

Why It's So Hard to Measure Knowledge Worker Productivity

Measuring the productivity of knowledge workers is exceptionally challenging. Here's why:

1. **Intangible output:** Unlike manual or administrative work, knowledge workers often produce intangible outputs, such as ideas, designs, or strategies. It's difficult to quantify the value of these outputs.

2. **Quality vs. quantity:** For knowledge workers, the quality of work is more important than the quantity of output. High-quality work may take more time and effort, but it's typically not easily quantifiable or comparable to other work.

3. **Creativity and innovation:** Knowledge work often involves innovation and creative problem-solving, which can be unpredictable and hard to standardize or measure. In addition, most creative efforts require numerous experiments and failures until a solution is found to a problem. The solution then has to measured against time frames that may exceed the knowledge worker's time on the job. As an actuary for a large insurance company told us, "If you want to measure the quality of any work come back in fifty years to see how well I did!"

4. **Collaboration and teamwork:** Knowledge workers collaborate with other knowledge workers, making it difficult to attribute productivity to individuals. A single knowledge worker's contribution may be a small, but still a critical part of a larger project.

5. **Non-linear work patterns:** Knowledge work is often non-linear, involving periods of research, brainstorming, reflection, and sometimes just walking away from the problem being solved. All of this may not appear as productive, but it's all still essential to the overall process.

6. **Customized tasks:** Knowledge workers often have unique responsibilities and work on customized tasks, making it challenging to develop standardized metrics that apply across different roles and industries.

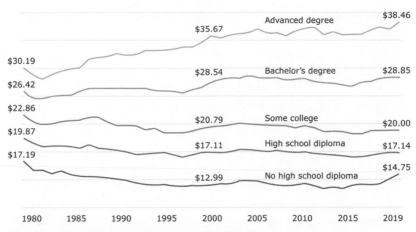

Figure 4.2 Median Wages by Level of Education

During the past twenty years the only groups to experience a growth in wages are those who have the education to qualify as knowledge workers, based on having a college degree, with advanced degrees beyond a Bachelor's being the only group to experience more than a nominal increase. Source: Congressional Research Service[11]

This gap can be interpreted in a number of ways. Although it's often used to illustrate a stagnation in wage growth due to factors such as globalization, declining union power, growing income inequality, financialization of the economy, and fiscal policies since 1970 that have favored the wealthy over workers, another way to look at this phenomenon is that productivity has started to outpace wage growth as many of the technologies developed by the companies we just mentioned (as well as many others), have started to make an impact on productivity. In the same way that it takes fewer farmers to till an acre, it takes fewer knowledge workers to perform most business activities.

Of course this sort of talk rings ominous notes when introducing a chapter on digital workers and the role they will play, since the implication is that digital workers will do to knowledge workers what farming automation has done to farmers (namely to put the vast majority of them out of business and to marginalize the rest, as shown in the wage gap in Figure 4.1). But that's only true if you discount the ability of human workers to create new sources of value which will ultimately employ many more people—something that we have historically underestimated.

Our perspective is that knowledge worker productivity will accelerate dramatically over the coming decades due to four core drivers: an increased ability for digital workers to offload the tedium of what knowledge workers do today, improved accuracy of digital workers over humans, the removal of most of the friction that exists in the partnerships that form today's business networks, and the resulting increase in the capacity of knowledge workers to innovate new sources of value.

Digital Workers

For the better part of the information age we've focused on creating more and more applications and putting this technology at the fingertips of knowledge workers. The result has been overburdened workers who spend far too much of their time thrashing among spreadsheets, email, data entry, document management, dozens of passwords that expire at different times, real-time chat/collaboration systems, and online search in an attempt to coordinate applications that were never built to work together. One recent study claimed that knowledge workers waste thirty-two days yearly juggling technologies.[12] That adds up to nearly $1 trillion in wages.[13]

 Digital workers collaborate as companions and co-workers in order to free knowledge workers to do what they do best—innovate and create value in entirely new ways, rather than be bogged down in tedious and repetitive tasks.

Digital workers collaborate as companions and co-workers in order to free knowledge workers to do what they do best—innovate and create value in entirely new ways, rather than be bogged down in tedious and repetitive tasks. They remove the tedium of knowledge work while creating new opportunities to leverage and amplify human capital. Unlike robotics in a factory—where human workers are pitted against technologies in a winner-take-all battle for jobs—the digital workers we'll talk about are anything but a zero-sum game. They have just the opposite effect: they create new value and innovation by amplifying the potential and impact of the only asset in the organization that can innovate—humans.

119

When technology creates new value, it also creates new employment opportunities. Consider that in 1800 the world's population had just reached one billion, with the US accounting for a minuscule 5 million. At that time nearly 90 percent of the US labor force (4.5 million) toiled in agricultural jobs. Today only 1.3 percent of the US labor force (2.2 million) performs this type of work,[14] yet it feeds more than 600 million people globally.

Today a single US farm worker produces the equivalent of nearly 200 farm workers in 1800. Yet, despite that radical increase in productivity, plow operators, soil tillers, and produce pickers do not fill the ranks of the unemployed.

A modern-day farmer uses GPS, AI/ML, thermal scanners, drones, satellites, robotic tractors and harvesters, process automation, analytics, automated supply chains, and sophisticated logistics and distribution systems that would have been unimaginable just twenty years ago.

While it may be easy to say that technology simply replaced human workers, who then found other industries that would employ them, that's not entirely correct. Some of those workers did find new jobs in new industries. However, dramatic increases in worker productivity always deliver the same inevitable effect. They foster innovation and create new business models that produce new economic opportunities. New industries are born out of these periods of tumultuous innovation. This, in turn, leads to expanded employment through growth in the economy and the job market. In short, technology always ups the game for humans by creating new ways in which we can create value.

Despite that, we underestimate how much more often knowledge workers will need to adapt to new skills and capabilities. McKinsey Global Institute estimates that 14 percent of the global workforce will need to switch occupational categories by 2030.[15] Fifty percent of current work activities can be automated by adapting currently demonstrated technologies. In its twentieth CEO survey, PwC found that 77 percent of the CEOs interviewed see the scarcity of key skills as the biggest threat to their business.[16]

The other issue that nearly every organization relying on knowledge workers is facing is that of job churn, which has reached unprecedented levels. According to a Korn Ferry survey of nearly 700 professionals, appropriately named, "I'm Outta Here," almost a third said they were thinking of leaving their job even though they didn't have another one lined up. It's what has come to be called the Great Resignation,[17] and it's the opening salvo in an era of knowledge worker scarcity brought on by a perfect storm of turnover and new attitudes about work.

According to the Bureau of Labor Statistics the national average turnover rate in 2021 was 47.2 percent—the highest it has ever been. That means that the median time employees stay in a job is four years, with managers averaging about five years. The cost of that turnover is staggering: according to Catalyst, by 2030 the US is expected to lose $430 billion due to low talent retention.[18] This is not just a US phenomenon—according to Catalyst, China will lose nearly $150 billion as a result of low retention rates.

As employees leave, they often take with them vital knowledge which is often not documented anywhere; the process leaves with the people. Digital workers can contribute to continuity of process knowledge . While there will always be a need for training new employees as they are onboarded, reducing that can add up quickly. Consider that, according to Gallup, a 100-person organization that provides an average salary of $50,000 could have turnover and replacement costs of approximately $660,000 to $2.6 million per year![19]

In 2022 the *Harvard Business Review* identified a phenomenon, especially prevalent among Gen Z (1995-2020) and Gen Alpha (2021 and beyond) known as "quiet quitting," which is characterized by employees opting out of tasks beyond the scope of their assigned duties, and an overall decrease in psychological investment in their work[20]. A Gallup poll showed that more than 50 percent of US workers admit to some form of quiet quitting.[21]

· ·

 Unlike Boomers or Gen-Xers, Gen Z and Gen Alpha have a low threshold of tolerance for work that they feel isn't leveraging their intellect and their capabilities.

· ·

Unlike Boomers or Gen-Xers, Gen Z and Gen Alpha have a low threshold of tolerance for work that they feel isn't leveraging their intellect and their capabilities. We can lambaste this behavior as entitled or simply spoiled, or we can look at it as a positive indication that this generation, which has grown up with 24/7 access to social media is recoiling at the absurdity of doing work that can be done through technology. For example, using AI tools such as ChatGPT to assist in doing research, writing basic programing code, data entry, schedule management. Digital workers that can do all of that and much more are not an optional or nice to have technology, for younger workers they are an essential part of the work environment.

On the other end of the age spectrum (as we discussed in Chapter 2), as life expectancy continues to increase, so does work-life expectancy—defined as the age at which knowledge workers stop working—with the two lines converging in the year 2100. The reason for this is not just a continued economic need for work due to a longer life expectancy, but rather a desire on the part of knowledge workers to continue to create and receive value for their knowledge. Unlike a skilled laborer or factory worker, knowledge work does not require the same levels of physical stamina, strength, and mobility at eighty-five as it did at thirty-five.

To cope with this perfect storm, organizations must scale and innovate faster and at a pace that is simply not sustainable with current knowledge work models

There are five ways that Digital Workers make that possible:

- They create a culture in which human workers do not feel threatened by technologies, such as artificial intelligence, but see them as colleagues in accomplishing tasks.

- By unburdening knowledge workers, they create an opportunity for them to achieve greater job satisfaction and success.

- Digital Workers learn and evolve similarly to human workers, and function as part of a team. Their collaboration enables ongoing evolution and increases their value to the organization.

- As Digital Workers evolve and learn they become permanent assets of the organization.

- Digital Workers allow human workers to amplify their value to the organization rather than being commoditized or replaced by technology.

What Is a Digital Worker

Digital Workers are AI that's enabled with skills to perform administrative tasks that would otherwise be performed by human knowledge workers, They have the capability to learn and refine these skills, and the ability to work in collaboration with human knowledge workers, in order to remove the tedium and friction that otherwise slows value creation.[22]

Digital Workers are AI that's enabled with skills to perform administrative tasks that would otherwise be performed by human knowledge workers, They have the capability to learn and refine these skills, and the ability to work in collaboration with human knowledge workers, in order to remove the tedium and friction that otherwise slows value creation.

As we describe what Digital Workers are, the natural temptation is to think of them as replacements for humans. This is the scenario envisioned by the doomsayers who make the case that humans will be replaced by an all-knowing AI.

To be clear, and it can't be emphasized enough, that's not a narrative that we are subscribing to. While AI is certainly part of how Digital Workers learns and perform tasks, they are not a replacement for human intelligence and creativity. In contrast, they function to encourage and enhance it. This is an important point. With the advent of conversational AI such as Generative Pretrained Transformers (GPTs), we are faced with a philosophical debate about how AI will impact the very idea of what makes humans intellectually unique. Some of these concerns center on the role of GPT in education, and are not unlike the arguments made against calculators in the 1970s or Internet search in the early 2000s— usually that these devices would cause damage by eroding the ability of students to do math longhand, or to do research. In short, it would make them lazy.

Decades later what we know is that human intelligence hasn't decreased because of tools that make the menial and the tedious easier. Instead, we have more knowledge workers than ever. In 1970 there were approximately 15 million[23] knowledge workers out of 78.5 million [24] total workers employed, or roughly 20 percent of the US workforce. By 2023 there were 100 million[25] knowledge workers out of 160 million[26] total workers employed, or 62 percent

The problem is that much of the conversation about AI uses too broad a brush. When AI is used to replace humans, rather than work alongside them, the results are often less than desirable. For example, the deployment of AI at MD Anderson Cancer Center illustrates what the use of AI to replace human intelligence can look like.

In 2013, MD Anderson invested $62 million in AI using IBM's Watson application. The objective was to create an Oncology Expert Advisor (OEA) which would make recommendation about patient cancer care. The project was ambitious. According to a press release by MD Anderson, the objective was "using the IBM Watson cognitive computing system for its mission to eradicate cancer." Four years later MD Anderson scrapped the project. Early failures in the use of AI are to be expected. However, there are some valuable lessons to be learned that apply to digital work.

Since Watson wasn't tied into MD Anderson's electronic records management system, it put even more burden on doctors and clinicians, and it circumvented the information technology group altogether. This perpetuates some of the fundamental problems with the deployment of many advanced technologies, not just AI—namely, that they act as disjointed parts of a critical process and only serve to further burden knowledge workers who are already stretched thin. What's especially interesting in the case of MD Anderson is that Watson OEA's clinical findings were the same as those of experts 90 percent of the time[27]—yet the project still failed.

Digital workers not only need to be accurate and intimately connected to the various applications and data sources that they will be using, but they also need to be able to work across and orchestrate these various connections while collaborating with the human workers they are freeing. In other words, effectiveness is about more than just being right 90 percent of the time. If that sounds odd, think of your many colleagues who are brilliant, but unable to work as part of a team. In the case of MD Anderson's deployment, according to a *New York Times* article, "physicians grew frustrated, wrestling with the technology rather than caring for patients."[28]

Ironically, the MD Anderson project started immediately after Watson's hugely popular win on the TV game show *Jeopardy*. Retrieving trivia for a game show compares poorly to the complexity inherent in medical care decision making. While Watson excelled at factual retrieval, it struggled piecing together those facts into a coherent care plan without the assistance of human intelligence.

IBM, and many early AI proponents and prognosticators, failed to recognize that much of what we call knowledge work is routine and procedural, and easily automated through existing technologies such a Robotic Process Automation (RPA). However, that same work requires

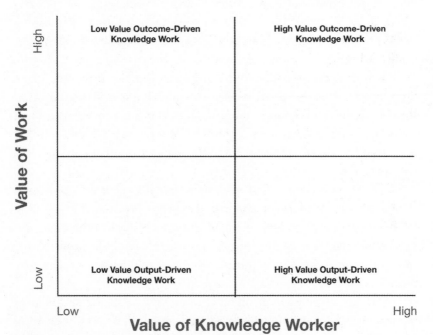

Figure 4.3: The Digital Human Workforce

Digital workers allow an organization to reallocate its high value human workers to tasks that have greater value—represented by the upper-righthand quadrant in this figure. Traditional automation is typically applied to the lower-lefthand quadrant. Today, however, knowledge workers end up occupying all four quadrants to some degree, diluting their impact. Digital workers can be used in the lower left-hand quadrant—where they work on their own or with traditional automation—and they can collaborate with humans in the remaining two quadrants (upper-left and lower-right).

integration with judgment and intuition, and, most importantly, the very human ability to manage uncertainty.

The other misinterpretation of what digital workers are is that they are simply human workers who have advanced digital skills. While this use of the term has been around for some time, it only perpetuates the growing burden on human workers to take on greater digital burden.

Digital Workers excel in systems where rules or patterns can either be defined or learned and where the outputs are standardized. This doesn't mean that digital workers are simply automated programs. A predefined program can never identify a new pattern and learn from it. Nor can it develop skills that evolve over time. Humans, on the other hand, excel where there is a need for innovation, new value creation, establishing bonds of trust and empathy, and where the rules are missing, broken, constantly changing, or simply unknowable.

Business is messy and includes risks and gambles that often make little logical or probabilistic sense. This unruliness drives innovation since it creates value where there wasn't even the known need for a solution. Think about your smartphone. Twenty years ago you couldn't have even conceived of 99 percent of the applications that you can't live without today.

And yet, when Apple first introduced the iPhone it was far from a slam dunk. One Wall Street hedge fund manager threatened to sell all of his Apple stock, which was selling at about $17/share at the time. The same held true for the release of the now iconic iPad, about which *PC Magazine* said, "There is, without a doubt, much disappointment surrounding the iPad."[29]

Humans are uniquely qualified at intuitively balancing and managing the messiness of innovation and envisioning new ways of creating value. The future isn't formulaic, it doesn't fit neatly into predefined processes and procedures, and it frequently departs from the patterns and behaviors of the past. It's shaped by forces that are both unknown and unknowable. Humans are inherently capable, thanks to millions of years of evolutionary pressure, at adapting rapidly to novel environments without the benefit of previous experience or knowledge. Uncertainty is uniquely challenging in that it defies our ability to predict based purely on the patterns of the past.

If we were to predict the future based just on knowledge of the patterns of the past, innovation would never occur. Innovation requires risk and failure, since by definition we are creating something that has not yet been experienced.

If we were to predict the future based just on knowledge of the patterns of the past, innovation would never occur. Innovation requires risk and failure, since by definition we are creating something that has not yet been experienced.

However, that takes intellectual bandwidth which is often being allocated in large part to tasks that barely leverage human intellect. According to research conducted by McKinsey, a startlingly large 40 percent of workers have indicated that they spend at least 25 percent of their time working on mundane and repetitive tasks such as sending emails and entering data. Not only are these activities time-consuming, they don't allow workers to focus more of their attention and energy on higher-return activities like building new client relationships or delivering responsive customer service. Digital workers are ideal for taking care of the mundane and repetitive tasks, not only freeing up human workers but performing administrative tasks with greater accuracy.

The bottom line is that either abdicating all decisions to AI in order to reduce the need for knowledge workers, or simply adding yet more software to the knowledge worker's digital burden, creates a digital façade: a thinly veiled attempt to continue business as usual rather than fundamentally reimagining the way we work.

Productivity at a Standstill

Although the information age ushered in an era of immense change, new business models, and new jobs for knowledge workers, it also had a counterintuitive impact on productivity.

In 1999, Peter Drucker himself wrote that "Increasingly, the ability of organizations—and not only of businesses—to survive will come to depend on their comparative advantage in making the knowledge worker more productive." Yet, nearly quarter of a century later, we still struggle with that same issue. Today's knowledge worker is deluged with distraction, administration, and interruptions. A study by vouchercloud.com on the routines of 1,989 UK workers found that the average office worker was only productive for two hours and fifty-three minutes. A similar study of 185 million working hours, conducted by RescueTime, found that the average knowledge worker—one who mainly works with information rather than manual labor—in the US was productive for only two hours and forty-eight minutes a day. We've built entire industries to employ people whose jobs depend on the existence and inefficiency of friction.

According to a study by McKinsey:

> About half the activities people are paid to do globally could theoretically be automated using currently demonstrated technologies. Very few occupations—less than 5 percent—consist of activities that can be fully automated.
>
> However, in about 60 percent of occupations, at least one-third of the constituent activities could be automated, implying substantial workplace transformations and changes for all workers.
>
> While technical feasibility of automation is important, it is not the only factor that will influence the pace and extent of automation adoption. Other factors include the cost of developing and deploying automation solutions for specific uses in the workplace, the labor-market dynamics (including quality and quantity of labor and associated wages), the benefits of automation beyond labor substitution, and regulatory and social acceptance.[30]

Where does the rest of the proverbial forty-hour workweek go? It's far too easy to chalk up the remaining non-work hours to informal chats around the coffee machine. The more likely scenario is that knowledge workers spend most of their time managing all the process-oriented tasks that are critical to eliminating the friction generated by the same technologies that were deployed to increase productivity.

 Simply put, we have strapped a technology millstone to the necks of our most valuable human assets, knowledge workers.

You'd be hard-pressed to find a knowledge worker who wouldn't welcome the prospect of a frictionless forty-hour work week, compared to how much time they spend wrestling with technological obstacles that stand in the way of getting their job done. Simply put, we have strapped a technology millstone to the necks of our most valuable human assets, knowledge workers. And we've known that for some time. In their 1994 groundbreaking book *Reengineering the Corporation*, Hammer and Champy made the bold claim that 90 percent of most white-collar work was dedicated to these non-productive tasks. The real work happens in 10 percent or less of the processes. Imagine what a knowledge worker could accomplish if we simply doubled that to 20 percent. Unfortunately, that's not the direction we've been going in.

In healthcare the number of administrative knowledge workers has increased by a whopping 3200 percent since 1970. Yet, the number of physicians has barely changed. (Figure 4.4) Much of those physicians' time is also spent in an administrative quagmire; the typical doctor invests one hour entering and managing data for each hour they interact with patients. Even more telling is that, according to the US Bureau of Labor Statistics, the growth of physicians and surgeons from 2021 to 2031 is projected to

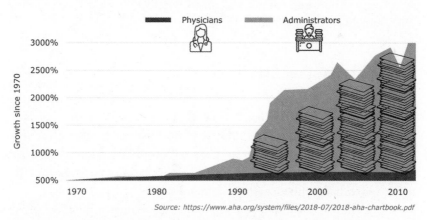

Source: https://www.aha.org/system/files/2018-07/2018-aha-chartbook.pdf

Figure 4.4: Growth of Physicians and Administrators, 1970–2013
During the period from 1970 to 2017 the number of healthcare administrators outpaced the 150 percent growth in physicians by an astounding 3050 percent. Even more telling is that the projected growth of physicians and surgeons from 2021 to 2031 is just 3 percent while the growth in administrative jobs is projected to increase by 28 percent. Source: Bureau of Labor Statistics

be 3 percent, while the growth in administrative jobs is projected to be 28 percent. At that rate by 2040 there will be more administrators in health-care than there are physicians and surgeons.

The burden this puts on doctors has severe consequences for both doctors and their patients. Being a doctor has always been an incredibly stressful profession. It's been known for over 150 years that doctors have a higher rate of suicide than the average population. Even in medical school, the second leading cause of death among students, after accidents, is suicide. It's estimated that the entire class of a medium-sized medical school is lost to suicide each year.[31] While we could argue that those individuals who make it through the demands and rigors of medical school and residency are the ones most able to take on that burden, we've clearly crossed the line over which the demands of the job exceed the capabilities of even the most resilient physicians.

In a 2018 survey of 6,695 physicians conducted by the Mayo Clinic, 54.3 percent reported symptoms of burnout, 32 percent reported excessive fatigue, and 6.5 percent reported recent suicidal thoughts.[32] And all of this ultimately trickles down to the quality of care the patient receives. Physicians' who reported errors were also the ones most likely to have symptoms of burnout, fatigue, and recent suicidal ideation.[33] To call that unsustainable is being generous to a fault.

The Digital Worker Ecosystem

Mary in HR is actively seeking experienced software engineers for numerous senior roles. She has been thoroughly researching job boards, such as *ZipRecruiter* and *Monster,* and evaluating professional profiles on *LinkedIn,* to find the best candidates for the positions. Mary is knowledgeable about all the required qualifications for each job and must take time to locate individuals who meet these demands.

Once she has identified and gathered a few hundred potential prospects, Mary creates a spreadsheet in which she records details from her search results. This necessitates her to standardize the information since not all sites categorize experience in the same way, as well as go through resumes to compile additional facts. Afterwards, Mary applies various weighting factors to consider each candidate's skills and capability set.

Following this process, she whittles down the list to select twenty of the most suitable applicants, who will then be presented to the IT leadership team for final ranking before any interviews are conducted.

Mary then has to vet the candidates for criminal records, social media posts, and prior employers. With all of that information, Mary can finally reach out to the short list of candidates to invite them to interview. However, before they come in, she must send each candidate a standardized form to fill out which contains questions from the IT leadership team that are intended to better identify the fit for each candidate.

Mary then conducts first-round interviews by looking at the IT leadership team's calendars to find dates that include as many of the team as possible. After the first-round interviews, she receives emails from each person who interviewed the candidate, and summarizes them. Lately she's been using the most recent version of GPT to create those summaries. The summaries are then sent to each leader with a simply thumbs up or thumbs down response, which she then ranks, picking twice as many final-round interviewees as there are positions to fill. If there aren't enough candidates then she has to go back to the start and find more, while she simultaneously proceeds with the final round of interviews for candidates who made the cut.

After the final round of interviews Mary sends her recommendations to leadership based on the leaders' final rankings. Once leadership approves her recommendation, she issues the offer letters to the selected candidates. If a candidate rejects the offer, she then goes to the next highest ranked candidate until all of the positions are filled.

At any one time Mary is working with several groups in the company, performing this same process simultaneously for each group. She takes great pride in her ability to manage the search and hiring process, and leadership across the company have often praised her for how well she does her job. She's been at this for ten years and the company has grown rapidly from a startup to more than 400 employees. She'd like to think that she has played an important part in that success.

Mary has just one complaint that she's wanted to bring up with leadership but has been too timid to raise. With ten years of experience she has a better understanding of the company's culture, and the kinds of people who fit the culture, that she can often tell from a short interview who is or isn't a good fit. If she spent more of her time doing first-round interviews, she could save leadership many hours of their valuable time as well as avoid much of the necessary back and forth to find new candidates when leadership rejects a candidate they've already put a great deal of time into vetting. But if she took more time to do first-round interviews she wouldn't be able to manage all of the other administrative parts of the process.

Then again, Mary was the person who identified and hired nearly all of the current management team, and they know that. Surely they'd see the value of her playing a more valuable role in building the company's talent. She gives it some more thought and decides to go to her boss and ask for several new hires to help her.

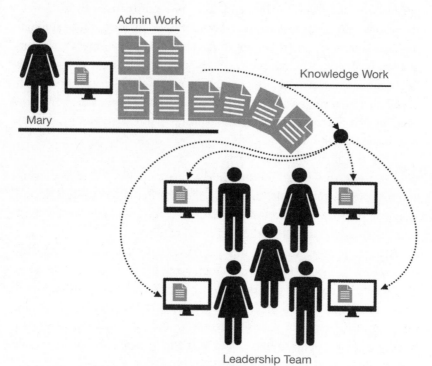

Figure 4.5: The Administrative Cascade Effect
The cascade effect occurs when the volume of administrative work exceeds the ability of one or more administrators. If it's critical for the work to be done within a certain timeframe, a portion of the work typically cascades to the next higher level of knowledge worker.

The conflict Mary is facing is similar to the one so many knowledge workers face: how to create more strategic value from their experience and know-how, while keeping the wheels on the bus from a tactical standpoint. You may also have noticed that Mary's difficulty in upskilling her own position has a negative cascading effect on leadership's productivity, since she could be offloading some of their work by being more involved in higher value activities. In addition, that last line in the narrative, "she'll go to her boss and ask for several new hires to help," illustrates how easily administrative tasks get baked into the very structure of the organization. Simply put, administrators create a gravity which attracts more administrators.

Let's take a look at how a digital worker might be able to change what Mary does.

In the same way that Mary would hire an administrative worker, she could also "hire" a digital worker who has the skills to work with a spreadsheet, draft letters, create summary documents, coordinate schedules, gather and update rankings. The digital worker would connect with each of the corresponding datasets and apps through APIs that have already been built to work in an HR setting. The digital worker would also engage with Mary in a conversational way whenever it encountered a task that it couldn't complete or didn't understand. That dialog might look like Figure 4.6.

Although Mary's example is fictional, companies such as IBM, Ampliforce, Automation Anywhere, and WorkFusion are already well underway in deploying digital workers.

Jeri Morgan is part of IBM's Human Resources team. She and her team work to ensure that the company's talent is developed and retained through a fair and timely promotion process four times annually. This process is incredibly important for keeping top talent within the organization, and it can take up to ten weeks of the twelve-week quarter to complete. This puts a lot of pressure on Jeri and her team, as they try to balance other job responsibilities such as strategic workforce planning and creating a focus on inclusion within the organization. According to Jeri, "[The process] was heavily reliant on collecting static data from various systems." Covering the North America region for IBM Consulting™, she had to pull data on 15,000 to 17,000 employees, from several systems, into

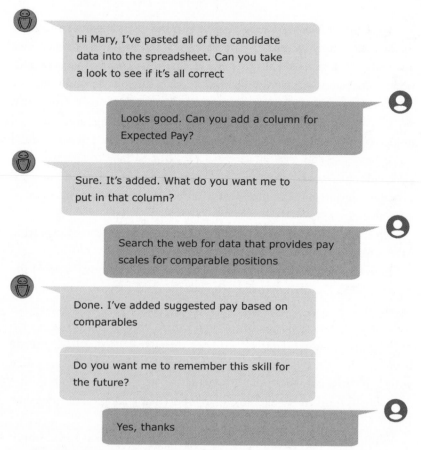

Figure 4.6: A Typical Dialog Between a Knowledge Worker and a Digital Worker

spreadsheets with about seventy-five columns of data. She would then share that data with the appropriate IBM Talent, HR, business managers, and leaders—hundreds in all. "This manual work was a huge obstacle of time and effort standing in the way of our *real work*: helping the business units evaluate the data and identify who was ready for promotion, who was getting close to being ready and who was not, in addition to helping them identify what's needed to get those that are not ready, ready for a future cycle.[34]"

Through the use of Watson Orchestrate, an AI-based digital worker solution, Jeri and her team were able to save 12,000 hours and five weeks.[35]

Marco Buchbinder, CEO of Ampliforce—which provides digital workers for a variety of industries such as healthcare and financial services—expects that eventually you'll be able to hire digital workers the same way that you can hire human workers off of *Indeed.com* or *ZipRecruiter.com*. These workers will have resumes, skills, and even references. They will live in the cloud and you'll hire them just as you do any contractor.

Outputs vs. Outcomes

There's another very important point to make here about the nature of knowledge work and how digital workers can help. When it comes to measuring knowledge worker productivity, it is important to distinguish between an output and an outcome. Outputs are the tangible products or services created by a knowledge worker, such as lines of code written for a software development project, or reports written for a research study. On the other hand, outcomes are the long-term impact or value generated by a knowledge worker's work, including increased revenue or customer satisfaction.

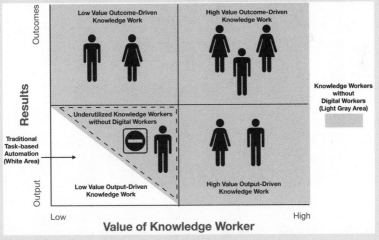

Figure 4.7: Knowledge Work without Digital Workers
In today's organizations knowledge workers are tasked with all but basis office automation, which inevitably they have to manage as well. This means that otherwise highly skilled or trainable individuals end up doing basic administrative tasks.

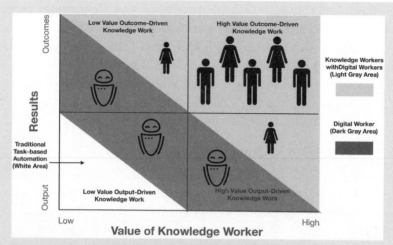

Figure 4.8 Knowledge Work with Digital Workers

With even basic digital workers knowledge workers can focus more time on higher value work which aligns with creative outcomes that drive innovation and long term value.

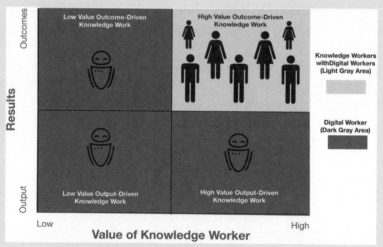

Figure 4.9 Knowledge Work with Digital Workers

With advanced digital workers, knowledge workers can focus exclusively on the highest value work and the creation of new sources of value. In this view of work humans no longer interface with technology but rather with digital workers who then coordinate and manage the automation of almost all of the tasks that today require knowledge workers to interact directly with computer applications.

Mary can track her recruiting process using both outputs and outcomes. Outputs could include the number of candidates she searches, the number of interviews conducted, and how many offer letters are sent out. Outcomes could be measured in terms of how well-suited the new employees are to their positions, and how successful they are at fulfilling their responsibilities.

Ultimately, Mary's goal is an outcome: to find quality candidates who will be an asset to her organization. What digital workers can do is help with outputs.

That's a key distinction to make. Work defined as output-driven is particularly well suited to a digital worker. Outcome-driven work is suited for knowledge workers.

Much of the conversation about AI centers on which jobs it will take away. That's a holdover from factory automation. It's much more likely that in the near-term digital workers will take on tasks, rather than entire jobs. Research conducted by OpenAI, OpenResearch, and the University of Pennsylvania found that "approximately 80 percent of the U.S. workforce could have at least 10 percent of their work tasks affected." And up to 49 percent of workers see half of their tasks as candidates for intelligent automation. The greatest impact was found in higher-wage knowledge work, notably roles which required programming and writing skills. What's not often discussed is that the tasks digital workers take on will create greater opportunity for knowledge workers to focus the time they gain on higher value work. With ongoing improvement expected in Large Language Models (LLMs) such as GPT-4 and GPT-5, the OpenAI, Open-Research, and University of Pennsylvania research projected that "these trends suggest a world where GPTs may be capable of executing any task typically performed at a computer." That last point is key. It's not difficult to imagine a future in which we no longer interface with computers but instead work directly with digital workers who become our primary interface to technology.

 It's not difficult to imagine a future in which we no longer interface with computers but instead work directly with digital workers who become our primary interface to technology.

While digital workers can help to offload much of the burden that knowledge workers currently face, they are still of limited value if they are unable to coordinate activities among themselves, across the entire spectrum of activities that make up a value chain. For example, the digital workers that manage inventory for a manufacturer should be able to communicate with the digital workers of multiple suppliers who provide the manufacturer with parts. This goes well beyond the conventional approaches already in place for automated ordering and invoicing between the supplier and manufacturer. The digital workers need to be able to respond to unanticipated changes in supply chains, market conditions, and interruptions due to unforeseen events such as natural disasters or pandemics.

This creates the potential to revolutionize supply chains by making them more efficient and resilient. Here are some examples of how digital workers can help accomplish this:

- *Automation.* Digital workers can automate low-level tasks like inventory management and order fulfillment, freeing up time for human employees to focus on more complex processes. This helps optimize operational efficiency and reduce costs.
- *Predictive Analytics.* Digital workers use predictive analytics to anticipate customer demand and respond quickly to changes in the market place. This allows companies to anticipate customer needs and be prepared accordingly, providing better service while reducing costs associated with over or understocking inventory.
- *Improved Visibility.* Digital workers provide real-time data that gives all stakeholders within the supply chain a clear understanding of current operations, allowing them to proactively anticipate potential problems before they occur.
- *Adaptability.* Digital workers can rapidly adjust their activities based on sudden changes in the market, helping businesses stay agile amidst fluid conditions.

However, doing all of this without integrating digital workers into the context of a larger digital ecosystem will only create processes that are further isolated behind the four walls of an organization. Realizing the promise and power of digital workers means that they need to be able to connect across the entire spectrum of activities, partnerships, suppliers, and customers in a value chain.

Driving Out the Friction

 While digital workers can help to automate tasks within an organization, the greater opportunity is to connect digital workers across digital ecosystems.

While digital workers can help to automate tasks within an organization, the greater opportunity is to connect digital workers across digital ecosystems. Consider that the typical Fortune 500 company has a supplier network that spans tens of thousands of partners. Research by The Hackett Group projects that on average companies have 3,000 suppliers for every US $1 billion in spend on products, materials, and services from suppliers. Proctor and Gamble has over 75,000 suppliers. Retailing giant Walmart counts over 100,000 suppliers.[36] These enormous supply chains create friction that puts an enormous burden on knowledge workers. Forbes reported that even simple products can have complex supply chains. For example, a single lasagna product that required over 1000 suppliers. That complexity creates risks that are invisible until they end up in a crisis.[37]

For example, when the 2013 European horsemeat scandal broke out, it was a shock to many consumers who had been buying and consuming products labeled as beef-based instant meals. It soon became apparent that there were significant flaws in the structure of Europe's food supply chains which allowed for mislabeling to occur on such a large scale. In response, governments and regulatory bodies put stricter regulations in place to ensure better monitoring of the production process, which in turn only increased the number of knowledge workers and systems that knowledge workers needed to manage.

Another source of friction comes from the proliferation of connected devices and systems which are not easily connected to communicate with each other. For example, consider that in healthcare, while over 90 percent of all physicians use an electronic medical record system, there are sixteen separate systems in use in the US alone,[38] none of which easily talk to another. Just having more devices and more things to connect does not equate to them connecting easily, if at all.

International Data Corporation (IDC) estimates there will be 50 billion interconnected devices by 2025. World-wide, the continuously expanding Internet of Things (IoT) ecosystem is enormous—expected to represent $2 trillion of economic impact in the next decade.[39]

Further evidence of just how dramatic this trend will become starts to stretch our imagination beyond the bounds of reasonable comprehension. Recall our prediction at the outset of this book that by 2100 there will be one hundred times as many individual computing devices connected to the IoT as there are grains of sand on all of the world's beaches. That creates an almost inconceivably large network of devices that will have the potential to connect virtually every object and person on the planet.

Ray Kurzweil, Founder of Singularity University, and Google's Director of Engineering, has taken that notion even further to suggest that the rate of increase in computing power and proliferation is not just exponential, but accelerating in its exponential growth, approaching what he calls "The Singularity"—a point at which we will have virtually unlimited power, storage, bandwidth, and ubiquity of computers and sensors.[40] To borrow a phrase we used in Chapter 3 on Healthcare, we could call this the age of "ambient computing." The implications of this accelerating exponential growth are beyond revolutionary; they disrupt the very foundation upon which we build business, economies, and society.

The world where everyone and everything could potentially be connected has arrived. And along with it comes an entirely new way to look at how businesses operate: Digital Business Ecosystems.

Digital Ecosystems

 Digital workers are the superglue that holds digital ecosystems together.

Digital Ecosystems are coordinated networks of strategically aligned and intensely collaborative communities. These hyperconnected communities tear down the boundaries between companies within industries as well as those between customers and suppliers. Digital workers are the superglue that holds digital ecosystems together. One way to think of digital ecosystems is as a sort of utility grid that connects business partners and their marketplaces. The ecosystem and digital workers operate in the background making sure that all the basic tasks needed to run a business get done. In the same way that you don't think much about all the nuances of generating, transmitting, rerouting, maintaining, and delivering power to a light switch when you turn on the office lights, a digital ecosystem is doing the same to make sure that the operational aspects of your business are running smoothly 24/7.

As Nicholas Negroponte—founder of the MIT Media Lab—predicted in 1984[41]: industries, products and services are converging and reforming as digital connections across industries and populations, at a rate that takes your breath away. In this new reality, businesses don't just change every so often, they change constantly, and therefore they need to be architected and built for change.

An article in *Forbes Tech*, "The Rise of Digital Ecosystems in the 'We Economy,'" described how ecosystems create a new era of digital orchestration:

> The new power brokers will be the master orchestrators that place themselves at the center of these digital ecosystems. These leaders will quickly master new digital relationships with their customers, end users, suppliers, alliance partners, developers, data sources, makers of smart devices, and sources of specialty talent. All will share the same goals: to grow new markets … and their individual businesses.[42]

The economic impact of Digital Business Ecosystems and their ability to accelerate the creation of economic value will be profound. According to Janus Bryzek (called the father of sensors), "the Industrial Internet has the potential to add $10 to $15 trillion to global GDP over the next twenty years. This is the largest [economic] growth in the history of humans."[43]

The fundamental premise of every digital ecosystem is simple, the cost and friction of maintaining a large vertically integrated infrastructure of non-core activities is greater, less resilient, more expensive, and less innovative, than the cost of coordinating an external value chain with the same activities among partners who have a core competency in these same areas.

Congratulations! Your New CEO Is a Digital Worker

While our expectation is that Digital Workers will be focused on administrative tasks, there's no reason why over time they may end up taking on increasing amounts of responsibility.

NetDragon, founded in 1999, has become one of China's most well-respected video game and mobile application developers. In early 2023, the company appointed a virtual humanoid robot powered by artificial intelligence as its new CEO. The AI, named "Ms Tang Yu," is expected to streamline processes, enhance the quality of work tasks, improve speed of execution, and act as an analytical tool to support decision making, while also playing an important role in employee development and ensuring a "fair" workplace.

Chairman of NetDragon, Dr Dejian Liu, said that the company sees the appointment of Ms Yu as a major milestone in its transformation into a "Metaverse organization," and will continue to develop the algorithms behind Ms Yu in order to transform into a Metaverse-based working community.[44] Clearly, NetDragon may be using Ms Yu as a way to gain media attention. However, limiting the longer-term prospects for digital work, especially given the exponential rate at which AI is advancing, only serve to limit our view of how we can shape the future. While the Metaverse may not end up as the catch-all concept that many had hoped for, it's clear that the move towards virtualized environments will transform the way we live, work, and play.

If you had to read that last sentence a few times to make sense of it, it's likely because it runs counter to the conventional wisdom that said that economies of scale would allow large vertically-integrated companies to do work at much lower costs and efficiency than smaller companies. That made sense when the only ways to connect with partners and customers were manual or proprietary technology interfaces, such as EDI (Electronic Data Interchange). These were not only siloed approaches that worked within closed networks, but were also heavily dependent on knowledge workers overseeing them. However, we are now entering an era when the availability of standardized models of integration—using cloud-based software that is shared across networks of businesses—can eliminate the manual work and the friction of more siloed approaches.

At the same time something else that's non-intuitive is changing; we are slowing the growth of population. Scale will still be needed to bring the modern world to what we are calling the Other Four Billion who live on less than $6 a day who do not yet have adequate access to healthcare, finance, or basic goods and services. However, even there the emphasis will be on building digital ecosystems that allow the smallest and most remote organizations to benefit from having the ability to leverage the same capabilities as much larger organizations. According to a study by McKinsey, "The integrated network economy could represent a global revenue pool of $60 trillion in 2025, with a potential increase in total economy share from about 1 to 2 percent [in 2020] to approximately 30 percent by 2025."[45]

Digital ecosystems can also be focused on the customer. An example is LEGO Group. In the early 2000s LEGO had initially pushed back on customers trying to hack its Mindstorms robotic product-building sets because LEGO wanted to maintain control over its product—having spent considerable time and resources developing the Mindstorms platform, LEGO wanted to ensure that it was secure. It also wanted to guard against any potential intellectual property issues that might arise if users were allowed to alter the Mindstorms code. All of this makes perfect sense if you look at it from a perspective of a closed—or, in this case, non-existent—ecosystem.

However, after customer demand grew louder, LEGO began to embrace a more open-source attitude towards Mindstorm's development. They released new programming tools and functions that made it easier for customers to create their own custom programs. Additionally, they launched an online community where users could share ideas, collaborate on projects, and ask for help. This helped to foster a vibrant community of hackers and developers who could use the platform to share and collaborate, as well as to provide LEGO with direct insight into how the marketplace wanted use Mindstorms.

The company has since embraced digital ecosystems for customer and community collaboration through platforms such as LEGO Ideas, where LEGO fans can submit ideas for new LEGO sets and have them voted on by the community. In a call with reporters in 2020, LEGO's CEO, Niels B. Christiansen, emphasized the point:

The entire LEGO ecosystem is actually, I think, only at the beginning. So, it's less about just creating an e-commerce store or an online store. It is really about this entire digital ecosystem and creating that future. And that's a long-term journey, that's a ten-year journey.... And we're just a couple of years into this.[46]

So, what might a LEGO digital ecosystem look like? Imagine that you could go to *LEGO.com* and submit a request to build a custom LEGO set in the same way that you might with a generative art AI program such as Dall-E—something along the lines of, "Create a Mediterranean villa in the style of Greek architecture with a fisherman in a fishing boat catching a large fish." LEGO could use generative AI to create an image of what your LEGO creation would look like. Once you'd fine tuned your LEGO creation, you could post it to find supporters who would back your idea by voting and commenting on it. If you gained enough support, a LEGO digital worker would then reach out to congratulate you. The digital worker would make sure that your design didn't infringe on any existing intellectual property (for example, a Disney character), and then notify you that your set would soon be in LEGO stores. LEGO's manufacturing and supply chain, along with its catalog of products, would all automatically be modified to accommodate your newly created set. Sound far-fetched? Well, pretty much all of this is already being done through LEGO's Idea platform and partners such as Bricklink Studio[47]. The only part of the narrative that's not there just yet is the interaction with the digital worker. Otherwise, all the pieces of the ecosystem are in place

Now imagine similar sorts of capabilities with other items that you buy, for instance, clothing, furniture, and appliances. You're probably getting the picture. Well-integrated digital ecosystems have the potential to radically alter the way we think of innovation by creating open environments in which innovation happens autonomically, as though it's part of a nervous system that can respond spontaneously and involuntarily to the marketplace.

We should pause for a moment here to explain that some of what may today pass for a digital ecosystem is better described as a walled garden. Companies such as Apple, Google, Amazon, Walmart, and Netflix are all creating the equivalent of proprietary ecosystems, which we prefer to call walled gardens. Walled gardens create large but closed environments that capitalize heavily on economies of scale. Think of Apple's App Store which is heavily vetted and controlled, and from which Apple receives a hefty thirty-percent royalty on sales.[48]

Key Opportunities and Imperatives of Digital Ecosystems

- Digital Business Ecosystems create higher levels of collaboration, co-creation, and innovation.
- Digital Business Ecosystems create the opportunity to expand capabilities around your business core without owning them (as in the case of Uber or Airbnb).
- Minimizing or removing existing friction (costs, inefficiency, latency, and poor resource utilization) create new opportunities for businesses to not only streamline existing processes, but also to free up resources for new innovation initiatives.
- Governance will take on a new and expanded role in a Digital Business Ecosystem, since the user-base, by definition, extends well beyond any single company, requiring strong profile-driven security and resource segmentation. For example, HIPPA requirements in the health industry, and regulatory requirements, such as Sarbanes-Oxley, in financial services will need to be incorporated into the ecosystems model.
- Ecosystems are fluid and dynamically adaptive to new business opportunities.

One thing is common among almost all of the above opportunities and imperatives: the importance of adopting a new view of the organization as an expansive network of relationships and alliances that need to be understood and managed, not from the inside out through ownership, but rather from the outside in as strategically aligned collaborators.

- An outside-in strategy, which supports collaborative business models involving complex networks of participants, will lead to a much more comprehensive view of the possible services and products that an ecosystem can deliver. For example, Amazon's initiative to partner with Boeing, to create an ecosystem model for package delivery, illustrates how otherwise separate companies can collaborate to identify new areas to create value for customers.[49]

In a digital ecosystem the level of collaboration blurs the lines between partners; in many ways, the digital ecosystems partner becomes part of the organization. Think of this in the same way that you might think about the hiring process for new talent. You don't think of the new employee as an outsider or a contractor who is simply lending talent to your organization, but rather as an insider who has privy to many areas of sensitive data and processes that would be hidden from the view of anyone outside of the organization.

For example, digital business ecosystem can take on the much larger role of re-orchestrating entire value chains to meet market needs and value chain capabilities. Companies such as E2Open are doing this across vast ecosystems—such as the suppliers of parts for the Boeing 787 Superliner—to reconfigure the value chain to best optimize potential partners and suppliers. This happens in an autonomic way so that the ecosystem responds to changes without manual intervention. The result is an intelligence that is now being built into the ecosystem and which respond immediately to markets.

This same phenomenon is also being seen in the automobile industry where players such as Covisint[50]—a business-to-business exchange founded by DaimlerChrysler, Ford Motor Company and General Motors and used by many automotive companies—have built enormous Digital Business Ecosystems that orchestrate thousands of suppliers, partners, and alliances across all of the major manufacturers.

One of the most important, but also least expected, benefits of these vast ecosystems is that the partnerships being managed and the data being collected about these relationships can be used to understand behavioral patterns across supply chains. Data scientists call this sort of view of digital behavior a "longitudinal view" because it cuts across a number of dimensions of behavior and data patterns. In healthcare, the longitudinal view is radically altering the way research into diseases is being approached by identifying patterns in data that would otherwise be invisible to researchers who are focused on just a narrow slice of the health care system. For instance, when you combine the data from healthcare providers, insurance payers, patient behaviors, and pharmaceuticals, you not only reduce the friction in the health care system, but you also start to see new unanticipated relationships. In manufacturing, similar patterns emerge in advance of supply chain disruptions, or as market demands change.

The problem has been that the patterns we know to look for are not the only patterns that lead to solutions and significant new value creation. So much of invention and discovery has historically happened as the result of accidental or serendipitous occurrences. Being able to make this sort of discovery systemic amplifies your ability to innovate and create new value.

 So much of invention and discovery has historically happened as the result of accidental or serendipitous occurrences.

Ultimately digital workers and Digital Business Ecosystems will demand an entirely new way of looking at how we work, partner, and innovate. What we're seeing start to evolve with early digital worker and ecosystem deployments is just the start of a new framework for organizations and supply chains that will reconfigure themselves and the work that needs to be done, in order to address new and unpredictable opportunities or challenges.

As digital workers and digital ecosystems evolve, the opportunities to create new business models and new levels of innovation will accelerate rapidly. The result will be an unprecedented rate of new value creation which will eclipse anything that's preceded it. It will need to, since the enormity of the challenges we face over the coming decades will be equally without precedent. The net benefit of all of this change is simple but profound: a level of collaboration, orchestration, and innovation that will make us cringe at how primitive and dependent on human orchestration business was before their advent.

Working from the Outside In

Throughout the last century there has been a slow but steady shift from the notion of standardized products and clearly delineated organizational boundaries (think of the Ford Model T where the product was "any color as long as it's black," and where every supplier was owned or controlled by Ford) to networks held together mostly by strategic alignment, where nearly every product is sold with a service or experience component. This same shift also typifies the move form economies of scale to economies of scope.

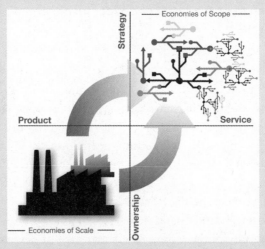

Figure 4.10 From Economies of Scale to Economies of Scope

Economies of Scale are built to produce standardized products within vertically integrated organizations, where one or very few companies own the resources used to manufacture and deliver the product. Economies of scope are built by orchestrating complex networks of partners, alliances, regulators, and customers in a digital ecosystem. This is a fundamental shift from the industrial era models to the era of Digital Ecosystem.

Rather than being focused on the "inside-out" processes and resources of any single organization, process management now needs to focus on the "outside-in," where resources are shared and distributed across an ecosystem.

The ecosystem model is already changing your industry, as it is every industry. So, how will your business have to change to accommodate this new reality?

DIGITAL WORKERS AND DIGITAL ECOSYSTEMS TIMELINE

2021–2030: Emergence & Early Adoption

During this decade, we'll witness the widespread use of AI-driven chatbots for customer service and RPA (Robotic Process Automation) tools for process automation. By 2023, advanced AI models like GPT become more prevalent in businesses, driving intelligent digital workers. The adoption of digital twins (the digital equivalents of physical objects, which we will talk more about in Chapter 7) for predictive maintenance and optimization of industrial processes starts taking place around 2025. By 2027, digital ecosystems expand to include data-driven decision-making, IoT integration, and smart cities.

By 2030, Digital workers and digital business ecosystems will become the new normal, replacing traditional approaches to work, process and supply chain management. Artificial intelligence (AI) technologies improve dramatically, resulting in AI-powered digital workers that can perform complex, highly specialized tasks on their own. The idea of interfacing with multiple applications in order to get tasks done will begin to give way to using digital workers as a simple conversational interface. The digital worker will take over interfacing with the individual applications needed to complete the task.

2031–2040: Growth & Integration

In the early 2030s, the development of advanced AI-driven automation for white-collar jobs—such as AI lawyers, doctors, and financial advisors—begins. By 2035, digital workers integrate into the mainstream workforce, working alongside humans. In 2038, decentralized digital ecosystems are implemented using blockchain technology, enabling trustless collaboration, which does not require that the parties in a transaction know or trust each other in order to have assurance in the validity of the transaction. We'll talk about this in more detail in Chapter 6.

By 2040, the automation of processes within digital business ecosystems is adopted widely across most industries as an efficient way to increase productivity and reduce costs. Digital ecosystems become commonplace as a wide variety of connected devices and services are used to manage data and automate processes. The use of decentralized technologies such as blockchain begins to replace centralized systems for data sharing and collaboration across digital business ecosystems.

2041-2050: Expansion & Optimization

The widespread adoption of AI-driven digital workers across industries leads to significant job displacement around 2042. By 2045, there is a transition to fully integrated digital ecosystems, resulting in seamless collaboration between humans and digital workers. Optimization of digital ecosystems using quantum computing emerges in 2048, leading to near-instantaneous problem-solving.

Machine learning and artificial intelligence also advance rapidly, allowing digital business ecosystems to dynamically adapt in response to changing market conditions. This leads to autonomous organizations, which are managed by smart algorithms and AI-powered digital workers, and which become commonplace and increasingly accepted by the public.

2051-2060: Autonomy & Adaptability

By 2052, self-managing digital workers with adaptable AI capabilities are developed. These digital workers are capable of learning new tasks without human intervention. In 2056, autonomous digital ecosystems capable of self-regulation and decision-making are created. An increased reliance on AI-driven systems to manage critical infrastructure, such as energy grids and transportation networks, is implemented in 2059.

2061-2070: Synergy & Symbiosis

The establishment of hybrid human-AI teams, combining the strengths of both, occurs in 2061. By 2065, brain-computer interfaces are introduced, enabling direct communication between humans and digital workers. In 2068, symbiotic digital ecosystems are created, in which humans and digital workers coexist and evolve together, driving continuous innovation and progress.

By 2070, Digital business ecosystems have become more interconnected and complex, reaching levels of performance never thought possible before. 90 percent of what was once thought to be knowledge work is now done by digital workers. Supply chains use quantum computing to reconfigure themselves in advance of events that would otherwise have crippled them in the 2020s. Much of innovation happens autonomically—without human intervention. The power of digital business ecosystems allows businesses to tackle global challenges that were previously unimaginable.

Humans are now almost exclusively dedicated to creative tasks and activities.

CHAPTER 5

The Future of Transportation: Mobility as a Service

"The future of mobility is an interconnected and seamless experience powered by technology."

—STEVE JOBS

GIGATREND—MOBILITY AS A SERVICE:
The end of the human driven and owned automobile.

The automobile is part of the fabric of the modern world. Not only is it a ubiquitous necessity for global socioeconomic infrastructure, but we build an intense cultural, personal, and behavioral bond with our vehicles. They define a person's identity. They are the backbone of commerce. As an industry, vehicle manufacturing is large enough to represent the equivalent of the world's sixth largest economy, employing over 50 million people and producing nearly one hundred million vehicles each year.[1] By the way, bumper to bumper in single file, those vehicles would form a traffic jam that could wrap itself around the equator eight times![2]

 Of all the things we do each day, driving and sharing our world with vehicles is the single riskiest thing most of us do.

In addition, of all the things we do each day, driving and sharing our world with vehicles is the single riskiest thing most of us do. Vehicles account for 1.3 million deaths each year, placing them as the tenth leading cause of death globally and the only non-disease related cause of death in the top ten. [3] However, if you adjust for the fact that there are only one billion vehicles globally, while all seven billion people don't risk acquiring any of the other nine diseases, you could make the claim that vehicle deaths are *the* leading cause of death for those who own or interact with an automobile.[4]

Yet, another aspect of how automobiles fit into the fabric of our lives is their relationship with an aging population. Increasingly, more people are having the very hard conversation—or worse yet, unilateral decision—of taking the car keys away from a parent. The automobile is perhaps one of the greatest statements of independence in modern society. When it's taken away, it takes with it not just the license to drive, but the license to live a full life, to socialize, and to enjoy personal freedom. But the risks of driving as we get older are well-documented. According to AAA, "With the exception of teen drivers, seniors have the highest crash death rate per mile driven, even though they drive fewer miles than younger people." With the Gigatrend of an aging population, which we discussed in Chapter 2, seniors are outliving their ability to drive by seven to ten years on average[5] a number that will only increase with time.

And lastly, let's not forget the impact of vehicles on global pollution and climate change. According to a study by NASA, vehicles are the single largest contributor to climate change.[6]

Given the enormous impact vehicles have on culture, risk, climate, the economy, employment, and nearly every other aspect of our society, we see the acceptance of autonomous vehicles (what we'll call AVs) as being the most significant milestone in measuring, understanding, and accepting AI and the devices that use it; to paraphrase an old song, "If AI can make it here, it can make it anywhere..." This is why we believe AVs represent one of the most visible and significant Gigatrends: the move to what we'll term Mobility as a Service, or MasS.

MaaS is so far removed from the traditional model of car ownership that our forecasts will likely appear outlandish, as they tread on some culturally and economically sacred turf. The automobile has become synonymous with personal identity. For most people, it is the first or second largest purchase and ongoing expense they will incur during their lives. Yet, unlike a home, the typical car is idle and has no utility for 95 percent of its useful life. According to a 2021 study by AAA, drivers spend on average 61.3 minutes a day in their car[7].

However, the transportation infrastructure of the modern world makes the personal automobile an absolute necessity. Nine in ten employees in the US need a car to commute to work. Even when public transportation is involved, the challenge remains for what is often referred to as the last mile problem: getting to and from public transportation still requires an automobile on one or both ends of the commute. Ride-sharing services have starting to change that, but their economics are still tied to business models that rely on private ownership of automobiles. They are an interim step in the right direction but, as we'll see, not sustainable in their current mode.

Does this thinking also apply in the developing world? After all, it wasn't so long ago that the same question was faced by the smartphone industry, with the surprising result that many developing countries, without significant infrastructure for telecommunications, leapfrogged developed countries when it came to deploying cellular technology. However, we see significant differences between the adoption of many prior technologies and MaaS.

Although technology convergence can experience exponential growth in developing countries, due to the lack of a prior infrastructure to anchor them to the past, MaaS requires the creation of significant new infrastructure, such as roadways and smart cities that can communicate with an AV. Just watch any *YouTube* video of traffic in a country such as Bangalore, India to appreciate the challenges of navigating streets that are crowded with all manner of vehicles, animals, people, and an apparently total lack of adherence to any consistent set of rules for drivers.

However, what is often missed in discussions about AVs in developing countries is that the same scenario we just described in Bangalore creates devastatingly higher rates of injuries and fatalities. For instance, vehicle fatalities in India are ten times those in the USA even though India has approximately 90 million fewer vehicles! When you consider that steep human cost, along with the relatively undeveloped rules of the road in a developing country, it is easier to make the case that a country such as India could lead the revolution to MaaS before a country that has a well-developed, significantly safer, and highly-regulated personal transportation model, and an economy in which the cost of individual ownership is less of a factor.

Over a two-week span in December 2022, a heavily modified F-16D Fighting Falcon fighter jet took to the skies no fewer than a dozen times to engage in high precision aerial dogfights like you might see in *Top Gun*. The fighter pilots came from two different efforts: DARPA's Air Combat Evolution (ACE) program and the Air Force Research Laboratory's Autonomous Air Combat Operations (AACO), program. Their execution was flawless, taking down their openers in every one of the dogfights. To be clear, these weren't virtual dogfights; the F-16 was a $100 million fighter jet. The only difference between it and any other F-16 was that its cockpit was empty. The plane was being flown by AI.

Pilot-less drones, or Remote Piloted Vehicles (RPVs), aren't all that uncommon in the skies over warzones today. In fact, pilot-less drones first appeared during World War I. According to the archive of the British War Museum, "Britain's Aerial Target, a small radio-controlled aircraft, was first tested in March 1917 while the American aerial torpedo known as the Kettering Bug first flew in October 1918. Although neither were used operationally during the war." One of the most famous of these early RPVs was introduced in 1935 during World War II. The DH.82B Queen Bee was a radio-controlled drone manufactured in the United States and used for target practice and training[8].

However, they are flown by human remote pilots hundreds or thousand of miles away. Our pilot-less F-16 was packing something completely different in its memory banks: AI algorithms complex enough to allow it to engage in a dogfight all on its own[9]. RPVs work well when they are engaged in missions where they are not likely to encounter opponents, since there is typically a three-to-four-second lag time in the round trip of information being sent form the drone to a remote pilot and any return commands to the RPV. That's about 3.5 seconds too long to be effective in air-to-air combat.

The most interesting, and counterintuitive aspect of how AI-piloted fighters will be used is surprising, but also telling, in the context of our discussion about how we will work with autonomous devices in the future. Although the AI-piloted F-16 easily won in simulated dogfights, the way the military talks about its use is very different than what you might be picturing. Rather than the image of skies devoid of human pilots, in which killer drones fight off each other, the role of these autonomous systems will be to work with human fighter pilots in collaborative air combat, where they act as a force multiplier for humans, amplifying human potential by allowing humans to focus on mission objectives and creative solutions.

This element of collaboration between human and AI is one of the most important elements of how we architect a future that best leverages autonomous devices and which creates the greatest opportunity for human innovation and creativity. We'll see this theme of collaboration repeated regularly in many of our Giga-trends. It's also an optimistic alternative to the common doomsday narrative that pits humans against AI in a winner-take-all battle for dominance.

The Road to Autonomy

 From a distance, driverless appears to be an all or nothing proposition—cars are either driven by people or drive themselves. The reality is much different.

From a distance, driverless appears to be an all or nothing proposition—cars are either driven by people or drive themselves. The reality is much different. There's a progression and evolution from human-driven cars to fully autonomous vehicles which is important to understand in any discussion about the road to autonomy.[10]

The US Department of Transportation's National Highway Traffic Safety Administration (NHTSA) has adopted the Society of Automobile Engineers (SAE's) five levels of automation, which range from a vehicle that requires total human control (level 0) to a totally autonomous vehicle under any conditions a human could also drive (level 5). Here's a quick summary of the five levels.

Level 0: (Here since the Model T) This is the way we've all learned to drive. You as the driver are in control of every system. It's worth noting, however, that even at level 0, we've had antilock brakes and computerized traction control since the early 1970s. There was a time when you learned to pump your brakes when skidding and you'd steer into a skid. In the 1980s, both systems were made standard safety equipment. This is a great example of how functions slowly make their way from driver to vehicle in an almost imperceptible manner.

Level 1: (Invented in 1990. In use since early 2000s) This level means that one or more systems assists in the steering or acceleration (and deceleration) of the vehicle. If you have adaptive cruise control, lane departure warning, or pedestrian braking, you are at this level. As the driver, you still have responsibility for being in full control of the vehicle and almost anything you do will instantly override the automated capabilities of the car. In fact, no system exists yet, at any level, in which the driver cannot override the autonomous features.

Level 2: (Invented in 1999. In use since 2003) This is where things start to get interesting. Some of us are already at this level. If you own a Tesla, a car that can parallel park on its own, or one which centers itself in a lane on the highway, then you are at level 2. At this level the driver can disengage by taking his or her hands off the steering wheel and feet off of the pedals, allowing the car to steer and adjust speed based on environmental factors, such as distance from other cars and traffic flow, staying within a lane. However, the driver still needs to be able to jump in at any time. And, once again, the vehicle still has to allow the driver to override its autonomous decisions.

For example, Teslas are designed to allow an override of the automatic emergency braking (AEB) if the driver turns the steering wheel, brakes, or presses the accelerator to full throttle. That should be a good thing, right? However, in March of 2017 Tesla was the target of a lawsuit which claimed that the Model S and X were accelerating at full throttle without any driver intervention.[11]

Oddly, the suit claimed that it wasn't the driver override that was an issue, per se, but that by allowing the car to accelerate at full throttle

forward (even if it was initiated by a fault in the computer), and not applying the AEB, Tesla was liable for the consequences of any resulting damage
or harm. The convoluted nature of this claim speaks to how uncharted
the legal territory is for AVs.[12] Should Tesla allow the driver to override
the AEB, and should the car correct itself if it makes a mistake? Tesla has
decided that the driver is always the final authority, which takes care of
most liability issues for now—but as we'll see with levels 3 through 5,
that's not a sustainable policy.

Level 3: (Invented and in limited use) This level is where the balance
of control shifts dramatically from driver to vehicle. You still need human
drivers in these cars, but the safety of the vehicle, under most circumstances, is up to the vehicle. However, there's a problem with level 3—it's
called the "handoff": that point when the vehicle needs to give control to
the human driver because it is no longer able to make the necessary decisions to drive the car safely. The handoff problem may well be one of the
most challenging in getting beyond Level 3. However, some manufactures
have made significant inroads with Level 3, notably Mercedes.

According to *Autocrypt*, "In May 2022, Mercedes-Benz became the
world's first manufacturer to get approved by German transport authorities
to legally operate its L3 Drive Pilot on the country's public roads, sold as
an option on Mercedes-Benz S Class and Mercedes EQS. This means that
those with L3 Drive Pilot are legally allowed to eat, draft emails, or watch
videos on the Autobahn. Still, given that L3 autonomy is conditional, if the
vehicle loses the environmental or locational conditions to operate at L3, it
will prompt the driver to take control within ten seconds. If the driver fails
to respond in ten seconds, the car will automatically turn on emergency
lights and decelerate to a full stop on the side of the road, then unlock the
doors in case first responders might need access to the cabin.[13]

It remains to be seen if Level 3 will be a viable solution for all AVs.
The fact is, humans get distracted. The better the system, the greater the
inattention of the human, because the more confidence they have in it, the
less frequent the handoff request will be and therefore, the less likely that
someone will be ready to take the wheel literally at a moment's notice in a
life-threatening situation.

All of this creates a perfect storm, which means is that a system that's
fully self-driving is needed, perhaps within a set of operational conditions,

but to rely on a human to take control in a challenging situation, one that the automation can't figure out, is just a very difficult path to go down.

Level 4: This is where the vehicle truly becomes autonomous in the way we'd expect to use the term. At this level the vehicle can basically handle anything that it was meant to do on its own. But the concept "meant to do" implies that the vehicle could have some serious problems trying to navigate a situation it is not meant for. For example, sedans aren't meant to drive through off-road terrain. The obstacles a vehicle might encounter, or the visual signals it perceives, may be well outside of its ability to assess and navigate.

Manufacturers call this acceptable envelope of conditions the "operational design domain" (ODD) of the vehicle. So, while a driver isn't needed within the ODD, if the vehicle finds itself forced off the road, or the driver wants to drive through a field of tall grass to get to a rocky cliff overlooking the Pacific, the vehicle is well outside of its ODD and the driver needs to take over. Of course, it's possible to imagine how different vehicles could have different ODDs. A Hummer may well take you all the way to the cliff autonomously. If you're feeling a bit uneasy about that, don't worry—we'll come back to it later in the chapter.

Level 5: Now we've arrived. At this level a vehicle is fully autonomous and performs at least as well as a human in any scenario, anticipated or not. (However, there is a bit of misrepresentation going on here, since by the time a Level 5 vehicle is developed it will undoubtedly operate much better than its human counterparts.)

Today we are somewhere in between Levels 2 and 3 in cars that are on the road with autonomous features. For example, Ford's BlueCruise, GM's Super Cruise, and (this may surprise you) even Tesla's Full Self-Driving are still in-between levels 2 and 3. All of these AVs require that the driver be alert and ready to instantly take control of the vehicle. In off-road testing we are somewhere between levels 3 and 4, which is an especially precarious place in the evolution of AI and autonomous vehicles. The reason is that at this stage we have to decide how AI and the human driver will coexist. On the one hand, this is a mechanical challenge of coordinating who does what, but on the other hand it's also a challenge of trust. Let's first look at the mechanical challenge, which is rather easy to solve.

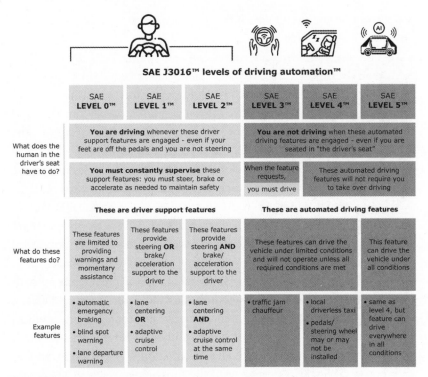

Figure 5.1: SAE Levels of Driving Automation.[14] Source: SAE.org

Since at Level 3 the vehicle can take over and the driver does not need to be engaged, it's only natural for the driver to really disengage, lose situational awareness, get lost in a phone call, eat a sandwich, perhaps even fall asleep. How does the vehicle then notify the driver that it needs help? The short answer is that in many cases it can't. If the situation is that dire, it's not likely the driver would have anywhere near enough time to assess and respond in any meaningful way. This is why many manufacturers of autonomous vehicles have wanted to completely skip over Level 3. However, this isn't as untenable as it seems.

Think of what it's like to drive with new student drivers (perhaps), when they first got behind the wheel. You probably drove them to a parking lot and then switched seats. They became the driver and you were the passenger. Did you then take them right from the parking lot onto the highway? Of course not. You first let them get a feel for the car while you also observed their level of competency. What you were doing was observing their behaviors.

Eventually your fledgling driver took the plunge and drove on the open road. But think carefully about that process. Since your house was probably not located at the foot of a highway onramp, the student had to drive along back roads, or perhaps through a town or city center, to get to the highway. You were probably thinking, "Which route would be the most manageable given their skill set and behavior at that point?" So, you likely planned out the least challenging route onto the least challenging highway. Effectively what you were doing was using an intuitively statistical model to determine the route that had the lowest probability of an incident or a set of conditions that exceeded the driver's abilities. If there was no such route then you, the experienced driver, probably drove part of the way.

Why not do the same with an AV? Using sophisticated maps of roadways, real time traffic and weather conditions, and a rating system that can be used to determine the skill set necessary for any route, an autonomous vehicle could easily calculate the probabilities of various risks along a variety of routes in getting you to your destination. Most of us are familiar with how a GPS will ask if you want the most direct route or the fastest route, one with highways or without. Why not add an option for an autonomous car to ask if you want your ride to be fully autonomous for forty minutes or partially autonomous at thirty minutes?

While it's tantalizing to think of AI as a technological overlord, a more accurate description is that of a collaborator who (yes, we said "who" and not "what," because we're anthropomorphizing AI intentionally) will work with us to determine which decision is in our best interests in a particular context. (We'll also look at this in Chapter 5 on the digital self.)

You're probably thinking, "Using probabilities and statistics to determine my fate is a frightening proposition." It seems that way, but measured against what alternative? If it's choosing between staying home or being in a vehicle, then, yes, you're absolutely correct. There is a greater likelihood of being involved in a vehicle incident if you're in a vehicle than if you just stay indoors (although even that isn't entirely true, since it's estimated that twenty thousand vehicles crash into commercial buildings each year in the US).[15]

The question we should be asking is: "which has the highest probability of safely transporting us: a vehicle being driven by a human, AI, or a combination of the two?" The answer is: some combination, depending on the situation. If we give ourselves the option to pick and choose among the three, instead of "either or," we've just minimized the risk to the lowest possible degree at any point in time and situation.

 We've been trusting far less sophisticated technologies with our lives for some time now.

You're still not convinced, and we can guess why: perception and trust. Few of us have ridden in an autonomous or semi-autonomous vehicle, and it's perfectly normal not to trust decisions being made by something we have no experience with. Well, guess what? We've been trusting far less sophisticated technologies with our lives for some time now. Level 0 and Level 1 vehicles already use antilock brakes, traction control, adaptive cruise control, proximity braking, self-parking, and lane departure warnings, among other computer-controlled functions that we take completely for granted.

While much of the talk surrounding AVs is about either safety or the cultural shift that will need to occur, we firmly believe that the overriding factor in the shift to MaaS will be an economic imperative, and one of the primary economic forces behind this imperative is higher vehicle utilization.

Factors Driving the Shift to MaaS

The relationship between utilization and the number of vehicles on the road is a simple one. As with any machine, the effective cost of ownership decreases as the use of the machine increases. If you pay $100 for a shovel to dig just one hole per day, the cost of the hole is $100/day. Dig two holes each day and the cost per hole, per day, is now $50. As we've seen, at a 5 percent average utilization, individually owned automobiles represent one of the most underutilized assets in a modern society. The relationship between utilization (as hours driven per day) and the number of vehicles needed is shown in Figure 5.2.

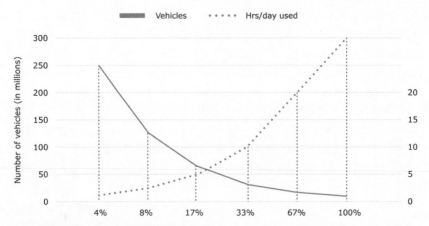

Figure 5.2: The Relationship Between the Number of Vehicles Needed and Vehicle Utilization

Utilization is also not just a mathematical issue. ICE vehicles are built to run a few hours a day, with a typical life of twelve years and about 200,000 miles. If they are utilized twenty hours a day, their useful life drops to one year and their maintenance costs skyrocket. While it's conceivable that an ICE AV could be economically feasible in the scenarios we are describing in this chapter, as the cost of ownership for EVs drops, the economics of EVs will far outpace that of ICE vehicles. Even if we set aside energy costs, EVs are simpler to maintain because they have fewer parts, about 15,000 as compared to 30,000 in an ICE vehicle. In fact, the drive train of an ICE vehicle has 2000–2500 parts and that of an EV has only eighteen to twenty.[16]

Ride-sharing services such as Uber, and ownership-sharing models such as ZipCar and Turo, are all helping to improve utilization rates. However, as we'll show, the current model of ride-sharing is unlikely to account for a significant enough jump in utilization to dramatically change the economics of owned and human-driven vehicles.

Our projection is that ride-sharing will increase utilization from the current 5 percent to as much as 25 percent. However, we see a hard stop at 25 percent utilization, due to the inherent limits of ride-sharing drivers; each percentage point of increased utilization is equal to about 14.5 minutes of increased usage per day for each registered car. Given that at this time there are approximately one million active ride-sharing drivers in the US, even if all these cars were used 100 percent of the time, the increased utilization would amount to less than 10 percent of all automobile hours driven (it's currently at between 0.05 percent and 1.3 percent).

As a result, we don't expect a significant uptick in utilization from the current model of ride-sharing. We're also suspicious of the long-term economics of a ride-sharing business model that relies on underutilized owner vehicles, given the current cost of ownership and maintenance for ICE cars; when all costs are accounted for, Uber drivers make less than or very close to minimum wage. The EV will lessen this burden on drivers and enhance the economics of owning a rideshare vehicle, but, again, even if this doubles, the net effect will still be an incremental change in the overall number of vehicles due to the inherent limitation of the driver over the car. The owner of a rideshare car cannot operate the vehicle more than a reasonable number of hours during the day. Even full time Uber drivers typically drive for 35 hours a week, resulting in a car that is still underutilized at least 75 percent of the time.

Without a significant reduction in ownership costs, we do not see ride-sharing through privately owned cars—by individuals—as a viable long-term business model for ICE vehicles. It remains to be seen if this could be altered significantly through the lower overall maintenance costs of an EVs, but we suspect that would again be an incremental change.

One of the greatest factors that will cause EV sales to ramp as quickly as we are projecting for 2026 to 2034 (Figure 5.3) is the anticipated drop in the cost per kilowatt hour for batteries. The cost of an EV is intimately linked to its battery, with about a third of a vehicle's cost being attributed to the cost of the batteries[17]. For example, we can extrapolate the cost of a Tesla Model 3 by calculating the cost of the batteries, and then the total vehicle cost as a multiple of battery cost—which is just over 3x if batteries make up one third of the cost.

Vehicle Cost = Dollar Cost per Kilowatt hour x Total Vehicle Kilowatt hours x 3

Since this formula works based on the ratio of battery cost to overall cost today, we expect that it will have to change as battery costs drop and the remaining component costs do not. However, we can still project costs

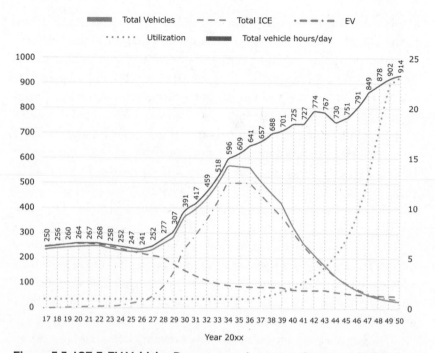

Figure 5.3: ICE & EV Vehicles Decrease as Autonomy Increases Utilization

The long-term trend towards increased hourly automobile usage. Through the early and mid 2020s we expect to see little change in the overall number of vehicles on the road. In large part that is due to a swapping of existing ICE vehicles with EVs during that same period. However, this will be followed by a steady projected decrease in ICE vehicles and a concurrent rise in EVs, with the number of EVs on the road surpassing the number of ICEVs by 2030. We project that EVs will then rise steadily and peak at just over 500 million EVs in 2034. A plateau for EVs and total vehicles is then expected to last for the following two years. This is the result of a sudden spike in utilization starting in 2034.

out in today's dollars, based on a model in which battery costs decline even though components costs may remain static.

Without this increase in component costs, a lower boundary for total vehicle cost is shown in the dashed line in Figure 5.4. There is an argument that could be made for total costs of a low-end EV, following this lower total cost trajectory, due to the ability of manufacturers to better control the component costs and thereby provide greater incentive to spur the appeal of EVs in the short term.

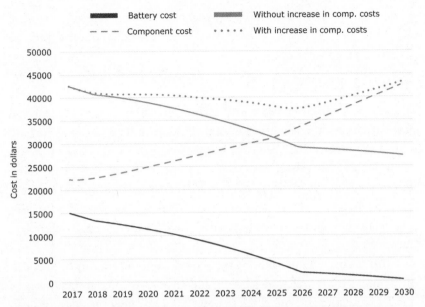

Figure 5.4: Projected Decrease in Battery Costs for a 60-kWh Battery Pack Along with the Anticipated Increase in Component Costs

The projected decrease in battery costs for a 60-kWh battery pack, along with the anticipated increase in component costs through 2030. The increase in component costs is anticipated due to both inflationary and demand increases in materials of 3 percent year over year. This yields a total cost that remains relatively stable (the double top line).

We should note that one of the unknowable variables in projecting battery costs is that of commodities, such as lithium and graphite, which make up approximately half of the cost of an EV battery. These costs can be impacted dramatically by geopolitical tensions, conflicts, and supply chain challenges over which manufacturers have little control but ample potential for significant impact on higher costs. Lithium mining also raises environmental and social concerns, which can both impact its economics and acceptance.

Closing the Gap

In the final analysis, it seems clear that the impact of EVs will be significant and disruptive from the period starting in 2025 through 2050. We call this period the Transition Gap and it represents the whole-scale turnover from ICEVs to EVs. We project three periods of distinct disruption during the Transition Gap.

The Handoff

The Handoff will take place from 2022 through 2029. During the Handoff it will become increasingly apparent that EVs are not only gaining, but will eventually replace ICE Vehicles. In the early part of the Handoff, traditional legacy ICE Vehicle manufacturers will need to already be prepared to compete directly in the EV market. No industry of the industrial era has ever faced a test on this scale: a well-established product used this broadly, requiring this level of consumer investment, experiencing a complete turnover.

This means not only altering the product, but the entirety of the business model, for car sales, ownership, and disposition. Today that business model is segmented into three distinct markets; new car sales, dealers, automotive repair shops, and used car resale. The only significant change in that model over the life of ICE vehicles has been the introduction of certified pre-owned (CPO) cars. One of the greatest challenges for traditional ICE Vehicle manufacturers will be reengineering this business model into a MaaS model. Although the utilization rate for all vehicles does not begin to increase until 2036—well after the Handoff—the initial groundwork for a MaaS model will be the use of automobiles as a service; where the owner will pay an agreed-upon price to the manufacturer for the use of the automobile, its maintenance, and its disposition.

 Not having a solid foundation for a MaaS business strategy will have the same effect on traditional automobile manufacturers as digital photography had on standalone camera manufacturers.

This radically alters the current infrastructure of dealers as well as the used car market. Reengineering the product will be a relatively simple exercise when compared to reengineering the overall marketplace. While ICE Vehicle manufacturers have committed to EVs—for example

Goldman Sachs has projected that half of all global new car sales will be EVs by 2030[18]—not having a solid foundation for a MaaS business strategy will have the same effect on traditional automobile manufacturers as digital photography had on standalone camera manufacturers.

Although the camera industry experienced a rapid spike in demand and sales from the early 2000s through 2011, it then fell precipitously as the smartphone evolved. Today the consumer stand-alone camera market is all but dead outside of professional photographers. Unlike companies such as Samsung, which had the ability to benefit from smartphone sales while they simultaneously participated in the decimation of their standalone digital camera market, automobile manufacturers do not have a similar option.

The Plateau

The second period of disruption, the plateau, will last from 2030-2036. During this time those manufacturers that are not prepared to first move to a life-cycle ownership model, and then a full MaaS model, will start to face monumental hurdles as EVs catch up with and eventually overtake ICE Vehicles. These laggards of the industrial era vehicle manufacturing industry will not survive much beyond 2036-2039, when MaaS utilization trends begin to accelerate rapidly and enter the final period of disruption, during which the EV/AV model has proven its economic and social acceptance and benefits. Not coincidentally, California and the US government both have mandates in place that target 2035 as a critical year for ICE. In the case of California the mandate ends the sale of ICE vehicles[19]. An executive order signed by US president Joe Biden mandates that 50 percent of all vehicles sold US by 2030 have zero emissions and that all of the government's 380,000 vehicles produce zero emissions by 2035.[20]

The Take Off

The third period of disruption, the Take Off, starts after 2036 and lasts until 2050. During this time frame, new sales of ICE vehicles come to a halt. By 2050 the number of ICE vehicles on the road will have already dropped at a precipitous rate to nearly 5 percent of the vehicles on the road in 2023, and insurance carriers will make covering human-driven automobiles prohibitively expensive. Something else will also begin to occur that takes most people by surprise when they first see it. The total number of vehicles will drop dramatically while the total number of hours driven increases almost as rapidly, due to the increase in the utilization of AVs.

 By 2050 the number of ICE vehicles on the road will have already dropped at a precipitous rate to nearly 5 percent of the vehicles on the road in 2023.

A Wildly Distributed Future

Something else worth considering in the context of this radical shift to EV/AV vehicles is ownership. This is especially critical to understand in the context of delivering MaaS on a global scale, to support 10 billion people.

As the MaaS model evolves, so will some of the most basic tenets of ownership through the use of technologies such as blockchain (see more about blockchain in Chapter 6 on identity), which provide for an immutable record of ownership as well as the elimination of the many layers of administration involved in traditional buy/sell business models and bank financing—most of which are not even an option in many developing parts of the world. Let's use ridesharing as an example.

Today Uber relies on owners of cars to provide ride-sharing services to clients. What makes this model work is the idle capacity of owned automobiles, which we've already talked about. That's an enormous waste of value and resources, which is why Uber's model is a great way to leverage latent assets and people, while addressing a fundamental need of a modern urban ecosystem—the need for frictionless mobility.

When most people try to project the AV model into the future, the natural inclination is to imagine fleets of robotic cars. This is the model that companies such as Zoox have in mind for their fully-autonomous vehicles. Just as you'd summon an Uber or Lyft, you can arrange for a Zoox AV to show up (without a human driver) and transport you to your destination. That may be a valid model for the near term—the handoff and the plateau—but in our view, it perpetuates the industrial-era business model based on economies of scale. It would certainly be more efficient from the standpoint of resource utilization, since the cars wouldn't be sitting in a garage or a parking lot 95 percent of the time. However, there's still a corporation with employees, management and executives, offices, and equipment to factor into the equation. Additionally, the competitive landscape would be limited since enormous initial investment would be required to build large organizations of this sort. We'd like to propose something that's a game changer.

 What if autonomous cars were non-human legal entities in which many people had a stake, not unlike a public corporation, which has many owners?

What if autonomous cars were non-human legal entities in which many people had a stake, not unlike a public corporation, which has many owners? We'd ask that you stop here and think about all the reasons why that wouldn't work. We're going to guess that your list may include: individual AVs would be much more expensive assets since they could not achieve economies of scale; AVs could not maintain themselves; if riders were unhappy there's nobody to complain to; what happens to an AV when it's no longer viable; who's to blame if the AV is involved in an accident?

All good points. However, technologies such as blockchain can address every one of these concerns by allowing cars to collaborate with each other and to form coalitions with buying power, clout, and economies of scale; blockchain also enables transactions for self-service to be conducted with other human or non-human entities, such as an automotive repair shop; the AV can even sell itself off for parts and distribute the proceeds to its owners when demand for its services dips below a profitable threshold; and, just like a human, it can purchase insurance coverage and pay for damages or liabilities.

Depending on how profitable any particular AV is, you could move your stake from car to car based on which ones perform best. Pools of cars could join forces to create their own AV corporations and build in redundancy to increase profit margins and return to owners, they could even build a brand image for themselves. And, yes, digital workers could be handling almost all of the administrative aspects of this business.

While the notion of cars that own themselves may seem far-fetched, there is no practical reason why this cannot be done. The technologies needed to do this exist today. Refinement of what we've described will no doubt be needed but there is nothing extraordinary about what we're describing. In fact, in developing parts of the world, where individual ownership is economically inconceivable, or where the overhead needed to introduce an industrial-era model is economically unattractive, this may be the only economically viable model to supply the transportation needed to build a thriving global economy.

A Radical New Vision of Transportation

While we have no doubt as to the long-term trajectory of MaaS, we are just as sure of the disruptive threat it will pose to a century-old industry that is well-entrenched and ensconced in an employment, business, and cultural model that may seem immovable. However, the economic factors that will drive the changes we have outlined will be impossible to ignore.

- Insurance companies will need to adjust models for insuring human-driven vehicles, making car ownership a financially infeasible model for individual owners.

- The automobile will be transformed from a form of transportation from point A to point B into a form of entertainment and socialization, which will create a new platform for the delivery of content and media.

- Autos will function as vehicles for socialization in which people connect and gather. Some will be mobile conference and meeting rooms, others mobile restaurants. Commute time will cease to exist and along with it untold hours of lost productivity.

- The AV will finally allow de-urbanization and decongestion of urban city centers, which are today littered with automobiles that occupy valuable land. For example, in the typical large city 30 percent of the land area is dedicated to parking.

- According to the National Safety Council the cost of motor-vehicle deaths, injuries, and property damage in 2016 was $473 billion.[21]

- The evolution of EVs and AVs will vary significantly from geography to geography and country to country. While commercial TaaS infrastructure will likely develop quickly in developed countries, such as the USA, individual ownership-based MaaS is likely to take longer. The inverse is true of developing countries, such as India, which will have a higher economic incentive and regulatory latitude to move to MaaS.

- We expect that the employment disruption of MaaS within developed countries that rely heavily on both the manufacture of ICE vehicles and of transportation will lead to workforce restructuring and significantly fewer jobs in related industries.

- And lastly, let's not forget the impact of vehicles on global pollution and climate change.

As a result of these irreversible economic factors and new market opportunities, we expect a global shift to MaaS during the next thirty years with a timeline approximately as follows:

MOBILITY AS A SERVICE TIMELINE

2021–2030: EV & AV Revolution & Acceptance

During this decade the economics of EVs, the acceleration of AI and its use in AVs, the large-scale deployment of AVs in ride-sharing and commercial transport, and the emergence of irrefutable evidence as to the safety of AVs will start to make the insurability of human-driven vehicles more expensive and to diminish their attractiveness to even their most diehard proponents. At the same time the demand for transportation in developing countries will exceed the ability to supply traditional transportation through individually owned vehicles. EV's battery technology will dramatically improve the business model for EVs and their affordability. Most notably, EVs on the road will exceed ICEVs for the first time.

We also see this as the most critical decade for the evolution of MaaS within developing countries, which will need to decide on how to scale their transportation infrastructure to accommodate the needs of a burgeoning workforce, which will be growing substantially in age as well. With changing demographics, mobility will be critical to keeping an aging population an active part of the workforce and the economy.

This period will also create the final tipping point for acceptance that the safety of an AV far surpasses that of a human-driven vehicle. That will finally start to detach us from the cultural legacy of the automobile. For example, it's easy to imagine scenarios where parents will be glad to have their child in an AV rather than a car driven by a family member, a friend, a third party transportation service, or, in the extreme by another sixteen- or seventeen-year-old child! Since that will define the cultural framework for this generation of children who have never known a human-driven experience, it is entirely expected that they will see no need to become drivers. In fact, they will come up with myriad reasons why not to.

2031–2040: Mass Adoption of MaaS & Transportation Innovation

This decade will see the rapid exponential rise in MaaS and the beginning of its mass adoption. With EVs exceeding ICEVs in affordability, and the cultural attachment being broken, the tipping point for ICE and human-drivers will have been reached, as will an acceleration in the manufacture and use of EVs and AVs. However, while at the start of this period the number of vehicles on the road will increase, it will soon peak and then start to decline—slowly at first, but then accelerating towards the end of this period. In many ways we regard this period as the most critical global shift in establishing the final move from individually-owned vehicles to MaaS.

During this period, it's likely that we'll see a boom in ride sharing services as autonomous vehicles become more predominant on the roads and more people opt for a shared experience, rather than owning their own car. We can also expect to see improved transportation models for disabled individuals, as well as further advances in EVs and battery technology. This is also when we may begin to see the deployment of low-cost urban air mobility systems such as drones, that use multiple VTOL (vertical take off and landing) aircrafts to transport people from place to place.

2041–2050: Integration & Optimization of MaaS

This decade will be focused on the further integration and optimization of MaaS, as it becomes commonplace throughout our cities and towns. This is when we may see a shift from ride sharing to shared ownership models, where people can own a fraction of a vehicle that can be used by multiple individuals or businesses based on time frames or needs. We will also expect to see the emergence of new mobility options such as autonomous watercrafts and autonomous airborne vehicles joining land vehicles in the transportation mix. It is likely that most trips in this period will be taken using autonomous vehicles and various forms of public transit, with fewer privately-owned cars on the roads. The safety levels for AVs will reach unprecedented new heights, with the potential to exceed even levels of human-driven vehicles.

2051–2060: Ubiquitous MaaS Dominates Globally

The decade of 2050 to 2059 will be a period of transition as MaaS becomes ubiquitous and largely accepted as the default form of transportation. We can expect to see further advances in battery technology and the emergence of self-charging or renewable-energy-powered EVs, allowing for longer trips at lower costs. Additionally, we may see an increase in subscription-based models that allow people to access a variety of transportation options on demand. This could lead to more efficient use of resources and an increased ability for people to access different parts of their city or country, without worrying about high costs associated with travel. The safety levels for AVs should reach near perfection by this time, making them a reliable and safe form of transportation for all.

2061–2070: Collaborating AVs Deliver Mobile Meeting Spaces

By the decade of 2061-2070, the role of MaaS now centers on delivering mobile platforms for socialization, mobile restaurants, and business-focused meeting spaces. Commute time will cease to exist and along with it untold hours of lost productivity. Ownership shifts from individuals and commercial entities to Decentralized Autonomous Organizations (DAOs) that allow cars to collaborate with each other and to form coalitions with buying power, clout, and economies of scale. Blockchain also enables transactions for self-service to be conducted with other human or non-human entities, such as an automotive repair shop; the AV can even sell itself off for parts and distribute the proceeds to its owners when demand for its services dips below a profitable threshold; and, just like a human, it can purchase insurance coverage and pay for damages or liabilities.

CHAPTER 6

The Future of Identity:
Your Digital Self

*"The future of identity is about where humanity meets technology—
to create new experiences, new opportunities, and new values."*

—ANDREW NG

> **GIGATREND—THE DIGITAL SELF:**
> **The creation of your most valuable and inalienable**
> **asset—your digital self.**

From immersive and augmented reality to what we will call "hyper-dematerialization" in Chapter 7, one of the few constants is that identity will be central to defining our digital future. The evolution of identity, and the Gigatrend of a digital self, offers one of the most critical vectors for understanding the path forward, and what will undoubtedly be a cornerstone for how we create new sources of value.

 Today, our digital identities are liabilities, not assets.

Today, our digital identities are liabilities, not assets. The burden is on us to secure them, however we can, and to control how they are used. Yet we don't own them, and when they are compromised, whether stolen or otherwise misappropriated, it's we as individuals who suffer the consequences. This paradox is a holdover from our digital past, one that—as we'll discuss later in this chapter—is a critical design flaw from the inception of the Internet.

Yet that same flaw also underscores one of the most promising opportunities for our digital future, one already unfolding and actionable today—namely, the shift from centrally-controlled digital identities to a decentralized model in a "trustless" digital world, where the threat of identity theft is obsolete. In this new digital world, identity is no longer a liability but rather our most valuable asset—one that every human will have irrefutable rights to and pass on to his or her heirs. To understand that, let's begin by examining where are today and how we got here.

The Identity Flaw

Over the nearly thirty-year history of the commercial Web, we've seen a tectonic shift in the role of digital marketers and their relationship with consumers. These are the firms known collectivity as "FAANG"—Facebook, Amazon, Apple, Netflix, and Google, whom we'll reference throughout this chapter simply as "Web2"—a label that's less about these specific companies than the business practices they have in common.

Underlying the evolution from "Web1" (the first phase of the commercial Internet) to today's "Web2" has been a subtle but steady shift from empowering consumers, with expanding choices of access to products and information, to the monetization of their digital identities by Web2 companies that have evolved from content providers into data aggregators.

Of course, firms such as Amazon and Apple would argue that data aggregation is merely a means to connect consumers with better products, while Facebook and Google would say that's how they deliver more meaningful content. That may have been true of early Web2 data aggregation practices. However, the data being aggregated today isn't just the self-disclosed personal data that we voluntarily shared in Web1, in the hopes of a more personalized experience. It also includes the involuntary capture of everything we do, either on the Internet or through our digital behaviors.

Our digital self is the totality of everything we do online and much of what we do offline. It's our identity in the digital age—a frighteningly comprehensive "Digital Clone" of each of us.

Our digital self is the totality of everything we do online and much of what we do offline. It's our identity in the digital age—a frighteningly comprehensive "Digital Clone" of each of us. Yet despite well-intentioned policies and laws, such as the EU's General Data Protection Regulation (GDPR) and California's California Consumer Privacy Act (CCPA), there are today few meaningful protections in place to safeguard your digital self. Your very identity is now a currency you trade for questionable value; such as access to "free" platforms for user-generated content.

You could argue that this is nothing new. Consumers have allowed their attention to be monetized in exchange for content since advertising-driven media first emerged. The now oft-quoted (sometimes misquoted) adage "If you are not paying for it, you're not the customer; you're the product being sold" was first coined in the early 1970s, and was about TV advertising, not the as-yet-uninvented Internet.

So, what's different fifty years later? It's the fact that this exchange is now increasingly involuntary. The notion of "opting-out" is moot when the model transcends content consumption, and is instead a matter of every action we take being expropriated and monetized—not just through the digital interfaces we purposefully engage with, but through the capture of our every behavior in what will soon become an inescapable web of sensors, cameras, personal digital assistants, automobiles, wearables, and the many other devices online and offline.

Not for Us, But from Us: Our Digital Self in the Era of Surveillance Capitalism

In her book, *The Age of Surveillance Capitalism*,[1] Shoshana Zuboff summed up the state of Web2, "Surveillance capitalism operates through unprecedented asymmetries in knowledge and the power that accrues to knowledge. [They] know everything about us, whereas their operations are designed to be unknowable to us." The creepy reputation which "Big Tech" now suffers from has far less to do with more obvious actors, such as the now-defunct Cambridge Analytica, which was instrumental in shaping political sentiment during the 2016 US Presidential election. Instead, it's the much greater risk of omnipresent sensors owned and controlled by gigascale aggregators, such as Alphabet (Google) and Meta (Facebook), now among the largest and most powerful companies in history.

The Web2 titans who are at, or approaching, trillion-dollar valuations by mining your digital identity are the same companies who control the exponentially expanding array of sensors capturing data about you. The surveillance at hand may be involuntary, but we have welcomed it into our lives with open arms, in exchange for the convenience it offers. We've all had that moment when we start to notice digital ads linked to a private conversation we had, or some other action far less explicit than a Google search.

The surveillance at hand may be involuntary, but we have welcomed it into our lives with open arms, in exchange for the convenience it offers.

However, the end game for the data aggregators isn't focused on advertisements. The greater opportunity is to influence and persuade behavior through the understanding and manipulation of our digital self. This may sound sinister and conspiratorial, and indeed that notion is not entirely off base when viewed through the lens of efforts such as DARPA's LifeLog project. Although shut down on February 3, 2004—an ironic date as Facebook was launched the following day—the aim of LifeLog was to comprehensively capture every aspect of an individual's life in order to identify (in the words of DARPA) *'preferences, plans, goals, and other markers of intentionality.*"[2]

While short-lived during the Web1 era, LifeLog remains one of the most notable archetypes of "lifelogging," which is now both a commonly accepted term of art as well as the dominant business model of Web2. What was impractical in 2004, given challenges in passively capturing the huge volumes of data required, is now already well within reach of

Big Tech. For the last decade Google in particular has expanded its IP portfolio in many dimensions which have little to do with its cornerstone business of targeted display and search ads

One example is its 2018 patent for "Baby monitoring with intelligent audio cueing based on an analyzed video stream,"[3] one of the hundreds that Google/Alphabet has obtained over the last decade which are intended to expand the barter between consumer convenience and deep-learning behavioral tracking. Do you want Google monitoring your baby? Well, maybe. Would you have traded your privacy, and that of an occasionally sleeping baby, for a sense of reassurance of your child's safety? Any parent who says no to that is likely lying, and that's why the Web2 business model is so insidious and lucrative.

Faustian Bargain or not, we—at least the majority of us—will readily trade something as relatively abstract as data privacy for the more immediate benefits of safety, convenience, and the occasional ego post in exchange for a handful of likes, thumbs-up, and followers.

 Faustian Bargain or not, we—at least the majority of us—will readily trade something as relatively abstract as data privacy for the more immediate benefits of safety, convenience, and the occasional ego post in exchange for a handful of likes, thumbs-up, and followers.

However, Google is not in the child-safety business—it merely offers a data collection tool by another name for a very different purpose. The "markers of intentionality" (in DARPA's vernacular) are today found in the Web2 era's shift from persuading behavior through targeted information—where the decision to act still belongs to the individual—to compelling behavior through data-driven automation, at a quickening rate too fast for us to even notice. At that point, the question pivots from "Why did I see that?" to "Why did I do that?"— that is, if we question it at all.

The business model of Web2 is ultimately built around behavior. It goes like this: first, facilitate the action taken by the consumer, rather than one merely suggested through an ad or presentation of information;

second, monetize that action through centralized control of their personal data, collected through prior behavioral tracking; third, repeat until you know the consumer's behaviors better than they know it themselves. But isn't that the objective of all forms of advertising? What's different with this model is that it happens without our explicit consent or knowledge, using our private personal data, which rightfully belongs to us, and in many cases contains details at a level we might never intentionally share with advertisers, or, for that matter, even close friends.

The reality is that, sinister or not, this sort of behavioral tracking is already underway, and again it is far beyond what ads you see. One of the emerging uses of the Internet of Things—the pervasive network of sensors and devices connected to the Internet—is the concept of ambient intelligence, which, in simple terms, is an environment that's aware of and responsive to those within it. This means systems are able to detect the needs of users without being asked and can provide them with various services through a combination of neural networks, big data, IoT (the Internet of Things), wearables, and the many device interfaces we all interact with every day, For example, your home heating system automatically regulating its temperature based on your presence in certain rooms, or your car adjusting audio, lighting, and ride comfort based on your biometrics, or your smartwatch anticipating your arrival to unlock doors as you approach.

If you are guided to an optimal outcome, or if workers are guided to the next best action, does it matter if data is captured more invasively than we might otherwise desire? Consider that it doesn't end there. What we're describing is not limited to your smartwatch, your Alexa, or your intelligent baby monitor. We are at an inflection point, where soon nearly every appliance or device in your life, every "thing" in the Internet of Things will also be a sensor. And most of these sensors will be far beyond your ability to detect, much less deter their data-gathering functions.

We are entering what futurist Peter Diamandis has labeled the trillion-sensor economy,[4] driven by the convergence of terrestrial, atmospheric, and space-based sensors, combined with machine learning and data networks—each listening, recording, watching, or otherwise tracking your every move, and the details of which, if aggregated, define you and your digital self with unprecedented accuracy and detail.

However, the challenge we face has far less to do with the sensitivity of the data which defines our identity, but with a less apparent issue, which is perhaps the only issue: who owns this data?

Under the Web2 model, our identity belongs to us only in principle. We each may have a right to the data which defines our digital self, and we may in theory have the right to revoke others' access to it, but we only benefit from it when we engage with the third parties where it is stored. While our digital self is the most valuable currency of the digital age, we ourselves cannot monetize it in any meaningful way. What's worse, while it's an invaluable asset for those who control it, for us individually it's a liability. When our identity is compromised, we individually pay the price. We each bear the burden when it's lost, through identity theft, imperson-ation, or other means.

 While our digital self is the most valuable currency of the digital age, we ourselves cannot monetize it in any meaningful way.

Web1	Web2	Web3
Supply Aggregators (Amazon, eBay)	Data Aggregators (Facebook, Google)	Decentralized Networks (Helium, Ethereum)
"Read-only Web"	**"Read/Write Web"**	**"Read-Write-Own"**
Valued-added via supply and demand aggregation by centrally controlled sites and platforms Focus is "one-to-many" audiences between publishers and retailers	Value-added via platforms for user generated content Focus is facilitating user interactions for the purpose of capturing & monetizing their data	Value-added via enabling ownership by of content and data by its creators Focus is decentralized networks enabling voluntary sharing of digital assets without compromising the identity or security of network participants
One word: **Commerce**	One word: **Behavior**	One word: **Ownership**

Figure 6.1: The Transition from Web1–Web3: How the Business of Model of the Web has Evolved Over the Last 30 Years

Over the last thirty years the Web has evolved from static website to user-generated content and social interaction, and is now entering the era of decentralized, trustless, and immersive spaces powered by blockchain and other emerging Web3 technologies.

Your own identity could indeed have value to you, and grow as an asset that you could leverage. That's especially critical when you consider that our behaviors tell much more about us than even we can typically comprehend, since we all have biases that create a highly subjective view of our behavior. For example, you may think that you eat healthy until you keep a diary and tally up the details of your diet.

The point here is that there is enormous value in your digital self that goes far beyond the obvious. The risk in any third party owning your digital self is that the knowledge it provides can easily be directed to cause you to take a particular action, not of your own choosing, but through the motivations of the highest bidder. We believe there's another way.

We've lived through two phases of the Web. Web1 was defined by publishing content online and the first wave of dot.com pioneers, such as Amazon and eBay, offering consumers access to a selection of products too immense and diverse to fit within a brick-and-mortar store. Their business models were based on supply and demand aggregation. The second phase is Web2, and, as we have discussed so far, it's focused on the capture and aggregation of our data. What's emerging now is Web3, also known as the Web of ownership.[5]

Web1 was described as the read-only Web, owing to the idea that we as consumers browsed pages published by website owners, but we could not change the content they provided. Web2 is called the "Read-Write Web" and it's based on the emergence of platforms such as Facebook, where we were given space to generate our own content—even though both the information and the data we left behind were the property of the platform owners. Web3 is the "Read-Write-Own Web." It's based on the notion that we as consumers own the content we generate, as well as the data. In the era of Web3, we own our digital identities, not the data aggregators of Web2.

 The promise of Web3 is a world in which we can leverage, for our gain, the data defining our identity and our digital self by shifting the point of leverage from the monetization of our behavior, to delivering better user experiences under our own control.

The promise of Web3 is a world in which we can leverage, for our gain, the data defining our identity and our digital self by shifting the point of leverage from the monetization of our behavior, to delivering better user experiences under our own control. Rather than manipulating our behavior without our knowledge or consent, the promise of Web3 is that it enables these benefits through anonymized interactions which do not require surrendering control or ownership of our personal data.

Our Data, for Our Benefit Not Theirs

Underlying the promise of Web3, is the transformation of our digital identities into personal assets which we own. This represents both a significant economic opportunity and a new platform for ushering in business transformation and innovation. A McKinsey Global Institute study, *Digital Identification: A Key to Inclusive Growth*, projected that the adoption of trusted, consumer-owned digital identity would add 6 percent growth to an emerging economy's GDP and 3 percent to an advanced economy's GDP by 2030.[6]

Today Web2 still dominates the Internet. Creating and maintaining a digital identity at the moment is centered on establishing a persistent account in a centralized repository with the same data aggregators focused on monetizing that data. Although there are specific identity services, such as Amazon's Namespaces, they are centralized, hackable, and not owned by you. Any identity created and stored in these systems can be taken away by corporate decisions, government pressure, a malicious actor, or just by accident. In the US alone, it's estimated that about a third of all citizens are victimized by identity-based crimes, costing over $50 billion annually and growing over 300 percent in the last five years,[7] according to Proofpoint Global Cybersecurity Awareness Survey.[8]

One of the most famous data breaches was the US Office of Personnel Management (OPM) in 2014, that leaked the identity data of over 22 million Americans, including sensitive information such as Social Security numbers, addresses, and employment history.[9],[10] Even the Web2 tech giants have not been immune to this type of widespread security breach. For example, LinkedIn[11],[12] suffered a breach where hackers stole the usernames and passwords of nearly 167 million users that were later confirmed to have been sold on the dark Web. In 2018, Facebook[13] revealed a breach that compromised the personal information of millions of users and allowed hackers to take over their accounts. In 2019, Google disclosed a security bug in its Google+ social network that exposed the private data of up to 52.5 million users and ultimately led Google to shut down Google+ for consumers.[14]

The threat of identity theft is the reality of today's centralized model, and it's not sustainable for our increasingly digital future. Imagine if starting your car, or receiving medication, or any other life-affecting, time-critical action was dependent on authenticating with one of these centrally controlled services. In fact, it's not difficult to imagine at all. Today these functions require a form of identity that we do not truly own. When obtaining certain medications, you're required to provide proof of identity, such as an insurance card, a driver's license, or another form government-issued ID. The same is true for opening a bank account or enrolling in government services. Haven't made the lease payment on your vehicle this month? Ford has a patent on a car that will return itself to the dealership—yes, it's repossessing itself—if you don't pay up.[15]

While Ford's self-repossessing car may be a first world problem, more than one billion individuals across the globe cannot complete basic life tasks since they lack the proof of identity necessary to obtain a government issued ID. What's needed is a decentralized, sovereign identity model, which operates not as a third-party service or a closed environment, but like the Internet itself.

Identity Beyond Web2

Historically digital identity has always been dependent on the service provider, as with the Amazon, Google, and Facebook examples. The service provider determines the digital identity and can decide what to do with it, and whom it allows on its platform. Think of Donald Trump being de-platformed from Twitter on January 8th of 2021.[16] Sovereign identity turns this on its head by putting ownership of identity in the hands of the consumer. While sovereign identity may not help you avoid getting banned from a social media platform it does allow you to have a validated online identity independent of the social media platform provider.

184

The identity layer now recognized and acknowledged as missing from the Internet's architecture was for years overlooked.[17] During the first phases of the Internet, the concept of identity was limited to that of a "user" who was granted access to a website. It's a very system-centric model—the opposite of a digital self with a portable, immutable identity which could be carried from site to site. There have been various standardized approaches for the authentication of identity, such as the OAuth or Open Authorization protocol which provides secure access between cooperating systems, but they still use a model where your identity is issued and controlled by a central authority. The same goes for using Facebook or LinkedIn credentials to log-in to another system.

Defining the core elements of identity in the digital world has been a matter of both aspiration and debate for well over a decade. One of the most notable contributions is the work of the late computer scientist and identity management icon Kim Cameron. In 2007, Cameron, then the Architect of Identity at Microsoft, proposed the Laws of Identity[18] as a set of immutable principles to ensure that the user controlled and owned their identity—what we are calling the digital self.

Kim Cameron's Laws of Identity[19]

LAW 1: *User Control and Consent:* Technical identity systems must only reveal information identifying a user with the user's consent.

LAW 2: *Minimum Disclosure for a Constrained Use:* The solution which discloses the least amount of identifying information and best limits its use is the most stable long term solution.

LAW 3: *Justifiable Parties:* Digital identity systems must be designed so the disclosure of identifying information is limited to parties having a necessary and justifiable place in a given identity relationship.

LAW 4: *Directed Identity:* A universal identity system must support both "omnidirectional" identifiers [recognizable across different systems] for use by public entities, and "unidirectional" identifiers [limited to a single system or context] for use by private entities, thus facilitating discovery while preventing unnecessary release of correlation handles [systems or entities able to recognize relationships].

LAW 5: *Pluralism of Operators and Technologies:* A universal identity system must channel and enable the inter-working of multiple identity technologies run by multiple identity providers.

LAW 6: *Human Integration:* The universal identity metasystem must define the human user to be a component of the distributed system integrated through unambiguous human-machine communication mechanisms offering protection against identity attacks.

LAW 7: *Consistent Experience Across Contexts:* The unifying identity metasystem must guarantee its users a simple, consistent experience while enabling the separation of contexts through multiple operators and technologies.

Like a digital Code of Hammurabi, these laws provide the framework for both the democratization of identity and a digital Rule of Law. Although it has taken time for these laws to materialize into something capable of overcoming Web2's ability to centrally control identity, what they have done is give rise to decentralized identity systems which use distributed ledgers (something we'll talk about more later in this chapter) to store user identity data. With this model, users can share only the data that they wish to share and retain the power to revoke access at any time. This notion has given rise to a movement known as self-sovereign identity, which today shows the greatest promise of enabling Cameron's seven laws and the idea of a true digital self.

Self-Sovereign Identity: Ownership of Your Digital Self

The notion of self and the irrefutability of our individual existence has long been a favorite topic of philosophers. However, Descartes wrote his famous posit, "Cogito ergo sum" ("I think, therefore I am") in 1637, making it relatively recent compared to the entire arc of human existence. Still, identity in the physical world, however nuanced in the mind of the philosopher, is nonetheless palpable. We exist because we know we've written this, and you exist because you know you're reading it.

That you are a person is unambiguous, but *which* person you are requires proof.

Your intrinsic identity is yours to claim. It is who you see when you look in the mirror, your beliefs, your values, your associations, and your behaviors. It's your extrinsic identity, that which proves to the rest of the world who you are, that's out of your control.

Your intrinsic identity is yours to claim. It is who you see when you look in the mirror, your beliefs, your values, your associations, and your behaviors. It's your extrinsic identity, that which proves to the rest of the world who you are, that's out of your control.

Extrinsic identity has required the cooperation of a third party, and for the better part of the last century, typically only governments have had the authority to grant the legitimacy of your immutable extrinsic identity, through a passport, a birth certificate, or a driver's license. In other words, you are who they say you are.

In today's digital world, your digital identity is largely intrinsic. One of the most oft-repeated mantras from the early days of the commercial Internet came from a famous 1993 cartoon in the *New Yorker Magazine* which showed a dog at a keyboard and read, "On the Internet, nobody knows you're a dog." That remains true today. In the digital world, you are free to be whoever you want to be.

In the digital world, you are free to be whoever you want to be.

There are few widely available means to demonstrate extrinsic identity digitally, so we find ourselves still relying on providing digitized photos of government-issued IDs to perform such basic functions as conducting a financial transaction. In fact, if you intend to become an Amazon seller you have to conduct a video interview in which, among other things, you physically hold up your government-issued identification and bend it to show that it has the properties of a physical ID.

Let's distinguish between the terms self-sovereign identity and digital self. Although the two may sound interchangeable, the notion of *self-sovereign identity* refers to the ability to irrefutably own your digital self, and to make your digital self as legitimate as your government-issued identity is today. While your digital self is the collection of all your digital, and real world, behaviors, and interactions, your self-sovereign identity makes it yours alone.

Self-sovereign identity also enables your digital identity to be universally accessible. In the same way that your government-issued passport is portable and universal, thanks to globally adopted standards, your digital identity should be as well. Yet, it must also be free of online vulnerabilities; in other words, it cannot be stolen, faked, or spoofed. Lastly, and most notably, it must not be reliant on a single government, corporation, or centralized authority.

A simple analogy would be to think of how today your medical records are the equivalent of your medical digital self. They are likely scattered about in the files and databases of dozens of providers and insurers. And each of these holders of your records has their own procedure for granting you access to them. However, without being able to demonstrate that you are the person to whom those records belong, using government-issued identification—the equivalent of self-sovereign identity—you would not be able to access, transfer, or otherwise use those records. And in the case of healthcare, you wouldn't have immediate access to that data.

 The right to our identity is one of the most basic human rights. However, today our identity remains largely under the control of third parties, whether governments or commercial enterprises—and, according to the World Bank, even that isn't afforded to one billion people.

The right to our identity is one of the most basic human rights. However, today our identity remains largely under the control of third parties, whether governments or commercial enterprises—and, according to the World Bank, even that isn't afforded to one billion people.[20]

When we have control over our own identity, we ourselves determine who we are, we can exercise property rights, we can accumulate wealth, and we can pass it on to our children. Without it we are anonymous, impoverished, and have little to no chance of improving our situation. This is the notion of self-sovereignty identity, the ability to own who we are, as well as to control what we share about ourselves, to be the beneficiaries of our identity, and to protect our privacy and the security of our personal data.

Origins of Self-Sovereign Identity

The concept of "self-sovereign identity" was first proposed in 2013 by self-proclaimed digital identity strategist, Christopher Allen. He defined self-sovereignty as "the ability to control and manage one's own digital identity characterized by four core attributes: transparency, privacy, security, and self-ownership."[21] He also proposed a road map for self-sovereign identity based on four pillars: 1) self-asserted identifiers, 2) self-asserted claims, 3) authentication, and 4) access control. Since then, instances of self-sovereign identity have evolved significantly to become a viable means for allowing people to control their own data and transactions. While still evolving, it is already used in a variety of applications, such as online banking, online voting, healthcare management, e-commerce platforms, and more.

Self-sovereign identity is not a specific system, per se, but a protocol which allows your digital identity to be enforceable in any situation, both offline and online. It also ensures that identity can neither be granted nor revoked by a single central authority. Self-sovereign identity is one of the foundational principles of Web3, premised on the notion of individual ownership.

Self-sovereign identity is also not a proprietary or standardized set of technologies, but an approach for leveraging the technology of Web3 to enable both individual ownership of your digital identity and to ensure its portability without reliance on a single, central authority. This approach is based on three technologies:

- Distributed ledger: A decentralized record of information that is stored across a multiple computers or nodes (typically but not necessarily blockchain) in an immutable write-once model that is nearly impossible to alter, hack, or fake.

- Decentralized Identifiers (DIDs): Cryptographically verifiable identifiers created and owned by individuals independent of any centralized issuer or authority, yet devoid of personally identifiable information (PII) which could otherwise be compromised via unauthorized access, acquisition, or disclosure without the owner's consent.

- Verifiable Credentials (VCs): Digital cryptographically-secure versions of paper and digital credentials (such as a token) that people can present to verifiers.

It's worth noting that self-sovereign identity isn't specifically dependent on blockchain. But it is dependent on storing data within a distributed ledger. Although all blockchains are distributed ledgers, not all distributed ledger technologies are blockchains. Still, blockchain is typically the way self-sovereign identity is implemented since it's the most mature and accessible example of distributed ledger technology.

As described by the World Economic Forum:

> In self-sovereign identity, the user has his or her identity information digitally signed by a trusted third party. When the user provides the identity information, he or she also digitally signs the information before providing it to the user of the identity information. The public keys (a form of cryptographic security) of the user and the third-party organization for verifying the digital signature are recorded in a distributed ledger, and the user of the identity information verifies the provided information using them. In this way, users can control their own identity information without relying on a specific central administrator. [22]

In the centralized model of identity (the first example in Figure 6.2), we are required to authenticate our identity with the organization which controls whatever we are trying to access (for example, logging into your email or Facebook). In either case, the organization that owns the system is the centralized authority that ultimately determines if you are who you say you are.

The centralized model is increasingly being replaced by Federated Identity models, where an identity provider (abbreviated as "IDP" in

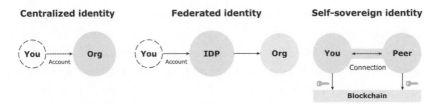

Figure 6.2: World Economic Forum's "The Three Models of Digital Identity"
Digital identity models have evolved from centralized models relying on a single entity for identity management and federated models allowing for multiple identity providers, to self-sovereign models offering individuals control over both their personal data and identity. Source: World Economic Forum

Figure 6.2) acts as the central authority standing between the individual and whatever entity or organization needs proof of their identity. Think of the practice of single sign-on—which you likely have in your work environment today—or using your Facebook or Google identity to log in to another website or application. The federated model is still centralized, although there are elements of portability. However, you still do not own your identity, nor do you control what information is shared between systems.

In contrast to both the traditional centralized and more recent federated identity models, self-sovereign identity is inherently decentralized. We as individuals hold the keys to our identity and the means to prove it. These keys (the Decentralized Identifiers or DIDs we just listed as one of the three technologies needed for self-sovereign identity) are written to a secure distributed ledger, such as a blockchain. The elements of decentralization with self-sovereign identity come from both the ability to share identity with any other party, as well as the fact that only the keys (e.g., unique identifiers) are exchanged, not sensitive personal data. Understanding this difference is critical to understanding the impact and new opportunities presented by self-sovereign identity.

The State of Self-Sovereign Identity

Although self-sovereign identity is still early in its maturity, there have been pioneering examples used to digitally validate extrinsic identity with the same legitimacy as government-issued IDs, without introducing vulnerabilities to identity theft or privacy concerns. Some of the first examples have been facilitated by governments and non-governmental organizations (NGOs) to help disadvantaged populations and other citizens to more easily take advantage of government services and other benefits. To be clear, in this regard self-sovereign identity is government sanctioned, not government-issued (where it would otherwise have equal authority to revoke an individual's means of proving their identity).

Having promoted the importance of digital identity for over two decades, the European Union (EU) has perhaps more than any other government body been at the forefront of advancing self-sovereign identity. In 2020 the EU launched an effort for self-sovereign identity to be incorporated into the European Blockchain Services Infrastructure to create a European Self-Sovereign Identity Framework, for individuals to store their own digital identities in a manner compliant with the existing EU electronic identification and trust services standard first mandated in 2014. In parallel, ID union is a cooperative effort funded by the EU to create an open, globally accessible self-sovereign identity.

Self-sovereign identity is often created and maintained through a cooperative effort between a number of participants in an ecosystem. Typically, this includes what's called the digital trust triangle of issuers, holders, and verifiers. Issuers decide which credentials will be granted, what these credentials signify, and how the data associated with the credentials will be validated. Holders may be people, companies, or other types of entities which are the owners of the identity; they ask for credentials from issuers, retain them when verifiers ask for them, and present them when the holder approves. Verifiers make requests for the credentials they want, and then use their own procedures to check the legitimacy and authenticity of those credentials.

For example, imagine attempting to access a banking website online. Giving the website your digital identity credentials, such as a username and password, is the first step in the identity verification process. Through communication with the digital identity issuer (for example, Google or Facebook), the website serves as an identity verifier, ensuring the validity of your credentials. The identity issuer then gives the verifier a token. The banking website gives you access to your account after receiving this token as identification. You, the identity holder, retain control over your digital identity throughout this process, enabling you to utilize your credentials on several platforms while still safeguarding your personal data.

 Despite how it is often perceived, the role of the blockchain isn't to hold any personally identifiable information.

As described earlier, distributed ledger technology, such as blockchain, represent one of the three pillars for enabling individual ownership of your own identity. Yet it is also important to note here that despite how it is often perceived, the role of the blockchain isn't to hold any personally identifiable information. Instead, personal data is kept only within what's called a wallet. This maybe either be a cold wallet (offline and not connected to the Internet) or a hot wallet (kept online). In either case, the only data shared is with connections you individually authorize. This removes the reliance on third-party identity services, and by leveraging the decentralized cryptographic capabilities inherent to blockchain, it allows service providers such as banks and governments, to store and manage their data decoupled from an individual's identity data. This is the benefit of decentralization, which is inherently more secure by separating sensitive personal data from the keys to access it.

So far we've discussed self-sovereign identity largely from the perspective of the individual and his or her own digital identity. However, there are benefits that can be realized at the enterprise level. Self-sovereign identity contributes to organizational risk management, through both greater data security and reduced risk of fraud, but most notably by reducing both the administrative overhead and inherent liability in storing customer data. It also enables faster onboarding of new customers or employees, by removing the effort otherwise required to independently verify an identity or employment credentials. For example, the costs of employment screening in the US exceeded $5 billion in 2022.[23] This can be significantly reduced through widespread availability of self-sovereign identity. Self-sovereign identity also offers the opportunity to empower marginalized populations that may not have access to traditional forms of identification.

Early-Stage Self-Sovereign Identity Use Cases

Supply Chains: Tracking the origin of products that are monitored on the blockchain, while instantaneously verifying parties and documents in the supply chain.

Expedited Hiring and Onboarding: Efficiently hire high-quality applicants by instantaneously verifying the educational and professional credentials like a university degree and professional certificates with self-sovereign identity, which saves days in comparison to conventional manual verification techniques.

Immutable Voting: Although not yet tested for public elections, self-sovereign identity is being explored with both shareholder and closed-organization voting (such as unions) where only members are permitted to participate and cast ballots; their names won't be made public, but their credentials will be connected to their DID, and because individuals may cryptographically demonstrate that they are who they claim to be and are entitled to vote, the organization can have confidence that they are who they say they are.

Eligibility Verification: Verifiable Credentials may contain information necessary to be eligible for government benefits, such as proof of age, veteran status, Native American or Indigenous ancestry, or proof of a handicap; consumers can use these credentials to apply for government programs or swiftly and easily prove anything about themselves, which allows VCs to speed up the verification process.

Know Your Customer Compliance (KYC): Verifiable Credentials can be used to speed up KYC compliance for anti-money-laundering practices throughout the customer onboarding process, as well as to offer additional services without having to go through the KYC process each time. For example, this may include the ability to leverage portable, decentralized Verifiable Credentials a consumer receives from one bank to expedite the KYC procedure when conducting a transaction with another bank.

Non-fungible Tokens (NFTs): Self-sovereign identity simplifies NFT ownership by providing decentralized and secure verification of ownership and authenticity.

Self-Sovereign Identity in Healthcare

 Self-sovereign identity enables secure and accurate medical histories which are instantly accessible, and which can be voluntarily shared with healthcare professionals.

The promise of self-sovereign identity's ability to provide patients, providers, and payers with a simpler, stronger, faster means of identification and eligibility verification is critical to healthcare. Self-sovereign identity enables secure and accurate medical histories which are instantly accessible, and which can be voluntarily shared with healthcare professionals. The promise is far more efficient and consistent care, based on accurate information about a patient's identity and medical history. This is especially important during crisis situations or difficult moments, such as the coordination of palliative care. There are few circumstances in life more stressful, distressing, and depressing than having to repeatedly fill out paperwork or find medical records during a medical crisis. Even worse is filling out paperwork equivalent to a mortgage application, amidst the shock and grief of the impending death of a loved one

In the U.S., the Health Insurance Portability and Accountability Act (HIPAA) was meant to ensure the creation of a secure and portable medical record, but it has fallen well short of this goal. In fact, HIPAA's privacy regulations, and the punitive threat to medical providers of a patient data breach, all but obviate its portability.

For example, in many healthcare facilities, notability hospitals and nursing homes, there is a reasonable expectation to demonstrate a recent negative COVID-19 test to enter the facility for either care or work. Today this is both a cumbersome and controversial process. Recently a global effort named the COVID Credentials Initiative[24] demonstrated how self-sovereign identity replaces a paper vaccine certificate with a unique identifier in a database accessible to any health practitioner. Today there is otherwise no standard means of evidentiary proof for COVID immunity, and certainly nothing portable, beyond physical vaccination cards which are easily faked.[25, 26]

Self-sovereign identity also has the potential to revolutionize health-care by providing patients with greater control over personal data. With it, patients are empowered to choose what data is shared, with whom, and when, allowing healthcare providers to quickly verify patient iden-tities, while simultaneously ensuring privacy. In addition, self-sovereign identity allows healthcare providers and payers to easily authenticate and authorize different users for different tasks, such as patient care or billing. This could help prevent bad actors from gaining access to sensitive data or committing fraud. Ultimately, self-sovereign identity makes the role of digital advocates (which we explored in Chapter 3) a crucial component in the future of healthcare, possible.

In addition to matters of personal privacy and easier access to medical records, an even greater economic opportunity for self-sovereign iden-tity in healthcare is found in claims payment and credentialing medical providers. This is a multi-billion dollar problem. To put it into context, the Center for American Progress estimates that in the US alone, the combined cost of excess billing and claims processing was $248 billion annually, with at least $100 billion attributable to overhead from identity verification.[27]

Accurately credentialing healthcare practitioners is also critical for ensuring both patient safety and preventing medical fraud. Healthcare identity credentialing typically involves verifying a healthcare provider's education, training, and professional experience, as well as conducting background checks and verifying licenses and certifications. Consider the infamous Zholia Aliemi forgery case, in which she was alleged to have earned over £1.3m in the U.K. posing as a psychiatrist for years, despite having no medical degree.[28] There are many other cases in the U.S. and globally, involving either services performed without appropriate cre-dentials or bills paid where no services were provided. Fraud preventable through validation of the provider's identity is estimated by the National Heath Care Anti-Fraud Association to exceed $68 billion annually in the US alone.[29]

Digital Identity for Emerging Markets and Vulnerable Populations

One of the least often discussed benefits of sovereign identity is also one of the most significant. The World Bank estimates that there are more than 1.1 billion people worldwide who lack the means to prove their identity. That puts these individuals, who are already at risk with little to no financial resources, in a position where they can easily be taken advantage of. One example of efforts to correct this using self-sovereign identity was the Kiva Protocol, developed by Kiva, one of the world's largest microlenders to developing economies. As Africa's first blockchain and decentralized identity platform, it was used to create identity for building credit history in Sierra Leone, until its relatively quick retirement on June 30, 2022 (it was designed as a proof of concept, not a longstanding program).

The challenge that the Kiva Protocol sought to address is that a large portion of the African continent's population lacks a formal, verifiable identity, instead conducting transactions with informal means of identification—sufficient for their local village lender, but not for opening a savings account or gaining access to more formal lending services. The Kiva Protocol was successful with lenders and investors, funding over $223 million in loans in 2021, and impacting the lives of over 550,000 individuals. It proved the viability of microloans as a means for global financial inclusion, but equally importantly it demonstrated that the identity verification process need not be cumbersome.

The adoption of self-sovereign identity technology has the potential to revolutionize the way emerging markets manage digital identities.

The adoption of self-sovereign identity technology has the potential to revolutionize the way emerging markets manage digital identities. Across emerging markets, the digital economy is growing far faster than traditional offline economic sectors. With this come immense opportunities as connectivity increases and distance evaporates as a barrier for commerce and trade. The ability to store personal data securely and access it in an instant, with the right authentication and authorization, will make emerging markets more competitive in the global economy.

This notion of a transaction occurring without an intermediary or centralized party to verify identity is not limited to emerging markets. For emerging market entrepreneurs to operate in the global economy, there is a threshold of trust which may be impossible to overcome on their own. You implicitly trust Amazon because you have confidence in its customer service policies. You know that you will receive what you ordered and can return it at zero cost. Amazon has invested heavily to establish this level of consumer confidence at a scale that no individual entrepreneur or small business can afford.

Presumably, you would have far less confidence sending an envelope full of cash halfway around the world in the hopes of receiving your desired purchase in exchange. However, with a smart contract the transaction is secured by the implicit trustlessness of Web3, through a technology such as blockchain.

In its simplest form, a smart contract is an executable agreement stored on a blockchain, which runs only if predetermined conditions are met, such as the terms agreed to for releasing payment for a product or service.

In its simplest form, a smart contract is an executable agreement stored on a blockchain, which runs only if predetermined conditions are met, such as the terms agreed to for releasing payment for a product or service.

Ensuring access to a secure immutable digital identity is essential to realizing these new economic opportunities for entrepreneurs, small business owners, and individuals.

In the same way, self-sovereign identity offers the potential to streamline and simplify government by reducing bureaucratic red tape and allowing for faster and more efficient delivery of public services. Both are critical to assisting vulnerable populations who lack the means to navigate government channels. In addition, the bureaucratic overhead of governments in emerging markets is typically greater than those in developed markets, putting access to basic services further out of reach of the populations who need it most. Allowing governments to easily verify the identity of individuals and businesses reduces the risk of fraud, money laundering, and other types of financial crimes commonly associated with the less mature regulatory environments of emerging market economies. This will create new opportunities for not only accessing government services, but also the formation of new businesses, which can often be a cumbersome process.

This supports why the McKinsey Global Institute cited benefits of 6 percent GDP growth for emerging market economies from a secure and reliable means to manage digital identities. By providing individuals with the ability to prove their identity in a secure and reliable way, self-sovereign identity can help vulnerable populations access critical services such as healthcare, financial services, and even education without fear of being taken advantage of or being exposed to fraud or abuse. We've already seen the success of the Kiva example, with over 550,000 individuals gaining access to microloans, despite lacking sufficient government-issued identification to do so much as open a bank account.

Digital Identity, E-residency, and the Digital Nomad Visa

Another notable movement related to the growing trend of government-promoted self-sovereign identity is the increasing number of nations offering e-residency visa programs. In 2014, the Republic of Estonia was the first nation to offer e-Residency, with participation to date of over 30,000 individuals from 139 countries. Estonia touts the benefits of its program as offering entrepreneurs a digital identity which allows them to launch an EU-based company from anywhere in the world, while leveraging Estonia's EU-wide financial and legal systems.

Since the success of Estonia's program, over twenty countries have launched e-Residency programs of their own. This list includes Portugal, which offers not only digital identity but also access to government services, including its national healthcare. Outside of Europe, the United Arab Emirates launched the "Dubai Virtual Commercial City," or DVC as it's more commonly known, allowing foreign nationals to incorporate businesses in the Emirates without relocating. Similar to the EU programs, what appeals to entrepreneurs is leveraging the protections of a stable regulatory environment with comparatively favorable tax rates, ranging from typically 20 percent for EU-based e-residency (as in Estonia and Portugal) to 0 percent for the UAE's DVC.

Although these e-residency programs are all premised on a government-issued identity from a central authority, they nonetheless follow an important trend emphasizing freedom and the power of individuals. Governments now compete based on how friendly they are to business in the bounds of their nation (virtually or physically). Estonia, again, offers a compelling example of this. On June 13, 2022, an Austrian entrepreneur set the World Record for the Fastest Business Startup by incorporating an EU business through the Estonian e-Residency program in fifteen minutes and thirty-three seconds. Contrast this with the time to completion of new business formation in Russia—from whose grip Estonia escaped just a few decades ago—or India, in both cases often measured in weeks rather than minutes. Entrepreneurs in India as well as from any other developing nation can now be operating in minutes as legal EU business, with all the protections of local citizens, without ever leaving their homes.

What if these businesspeople do want to leave their current location? Another area where Estonia has demonstrated leadership is in the creation of the Digital Nomad Visa, which allows foreign entrepreneurs and digital nomads to live in Estonia for up to a year and legally conduct their business in the country. The Digital Nomad Visa provides access to the same remotely available business benefits of the e-Residency program, while also allowing local benefits.

E-residency and the Digital Nomad Visa, as well as the inevitable competing alternatives to be offered by other nations, have significant implications for the future of digital identity and self-sovereign identity. Where identity has traditionally been—and otherwise still is—tied to physical location, nationality, and citizenship, these programs enable individuals to maintain their own identity while still being able to operate globally. This also reinforces the ability of individuals to control and manage their own data, giving them choice over which countries to do business in and with whom to share their data.

Paired with the rise in the self-sovereign identity, where identity is recognized by governments but not dependent on a specific government authority for issuance, e-Residency programs can be transformative, especially for the more than one-billion individuals identified by the World

E-Residency	Digital Nomad Visa
+ Secure, government-issued, digital identity for personal, online authentification	+ Right for remote workers to temporarily stay in Estonia for up to 1 year
+ Remote entrepreneurs gain digital access to Estonia's e-services:	+ For digital nomads who can work online & independent of location:
+ Establish and run a company online	+ For an employer registered abroad
+ Declare taxes & access banking/payments	+ For their company registered abroad, or
+ Low-cost, minimal bureaucracy alternative	+ As a freelancer for clients mostly abroad
+ No right of citizenship, residence or travel to Estonia or EU	+ No right of ofcitizenship or permanent residence in Estonia or EU
+ Apply online at e-resident.gov.ee. Process takes 6-8 weeks	+ Apply at your nearest Estonian Embassy. Process takes at least 15 days
+ Receive your e-Residency kit at pickup points around world after verifying identity	+ Pick up visa at nearest Estonian Embassy. Standart visa rules & procedures apply

Figure 6.3: Key Distinctions Between E-Residency and Digital Nomad Visa
E-Residency is a program for digital identity, while a Digital Nomad Visa allows remote workers to reside temporarily in a country.

Bank as lacking the means to officially prove their identity, and therefore locked out of any meaningful commercial activity. However, with e-Residency they are able to participate in the global economy with the protections and benefits of the world's most liberalized economies (those with the greatest personal freedom as well as the protections of these freedoms), giving rise to a new level of individual empowerment.

The End of Passwords: Behavior as Identity

Passwords are a ubiquitous aspect of modern digital life, used to secure everything from email accounts to online banking. They are the first line of defense against unauthorized access to our sensitive information, and creating a strong password is crucial for protecting our online identities. However, they are still a notoriously insecure method of authentication, as many people still use weak or easily guessed passwords, leaving themselves vulnerable to hacking and other security threats. There are a finite number of ways identity can be verified for authentication purposes, and the worst possible way is typing in a random string of characters and symbols, which you have to recall, write down, or store in a password manager. So, what will replace passwords?

Let's suggest a radical new approach. Imagine using your behavior as your identity. Sound farfetched? It has already been done. Two promising and pioneering examples have been demonstrated as working pilots by the Department of Defense (DoD).

The first involved creating a pattern-of-life key.[30] Under this model, piloted in the mid-2010s, DoD personnel were liberated from having to walk around with a Common Access Card or "CAC" to authenticate their identity.[31] Instead identity was based on all of the unique characteristics of their behavior: the way they walked, the direction they took to work, the time it took them to commute to work. All of these factors collectively are added into a security key which defines unequivocally who someone is, and no bad actor can spoof the large number of behavioral instances that are being calculated. Each element of behavior adds variability, resulting in a mathematically impossible level of complexity to hack or fake an individual's identity.

The ability to fake or spoof identity within this model faces the challenge of what's called factorial probability, something that happens when a set of variables which are independent events create a range of combinations that are astronomically large. For example, there are twenty-six uppercase letters, twenty-six lowercase letters, ten digits, and thirty-three ASCII-printable symbols available on the standard keyboard. This totals ninety-five alternatives per character, resulting in nearly 800 billion combinations for a six-character password (or ninety-five to power of six). Expand this to eight characters and that is ninety-five to the power of eight, or nearly 7,000 trillion possible combinations. That is a staggering number, yet passwords are hacked all the time. Why? For one, few of us take advantage of the full diversity of all ninety-five characters and end up using a more easily hackable password, such as "1234356" or "password," which according to the National Cyber Security Centre are the first and fourth most common passwords. (We'd add that most of the slightly harder-to-recall passwords end up on Post-it Notes under a keyboard.)

However, even if the password is complicated enough to take advantage of the trillions of possible combinations, the problem with passwords is that they are stored in a central repository which itself can be hacked.

With the pattern-of-life key, the unique identity representing your password is constantly changing. As a result it cannot be retrieved from a central repository, as in the earlier example of the LinkedIn data breach, since even if it were accessed it would have changed before it could be used. The potential combination of unique identifiers would also be well beyond the limit of eight specific characters. Your pattern of life consists of hundreds of variables changing every day, each with hundreds of different alternatives. The potential combination of these variables is in the trillions of trillions.

Today the fastest brute force algorithm that is most commonly used for 'cracking' passwords is Hashcat, capable of making 100 billion attempts per second. One billion Hashcats working around the clock every second would take over 3,000 years to generate every possible combination of 100 independent behavioral variables.[32]

Could this not be accomplished by extending passwords to 100 characters? Sure, but think for a moment about how impractical that would be. Imagine having to remember the unique sequence of 100 characters, and repeatedly entering them every time you log into any system or service. Even then, we're back to a central repository of static passwords. What makes the pattern-of-life approach so compelling as a password alternative is the combination of non-hackability and not having to rely on creating unique passwords in the first place. Think of this concept combined with ambient intelligence and self-sovereign identity. Everywhere you go your movements are anonymously written to a unique pattern-of-life key. Using the Decentralized Identifiers of your self-sovereign identity, your identity is validated, but your unique data is not shared. It's unlike the cookies used in today's Web2, which track each click you make. Your office door knows to let you in, yet your identity is otherwise unknown to the mechanism which unlocks it. You capture and store each step within your own pattern-of-life blockchain, but there is no centralized system recording your behavior.

 In a behavior-based model every step you make is part of the increasingly precise definition of your identity, all of this metadata is securely decentralized, and only you hold the keys to unlock it.

In a behavior-based model every step you make is part of the increasingly precise definition of your identity, all of this metadata is securely decentralized, and only you hold the keys to unlock it. But simultaneously, each facet of your behavior is part of what defines and what enables intelligent systems to better adapt and optimize to support your unique preferences and needs. If all of this sounds a bit far-fetched, think about it this way: imagine that someone who looked, dressed, and sounded exactly like your spouse tried to convince you that they were your spouse. Would they be able to fool you into believing he or she was your spouse? Unless you're completely distracted and not paying attention, it's highly unlikely. The reason? You have made a mental map of every subtle micro-gesture that enables you to recognize your spouse is. Hundreds of inconsequential behaviors together create an unambiguous identity, yet it would be nearly impossible to document all of those behaviors. That's similar to the way technology for pattern-of life works, using a technology called tokenization.

Tokenization is a process that scrambles sensitive or confidential data into what are referred to as tokens. Tokens cannot be reverse-engineered to their original form; instead, they act as immutable proxies for the original data. This is a form of what's called hashing, which refers to methods for protecting data by obscuring it via an algorithm or mathematical formula. Hash functions are designed to be one-way, meaning it's computationally easy to create a hash from an input, but extremely difficult to reverse-engineer the input from the hash. Additionally, hash functions generate fixed-length outputs, regardless of the input size, which means information is lost during the hashing process, making it impossible to perfectly recreate the original input. For example, an SHA-256 hash of the prior three paragraphs would look like this:

34974E84D0DBC3DB7EC93B603B853604BEF6B35D
CD21054B62D5B40EFB86DBBB

If we simply deleted the second to last word in the third paragraph, "mathematical." The hash would look like this:

D666C0E078324BDB14DF7484154B44F7313F67D91EE451BD
B44CC4B814E03C99

If you look carefully at those two hashes you'll notice that their patterns have absolutely nothing in common. Now try to imagine reverse-engineering those hashes to get the same three paragraphs. The only way to "reverse-engineer" a hash is through a brute-force attack, which involves trying all possible combinations of inputs until the correct one is found. That's not just impractical, it's impossible with today's computers—the time required to brute-force an SHA-256 hash would take longer than the age of the universe.

Tokenization is one form of hashing which specifically replaces sensitive data with a token, which, like our hash above, has no value outside of the system in which it is used. Tokenization itself is not new and has become common practice in highly sensitive transactions, such as with financial services. In the contexts of behavior as identity and ambient intelligence, its role is to allow your identity to be anonymously validated through your interactions with your physical surroundings. Aggregated sensors feed into a sovereign token of who you are. The token presents the means for authenticating who you are, without divulging any sensitive data which could otherwise be used to compromise your identity.

Consider it in these terms. Today you may have a motion detector located near the front door of your home. You approach the range of the motion detector, and the light turns on. It does this whether you, or your neighbor, or your neighbor's dog approaches. It's activated by motion not identity. Now, imagine that instead of motion, the light has a sensor which is activated by detecting radio frequency identification tags (RFIDs). The light turns on when you approach, but not your neighbor, because it is linked to the RFID-emitting device you possess. When this happens, the light doesn't "*remember*" that you were there, but the event is added to the blockchain storing identity data.

The first half of this concept has been in practice for years, with RFID door locks and light activation in commercial use since the early 2000s. The second element is common today as well, in the form of *refresh tokens*,[33] which allow you move between systems without having to continually log-in. What is new here is two-fold. First, using something such as RFID for communicating your identity, then having lights, doors, and other items in your environment respond based on your identity. The second is your identity defined by your *pattern-of-life*: each interaction you make presents a number passed through a cryptographic algorithm, continuously updating your identity token.

Note that in this example the RFID tag is not specifically part of your identity. It is today the most common way for passively interacting with systems. Another passive means, which does raise the specter of privacy concerns, is facial recognition—already common on consumer devices such as the Apple iPhone, but less common in public settings such as hospitals. Less invasive and more common means of biometric authentication today are voice, fingerprint, retina, and vein pattern recognition. However, each of these require user interaction, whereas both RFID tag and video-based facial recognition can be done without requiring the individual to actively participate. But as we'll discuss in a moment in the context of deepfake technology, relying solely on voice or facial patterns introduces its own risks.

Every Soldier Is a Sensor

The second example from the DoD is an initiative from the U.S. Army called Every Soldier is a Sensor (ES2).[34] In the case of ES2, the role of behavioral identity is to validate the identities of soldiers in the field, as part of ensuring all necessary data points are in place for Mission Command to make the appropriate decisions when directing personnel in an operation or battlefield. Still in place and evolving today, ES2 is part of the shift towards network-centric warfare, where the intelligence leveraged for decision-making is derived increasingly from a priori sources—a broad spectrum of inputs ranging from satellite data to input from soldiers in the field, rather than dedicated reconnaissance.

It is not difficult to imagine the gravity of making a battlefield decision which may result in the loss of life. Even though the focus of that decision may be an enemy combatant, the risk of friendly fire and collateral damage (unintentional death or injury of non-combatants) weighs heavily on the minds of military commanders. To ensure that decisions of this magnitude are justified, the ES2 effort seeks to gain data from as wide a range of information sources as possible. The concept is to make every soldier a sensor, each providing input into an aggregate collection of decision-assisting data. The ES2 effort is a prime example of ambient intelligence, which will soon be fed by trillions and trillions of sensors.

On one hand, the idea of being recognized wherever we are and having every interaction personalized to our own preferences, without having to express our intent or expectations, offers an unprecedented level of convenience and efficiency, as well as safety—imagine no loved one ever at risk of being lost. Yet in the Web2 world of having all of our personal data aggregated by third parties for their own financial benefit, in exchange for our convenience, these benefits come at the cost of an Orwellian existence of continuous surveillance. This contrast between Web2 and Web3 vividly underscores the benefits of self-sovereign identity, where we control our own data and leverage it anonymously through privacy-protecting tokenization.

Protection Against the Rising Threat of Deepfake Technology

There's yet another aspect of identity that we need to talk about—Deepfakes. They represent a rapidly growing category of what's termed "synthetic identity fraud," with the cost in damages from individual cases ranging from \$243,000 to \$35 million each.[35]

 Imagine for a moment, watching a video of yourself committing the most unspeakable acts. You can't believe what you're seeing. You know with complete certainty that it's not you, but who else will believe that it's not?

Imagine for a moment, watching a video of yourself committing the most unspeakable acts. You can't believe what you're seeing. You know with complete certainty that it's not you, but who else will believe that it's not? That nightmare scenario is an increasingly likely reality given the rise of deep fake technology.

In 2020, a deepfake bot was uncovered on the social media platform Telegram, which was claimed to have undressed more than 680,000 women without their knowledge.[36] In a similar episode in 2022, a video of Elon Musk surfaced online, promoting a supposed cryptocurrency trading investment platform, BitVex, which promised up to a 30 percent return within three months. It was only after very careful scrutiny of the video that it was identified as a deepfake. (The scam was largely unsuccessful, garnering only $1,700 in deposits.)

Deepfake technology is an example of generative AI that allows the alteration of video and audio to make it appear as though a person is saying or doing something that they never actually said or did. The term "deep" comes from its origins in "deep learning technology" which learns the many nuances of an individual's voice and appearance, and then generates convincing replicas with generative AI models such as GPT-4.

The basic capabilities required for deepfakes have been around for several years already in the commercial world of video production, as well as more recently with consumer-oriented apps such as DeepFaceLab, Zao, FaceApp, and Wombo. But those are not yet capable of producing something of the quality needed to present a significant threat. Both the prevalence of deepfake-enabled fraud and the means to create them are now rapidly growing in both power, accessibility, and affordability. An example was Microsoft's early 2023 announcement of a new text-to-speech AI model called VALL-E which they claim can replicate an individual's voice with only a 3-second audio sample.[37]

 As deepfake technology becomes more sophisticated, the line between what's real and what's not will not just blur but disappear entirely.

As deepfake technology becomes more sophisticated, the line between what's real and what's not will not just blur but disappear entirely. It's fair to say that to the human eye, or ear, a deepfake will be indistinguishable from the real thing, a notion already true for synthetic identities created with commercial deepfake systems. Preventing the harmful consequences of deepfake technology represents a parallel area of growth, with firms such as Deeptrace, which employs machine learning to detect deepfakes, as well as initiatives such as the Deepfake Detection Challenge, launched a few years ago as joint effort by Amazon, Microsoft, and Facebook. Yet the history of technologies, such as AI, suggests that our ability to stay ahead of such rapidly evolving capabilities will be an exercise in futility.

Meanwhile, governments around the world are scrambling to prevent the use of deepfake technology for more harmful purposes, such as political manipulation. In 2019 China put forth expansive rules requiring consent as well as the use of digital signatures and watermarks on all videos.[38] At the same time, the U.S. also passed the Deepfake Report Act which requires the Director of National Intelligence to submit a report to Congress on the use of deepfake technology and its potential impact on national security. Several states, such as California and Texas, have also passed laws that prohibit the use of deepfake technology for political purposes.

The U.K. has taken a softer approach with a Center for Data Ethics and Innovation report on deepfake technology that made suggestions and recommendations on how the government should take a risk-based approach to regulating deepfake technology, while maintaining a balance between protecting citizens from its negative effects and fostering the innovation and creativity that it can enable. The Netherlands Authority for the Financial Markets has warned that deepfake technology poses a risk to the financial sector, and has called for regulations to hold individuals and organizations accountable for its misuse.

Despite all of this, we have to assume that there will be perfect deepfakes which are undetectable, not only to the human eye but also to detection algorithms. However, there's another approach to fighting deepfakes, which we discussed previously: immutable digital identity. Proving that "it wasn't me" will remain a challenge when deepfakes can evade even the best-trained algorithms. However, immutable digital identity removes both the risk of fraud and eliminates the incentive for its malicious use. For example, linking verifiable digital identity—stored cryptographically within a blockchain as with self-sovereign identity—to the digital media containing the deepfake can be used to prove its (lack of) authenticity and chain of custody. While this would not remove the embarrassment of the deepfake being seen, it would provide an indisputable way to prove it wasn't you, since only you can attach your own identity to digital media.

The Next Trillion Dollar Market Opportunity

If self-sovereign identity is worth 3 percent of US GDP growth, as McKinsey claims, where does that roughly $700 billion (in today's dollars, or

well over $1 trillion by 2030) come from? It's a mix of revenue genera-
tion and cost offsets. Self-sovereign identity offers a range of value-adding
opportunities for individuals, businesses, and governments, which include
selling the underlying capabilities themselves (roughly $200 billion
today) as well as reducing traditional identity and eligibility verification
processes in both government and commercial sectors ($600 billion by
most estimates).[39]

In its most basic sense, the core benefit of self-sovereign identity lies
in the ability to achieve and demonstrate individual identity, without
dependence on it being issued by governments or other third parties. Yet
this does require supporting infrastructure, which itself presents business
opportunities—offering the ability to provide users with secure access to
digital services without having to share any personal information deliv-
eries opportunity for service providers, as well as cost avoidance for
consumers and businesses.

Identify and Fraud

Of course, we can't talk about identity without talking more about fraud
and the ways in which identity can be monetized by its owners. Various
government and industry reports place the global cost of fraud at $5 tril-
lion annually, and the fastest-growing portion of this is associated with
identity-based fraud. This includes costs to businesses and consumers of
identity theft, which the US Federal Trade Commission cites as $56 billion
in 2022 and one of the fastest growing areas of financial theft.[40] Add to this
the cost of fraudulent insurance claims, which the insurance industry con-
sortium (the Coalition Against Insurance Fraud) cites as being over $300
billion in 2022, and if current trends continue, these numbers combined
will exceed $1 trillion in financial loss by 2030 in the U.S. alone. If just 10
percent of this is reduced through the widespread adoption of immutable
identities, the cost savings by 2030 is conservatively estimated at $100
billion, although we believe that this number could be far greater.

An analogy for the prevention of identity-based fraud is the role
of identity verification in both government services in general and in
healthcare specifically. As we mentioned earlier, according to studies by
the Center for American Progress, and backed by large payers such as

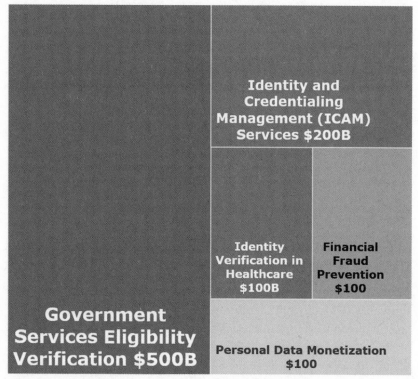

Figure 6.4: A Trillion Dollar Market for Digital Identity

The market opportunity for immutable digital identity is projected to reach $1 trillion by 2030.

UnitedHealth, the adoption of digital identity would address what is currently estimated as a $100 Billion annual cost (in the U.S. alone) from the overhead of identity verification.[41] In most nations, and the U.S. is no exception, the majority of government services are means-tested and specific to an individual as well as to their unique circumstances. In each case, enrollment into government programs which provide services to consumers—such as Medicare, Medicaid, and other forms of assistance which currently total about $5 Trillion in the US across federal and state programs—requires what is most often a manual process of identity and eligibility verification.

It's estimated that for many programs the cost of eligibility verification is as much as half of the cost of the total program, and in more mature

211

programs it is often as much as 10 percent of the funds spent through the program.[42] This also does not include the cost of fraud itself, the core driver of eligibility verification in the first place. For example, the Centers for Medicaid and Medicare spends over $50 billion annually on improper payments for Medicare alone, according to the U.S. Government Accountability Office.[43] In light of this, the value of both streamlined, accurate enrollment and eligibility verification via immutable digital identity will conservatively exceed $500 billion—under 10 percent of the total cost of these programs—by 2030.

But there's another side to the issue of fraud that will soon go well beyond the cost to an economy that we've outlined above, the economic value that can be created through your ownership of your digital self.

Cashing In On Your Identity

Because individuals have full control over the data they store and share through a self-sovereign identity model, it creates new revenue streams and opportunities for monetizing their data.

In a notable pivot from the Web2 model, the revenue from the value of identity flows to the owner of the digital self, rather than a third party. The impact of this on individuals and the global economy may be one of the most unexpected ways that we will create value in the future.

> **The revenue from the value of identity flows to the owner of the digital self, rather than a third party. The impact of this on individuals and the global economy may be one of the most unexpected ways that we will create value in the future.**

Throughout his career and notably in his book *The Mystery of Capital*, economist Hernando DeSoto argued that property rights provide a key leverage point for economic development, by allowing individuals and businesses to establish a legal and indisputable claim to assets, to then use them as collateral for loans, and transfer them to others. Thus property rights serve as the foundation of a capitalist system that incentivizes investment, innovation, and risk-taking, all of which are critical drivers of economic growth.

Through the lens of DeSoto's work, consider how the ownership of our digital identity offers the same path for economic growth and prosperity over the coming decades. As discussed throughout this chapter, our personal data has become such a valuable asset that Web2 giants such as Google, Facebook, and Amazon have evolved into some of the highest valued firms in the world through collecting and analyzing it. This has happened in large part because we are not able to own our personal data. In contrast, enabled by blockchain and other Web3 capabilities, the ability to create and enforce ownership rights of our digital identities in a decentralized, transparent, and secure way will enable new business models and economic opportunities.

One example has been the emergence of NFTs as investment vehicles. NFTs, or non-fungible tokens, are unique digital assets stored on a blockchain and used to represent ownership of intellectual property. They are most frequently associated with creative works such as art, music, or videos, but they may also be used for any claim of ownership. NFTs are *minted*,[44] meaning they are recorded onto a blockchain, which then can't be modified or overwritten. This provides the basis for the NFT to establish immutable ownership in a portable and decentralized way, that is *non-fungible*—meaning that each NFT is unique unlike an asset such as a dollar bill, which is fungible, meaning any dollar can be exchanged with any other dollar. This allows NFTs to be bought and sold as tradable assets. Extreme examples of this emerged during the 2021 NFT bubble[45], including the $69 million sale of Beeple's digital artwork *Everydays: The First 5000 Days* at a Christie's auction, and the $2.9 million sale of Jack Dorsey's first tweet. In each case, it wasn't the assets themselves being valued—Dorsey's tweet was free for anyone to see or copy—but rather the ability to claim and prove ownership of the digital item is what is valuable, and gives the owner the right to monetize or resell that content.

NFTs change the way that intellectual property is controlled and protected by providing a new way to establish ownership and authenticity of digital assets.

NFTs change the way that intellectual property is controlled and protected by providing a new way to establish ownership and authenticity of digital assets. This enables creators to more easily monetize their work and retain control over its use and distribution, while also providing a transparent and immutable record of ownership. Additionally, NFTs can provide new mechanisms for enforcing intellectual property rights, such as through "smart contracts" that automatically ensure proper attribution and compensation for the use of digital assets.

For example, content creators can receive payment for their work without the need for intermediaries or advertising revenue. This creates a more direct and transparent relationship between creators and their audiences, but it also demonstrates one of the most transformative financial models of Web3: microtransactions and micropayments, including those for a fraction of a US cent. These "smart contracts" are self-executing digital contracts which enable secure and transparent transactions by recording the terms of an agreement on the blockchain, which when combined with micropayments, enable decentralized transactions. Transactions are conducted in a way which is *permissionless, trustless,* and, what in cryptographic terms is often described as *knowledgeless*—meaning that payments can be received and recorded without requiring any specific effort on your part. Rather, each transaction is recorded as a new block on the blockchain, which is then verified by a network of nodes to ensure that it's valid and accurate. This enables a transparent and immutable record of all microtransactions, which can be easily tracked and audited by anyone on the network. As a result, content you create can now be traced back to you when it's reused—anything from a book you've written, a poem, a piece of computer code, an image, a formula, or even a sentence. As that content is traced back to you, any monetization of that content will also flow back to you.

To make sense of this, think of two revenue models in existence today. The first example is Bitcoin mining. Although bitcoin mining is somewhat complicated and obscure, we picked this example because it is the most likely scenario for not only how financial exchanges will be conducted in the future, but how all forms of ownership will be managed. Most important, this is how you'll get paid for leveraging your digital self.

Bitcoin is a cryptocurrency which runs on a decentralized computer network used to track and store every transaction. Bitcoin miners are the people who create bitcoins by validating each individual transaction. This is done by solving a cryptographic (mathematical) puzzle using a hash function called SHA-256 (the same hashing method we explained earlier in the chapter). In exchange for a micropayment of a tiny fraction of a Bitcoin, miners compete for each transaction by being the first to solve the math problem or cryptographic hash. (This is why computing power is in such demand in Bitcoin mining—whoever has the greatest computational capabilities within the network will most likely complete the hash first.) The role of miners providing computing capacity is "permissionless," as they do not provide approval for any given transaction, and "trustless" as there is no way to compromise the transaction, even by attempting to destroy the data of the blockchain, as it is simultaneously encrypted and replicated.

The second example to consider is how personal data is monetized today in Web2 the model. Most commonly, the action monetized is your clicking on an online ad. But why are you seeing the ad you clicked on? Typically, it's an ad presented in an exchange model, where ads are served according to the highest bidder, in an auction-based transaction conducted in microseconds. This is a zero-knowledge transaction, meaning the bidding advertisers have committed to prioritized demographics, but know very little about you specifically—for example, your age, sex, location, or income band—unless you click on the ad (or engage in whatever the call to action is) or if you have a cookie[46] passing your data. The cost of the ad, in this case, may be as much as $500 or as little as $0.01, depending on the circumstances of the bid and the value of your demographic details to the bidding advertiser.

Now imagine if we were to combine those two models—bitcoin mining and pay-per-click exchanges—but with a twist. You, not the data aggregator, own your data. You're still shown advertisements, which are uniquely tailored to you based on the details provided by your digital identity token. You may still see embarrassingly precise contextualized ads, but neither the advertiser nor the ad exchange know why they are so relevant to you or your personal interests. Your privacy is preserved, and in a further twist, you are paid for your ad. The Web2 data aggregators no longer hold the leverage they once did. That leverage has shifted to you, the owner of your own data.

Let's go even further. What if this scenario was carried out for every transaction you do online? Not simply as a new model of opt-in advertising, but where every interaction is a microtransaction. Each one is an exchange of value, in a globally decentralized, peer-to-peer model, where you are compensated for your data, your cooperation, your content, and other monetizable dimensions of your digital identity—notably without the Web2 intermediaries in the middle. What this requires is the immutability best offered through digital identity, combined with the ability of a permissionless and trustless model of zero-knowledge micropayments. It would be highly impractical to negotiate payment terms on a transaction-by-transaction basis, since every transaction would fall below the threshold of practical value for either party. But similar to Bitcoin mining, in the aggregate, the combination of microtransactions for micropayments adds up to considerable value. In this model, digital identity has shifted from what may be your greatest liability, to becoming your most valuable asset, and perhaps your greatest source of revenue.

 Digital identity has shifted from what may be your greatest liability, to becoming your most valuable asset, and perhaps your greatest source of revenue.

Earlier we discussed how your digital self can work on your behalf, generating income just as you would through your own work. What we just described above is how identity can be monetized through your behavior and the choices you make, at the same time allowing your data to be leveraged by third parties for research and other purposes, yet without compromising your privacy or security.

In addition to monetizing our personal data, there is an emerging secondary market for enabling immutable digital identity. Because digital identity is decentralized, it is today still wallet-based, not unlike the earlier stage of the cryptocurrency market in which critical data could be easily and permanently lost. Then Bitcoins were stored locally in what are called cold wallets, which are disconnected from the Internet. Since the wallet contains the immutable record of the Bitcoins, if they were lost they were lost forever. But the portability of wallets has evolved, benefiting from Bitcoin's growing adoption and the maturing blockchain.

There are now *hot wallets* with both privacy protections as well as the security of backups to prevent data loss. We can imagine the same evolving for digital identities. We can see this already with Barclaycard who teamed up with Evernym to explore the benefits of using digital identity for secure customer onboarding and payment validation for retailers.[47] Also Korea's three largest mobile telecom providers (SK Telekom, KT, and LG U+) have teamed up with Samsung to provide a digital identity service called *PASS* which allows users to use their mobile phone to prove their identity with the same authority as a government-issued ID.[48]

The future of immutable digital identity will combine increased individual ownership and control over personal data with the move towards decentralized solutions that enable users to maintain ownership and control over their personal data, while still providing the convenience and accessibility of centralized services. This enables ownership and control over who has access to our personal data and how it is used, while also providing a secure and transparent record of identity verification and authentication.

The role of blockchain and NFTs in digital identity will provide a tamper-proof and transparent record of identity and ownership, enabling service providers to verify and authenticate your identity without requiring you to share sensitive personal data. By establishing trust and enabling fast and efficient payment processing, our identity as currency will create new opportunities for incentivizing user behavior and driving engagement in online communities and marketplaces, as with the pay-for-click model described earlier. This will be increasingly relevant within the immersive spaces referred to as the Metaverse.

Your Meta Identity

Within immersive environments, entertainment platforms will increasingly mix fantasy and reality along with a growing number of options for virtual property, assets, and travel. While still in its infancy, we have already seen the launch of virtual properties, such as Millennium Hotels and Resorts' recently opened by M Social Decentraland,[49] credited as the first hospitality group to open a hotel in the metaverse. This virtual hotel blends real and virtual experiences which guests can virtually explore with an avatar; the VR hotel is said to mirror physical Millennium properties. Similarly, Emirates airline is launching what it's calling "signature metaverse experiences" for customers[50], as well as developing NFTs both for utility and collectible purposes.

The combination of AI and the metaverse will deliver hyperpersonalized experiences, both unique for each user and far more accessible than ever possible in the physical world. As immersive environments and the metaverse overall matures, standardization will eliminate the current need for (nominally) expensive equipment and the development of specialized content.

As the metaverse evolves as a platform individuals will interact with each other in virtual spaces for business as well as pleasure, and having easily verifiable and portable digital identity will be critical to allowing them to interact as they do in the physical world. They must be able establish trust with each other and transact with the confidence that they are dealing with legitimate and trustworthy individuals, even though our appearance in the metaverse may bear little resemblance to who we are in the physical world.

Just as with social media today, in the metaverse we will each choose our own identity and appearance. Even if we pick our legal names as usernames, by default any username is a pseudonym. Immutable digital identity will eventually be critical to the metaverse, offering the ability to not only define our own identities but prove them with immutability.

As we project this notion forward in time, the lines which separate physical and digital identities will continue to blur, particularly with the growing trend of government protections for digital identities. Given the ability to obtain immutable, government-sanctioned digital identity with the same protections offered by government e-residency and digital ID programs, combined with the pseudonymity inherent in the metaverse, we're not far from the rise of the pseudonymous sovereign citizen. This model would enable pseudonymous participation in government services and transactions, even voting or accessing healthcare, complying with governing laws and regulations with privacy and security intact.

As we'll discuss in the next chapter on hyper-dematerialization—the increasing digitization and virtualization of physical things—the way we live, work, and play in the future will take place in an increasingly digital world. As immersive spaces grow in realism and accessibility, immutable digital identity increasingly becomes a cornerstone of this digital future. The reliability of our identity will determine our ability to prove who we are, to enable secure transactions and interactions, to profit from the value of our ideas and work in ways never before possible, and most importantly to create mechanisms for new value that can be delivered not just to the half of the world which today can benefit from a digital self, but the other half that has barely begun its digital journey.

YOUR DIGITAL SELF TIMELINE

2021–2030: The Rise of Trustless Digital Identity

The dominant brands behind Web2 seek to stay in business, paradoxically rebuilding trust by offering new trustless capabilities, such as shifting from data aggregator to data facilitator, managing personal data in decentralized blockchains—with access control by the data owner (you) via tokenized digital identity, the business of collecting and monetizing user data will become obsolete, as digital identity rapidly heads towards becoming the global norm, having shifted from the domain for "netizens" and "hacktivists" to being a value-added benefit offered by commercial enterprises, governments, and NGOs.

The pay-per-click business model is replaced with paid-per-click as the data aggregators now serve as trustless intermediaries for individuals who seek to monetize their own data. Rather than selling your data, they broker exchanges for you to monetize it (following the same secure yet permissionless and automated described earlier as a convergence of pay-per-click and Bitcoin mining).

Forget your password? Not to worry. Before this decade is out passwords will be long since relegated to the antiqued world of Web2 and centralized identity stores. Before the end of this decade identity and verifiable Credentials become inseparable. For anyone born after 2015 the notion of "logging in" about as much as sense as payphones do to Gen Z.

2031–2040: Biometrics & Fluid Identity

By 2031, digital identity has become an integral part of our daily lives. Biometric authentication, such as facial recognition, fingerprints, and voice recognition, are now far more prevalent and widely accepted. Governments and businesses have increasingly adopted common standards for digital identity verification, making it easier to conduct transactions online.

Your Alexa knows you, but also knows me, and not because there's a unique record of either of our identities at Amazon.

The idea of using the same device day after day now seems as antiquated as a Rolodex. With self-sovereign identity, now long since the norm, your identity is authenticated by sensors, a device, or a system through tokenized anonymous means. Your history and persona are also connected to the vehicle you are driven in (whether you own it or not). In fact, each trip you take is not only part of your history, it is added to your blockchain to define your unique identity stamp.

Your identity now has the quality of provenance with autonomy and continuity wherever you go. It is your digital twin, as a whole and immutable entity. It consists of every action you have taken, but is only visible to you. You are old enough to remember how mobile computing freed everyone from their workstations and allowed you to work from anywhere. Now you take all of that for granted. The idea of repeatedly using the same device over and over seems like a quaint and horribly inefficient tradition. The portability of digital identity both enables as well as offers the model for how computing is done.

2041–2050: The AI-Enhanced Digital Self

In the 2040s, digital identity has become even more ubiquitous, with most transactions and interactions occurring online. Physical forms of identification, such as passports and driver's licenses, are now increasingly less common. Instead, our digital identities are portable and secure, able to be accessed and verified with immutability, and increasing standardization and makes it easy to securely share personal data across different systems and platforms.

By 2041, your digital self never sleeps, never quits, and never stops working—both for you and on your behalf. By the time you awake on a given weekday, you have already answered over 1,000 emails. Just kidding! Email has been extinct for years. The vast majority of correspondences are handled by your digital self, which everyone appreciates since advances in generative AI have made your digital self far more pleasant, thoughtful, and responsive than the physical you. You might as well go back to bed. Before you do though, your ten-year-old daughter poses an exceptionally erudite question, "What does 'online' mean?" You struggle for an answer as it has been years since you had this type of conversation. For anyone born after 2020, the once clear line between the online and the offline world is blurry at best.

2051–2060: Identity-Driven Digital Economy

By the middle of the century, digital identity has become deeply integrated into the fabric of society, inseparable from everyday devices and services, such as smartphones and home automation systems. The use of biometric data, such as fingerprints and facial recognition, have become the primary means of authenticating identity. Identity is now the common means of accessing nearly all services and transactions, from transportation and hospitality to entertainment and shopping. It is now used not only for financial transactions and online communication, but for healthcare, education, and government services. Three billion individuals now have self-sovereign identities, a growing number of them without any government-issued ID other than the record of their birth (if that).

Digital identity is now a $5 trillion industry in the U.S. alone, and the role of identity is at the center of everything we do in the digital world. It is the primary means for how payments are made and recorded, even how work is performed. The lines of demarcation we once used to categorize tech sectors (such as AI, financial systems, cryptosecurity, automation, identity management, and others) have blurred to the point that the categories as we know them today are already unrecognizable.

2061–2070: Seamless Identity Integration & Immortal Identities

In the 2060s, digital identity further transforms society in ways we couldn't fully anticipate even a decade before. Because it is now possible to effortlessly transfer our digital identities between different devices and platforms, we move seamlessly between the physical world and an interconnected digital world. Concerns about privacy and the potential for abuse of personal data, have led to several new regulations and protections. By 2060, the fastest-growing nationality is the pseudonymous sovereign citizen, which now totals over one billion. Our digital self is now seamless integration of our online and offline identities, a palpable and tactile replica of our physical self.

You are old enough to remember such matters as "bills" and "paychecks" and having a single job. However, these are odd notions for anyone just entering the workforce in 2060. The daily exchange of micropayments and microtransactions would be impossible for anyone human being to manually track. Every day you receive thousands of payments through your digital self, working on your behalf, leveraging your data, your know-how, your personal and intellectual property. Each transaction is part of your blockchain, but can only be understood in aggregate.

By 2070, decentralized digital identity is an essential part of the digital infrastructure that underpins modern society, replacing any former use of centralized identity systems. Now fully interoperable across all platforms and systems, it has become so ubiquitous that it's impossible to imagine a world without it. The use of quantum-resistant cryptography is now widespread, ensuring even greater security and privacy for individuals and organizations.

It has now become possible to store our consciousness digitally, allowing our digital self to live on beyond our physical bodies. However, the ethical and societal implications of such developments remain uncertain, with many unsettled debates about the nature of identity in a world where digital and physical realities are deeply intertwined.

CHAPTER 7

The Future of Things:
Hyper-dematerialization

"Dematerialization is less about getting rid of physical objects;
it's about redirecting the energy to where real value lies."

—BRUCE NUSSBAUM

> **GIGATREND—HYPER-DEMATERIALIZTION:**
> The transformation and convergence of the things that
> were previously separate, discrete, and most often
> physical technologies, into primarily digital or virtual
> equivalents

So far, we've addressed the changing nature of global demographics, the rise of Ambient Care, how digital workers will perform the vast majority of today's knowledge work, the shift to mobility as a service, and the emergence of the digital self. In each of these five Gigatrends, we've offered an optimistic lens through which to see the future. However, while we're optimistic, we're not naive. Clearly, we have many challenges beyond the ones we've already discussed that we'll need to overcome during the remainder of the twenty-first century.

We'd like to close the book, and the final Gigatrend, with what we believe will be the defining social achievement of the century: bringing online what we'll call the other four billion, the bottom half of the world's population pyramid that today lives on less than six dollars per day. This effort is something that will require an entirely new set of technologies to scale the caring, feeding, housing, educating, and powering of four billion additional people.

In this chapter, we'll look at the Gigatrend that will, in many ways, act as the foundation for a future that will be much wilder than anything we may have imagined so far: *hyper-dematerialization*. Yes, it's a mouthful, so let's break it down into simple and understandable terms by looking at the evolution of a familiar piece of technology: the smartphone.

Adjusting for inflation, the price of leading brand smartphones (such as Apple or Samsung) today is roughly half that of a mobile phone in 1993. Yet the number of capabilities we now take for granted in even the most basic smartphone would have cost orders of magnitude more to even acquire separately in 2003—and it would have meant dragging around a backpack full of different devices that today fit comfortably in the palm of your hand.

Today you have the equivalent of a digital camera, a video recorder, a Global Positioning System (GPS), a personal computer with nearly the same processing power as a laptop, a Personal Digital Assistant, a gaming console, a digital music player, video conferencing, radio, encyclopedia, television, pedometer, alarm clock, stopwatch, lap timer, compass, flashlight, calculator, oxygen sensor, EKG with basic diagnostics, and various other functions which once were all standalone devices. All of this is in addition to the basic function of a phone, which is now text and streaming video in addition to voice.

Just by way of comparison, because we are as curious as you must be at this point, the cost of all of the components that go into today's smartphone would have cost roughly $137,000 in 1985 or $400,000 in 2024 dollars.[1] It also does not include the cost of the computing power in 1985, which would have required a $32 million Cray supercomputer.)

This is the essence of what we're calling hyper-dematerialization: the transformation and convergence of the *things* that were previously separate, discrete, and most often physical technologies, into primarily digital or virtual equivalents. Of course, this continues to include some physical components, such as a processor, sensors, camera lens, screen, and data storage, which are all necessary for delivering its capabilities.

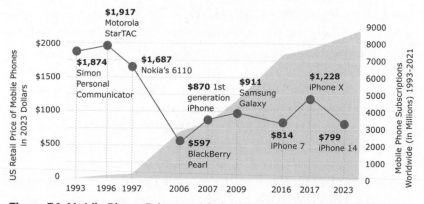

Figure 7.1: Mobile Phone Prices and Subscriber growth 1993–2023
The effect of hyper-dematerialization is seen in the decrease in mobile phone price despite significantly expanded capabilities.[2]

But it's the hyper-dematerialization of many more components and how these combine into a digital ecosystem (both within the phone as well as connected services in the cloud), which enables the broad spectrum of capabilities offered by a single smartphone today.

The other aspect of hyper-dematerialization, that's important in our discussion, is that as these previously separate physical devices converge in digital form, we are increasingly less likely to pay for them separately—they have been effectively demonetized.

The plot twist here is that while hyper-dematerialization clearly has benefits for and has been used to spur the economic prosperity of the developed world, its most profound impact will be in addressing the challenge of bringing online roughly half of the world's population that lives on less than US $5.85 a day[3] and can barely be considered as part of the global economy. Adding these four billion people to the global economy will put enormous pressure on the resources needed to feed, house, care, power, and deliver services to them.

There are two apparent and distinctly different ways to handle that challenge. One is to keep half of the world's population impoverished. As abhorrent as that may sound, there are, unfortunately, those who would claim that there is economic incentive to do so, since the circumstances of this population make them easy for exploitation and low-cost labor. The other is to find a way to radically alter the cost and ecological impact of bringing them into the economy of the twenty-first century.

Rather than having to choose between food, energy, housing, and the impact these will have on the planet, hyper-dematerialization presents a third path; a world where the cost of meeting the basic needs of every person is dramatically reduced, while simultaneously supporting net-zero targets of decarbonization. If this sounds as though it's an impossible goal, think back to how the smartphone's ability to hyper-dematerialize so much capability, and to make it affordable, radically impacted the lives of so many marginalized people around the globe without the additional cost, natural resources, or carbon footprint of all the devices the smartphone replaced. At the same time, it made the access to all of these capabilities affordable to people who would otherwise never have been able to afford them separately.

We're the first to admit that it's a lofty goal to put so much on the shoulders of one Gigatrend. But as with all of the Gigatrends we've discussed, there is a synergy between them that, as Nobel economist Paul Romer would say, does not add up, but multiplies.

Some of what we're about to propose will stretch the boundaries of what you may consider possible. Do you recall our discussion about the cone of possibility that we introduced in Chapter 1? Well, we're planning to step well outside of its confines. However, we are firmly of the opinion that without the benefits of hyper-dematerialization, and the future we're about to describe, we will not be able to deliver on the ultimate promise of each of the Gigatrends we've talked about at the outset of this book—a world in which the dignity and potential of each individual are protected.

Before we look at the many possible ways that hyper-dematerialization will play out, keep in mind that while the objective is to provide a way for the other four billion to become part of the socio-economic mainstream, what we're also discussing in this chapter is the bridge that will need to be built for the world to make the crucial shift from economies of scale to economies of scope. So, let's begin there.

From Scale to Scope

The combined challenges of caring for, feeding, housing, educating, and powering the most vulnerable populations of the world is daunting enough on its own, but even more so, these issues are so entangled that tackling one worsens the others. For example, feeding and sheltering billions of additional people threatens to accelerate global warming a time when governments worldwide fight an already escalating battle with climate change.

Solutions to date have approached these challenges as a zero-sum game, because industrial-era models based on economies of scale create enormous waste and friction. The evidence is in the tremendous increase in waste over the past several decades. By waste, we're referring to the volumes of physical trash, landfill, and the objects that we discard as individuals, organizations, and institutions.

According to research by the World Bank, the amount of waste produced globally has increased from 1.3 billion tons a year in 2012 to 2.2 billion tons projected by 2025. To put that into perspective, we are each producing 55,000 pounds of waste each year, or our body weight in waste every day. That's an increase of $170 billion in global costs.[4] With waste and inefficiencies on this scale there's little room to accommodate change just by scaling the same industrial era models that created this situation in the first place.

 To put that into perspective, we are each producing 55,000 pounds of waste each year, or our body weight in waste every day.

The solution to these challenges is to fundamentally rethink the way we build and deliver products and services, with what we've called economies of scope. Recall that in Chapter 1 we defined and economy of scope as one in which the friction of working with partners is eliminated through the use of technology. Economies of scope are built on three cornerstones: digital ecosystems, digital twins, and reusable resources.

Digital Ecosystem

Digital ecosystems, which we introduced in Chapter 4, are networks of interconnected digital platforms, applications, services, and stakeholders that are held together based on strategy rather than ownership. In the context of economies of scope, digital ecosystems enable organizations to share data, resources, and capabilities across different products, services, or industries. They foster collaboration and innovation, reduce barriers to entry, and allow companies to leverage shared infrastructure and services to achieve cost savings and efficiencies. While technology has increasingly facilitated digital ecosystems, the trend away from highly vertically integrated organizations has been evolving for the past fifty years.

Notable examples include: the breakup of AT&T into "Baby Bells," which paved the way for today's major telecommunications players and the Standard Oil breakup, which resulted in industry leaders like Exxon, Mobil, and Chevron. What these sorts of breakups have in common is that they allow the smaller entities to concentrate on their core businesses, reduce complexity, and improve market performance. The advent of digital ecosystems will accelerate this trend, playing an increasingly important role in shaping the future of business and driving the move towards smaller, more agile organizations with less waste and less friction.

We should add the caveat that the trend away from vertical integration is not universal. There are still instances where companies choose vertical integration—even newer companies without the legacy of pursuing an economy of scale. One of the most notable examples is Tesla. Tesla controls multiple stages of its production process, from raw materials to finished products, to its dealerships, allowing it to maintain control over critical aspects of its business—leading to cost savings, increased efficiency, and faster innovation. One key aspect of Tesla's vertical integration is its control over battery production. The company operates its Gigafactory in partnership with Panasonic, which enables Tesla to control the quality, cost, and availability of batteries—a critical component of electric vehicles that represents about one third of an EV's cost. Additionally, Tesla designs and manufactures its vehicles in-house at its own factories, allowing it to oversee the entire production process and maintain strict quality control.

Tesla also develops its software in-house, including the Autopilot system and over-the-air updates, fostering rapid innovation and seamless integration of software with its vehicles. The company has also built its own extensive network of Supercharger stations to support its customers and facilitate long-distance electric vehicle travel, addressing the lack of charging infrastructure, a common concern for potential buyers. Lastly, Tesla is the only player in the automobile industry that operates a direct-to-consumer sales model, bypassing traditional dealership networks and providing better control over the customer experience.

Tesla's vertical integration strategy has been instrumental in establishing a strong competitive advantage in the electric vehicle market, but it also comes with challenges, such as the need for significant capital investment and the complexities of managing a highly integrated organization. Tesla's approach makes sense given the enormity of the challenges a new car manufacturer faces in competing with monolithic competitors.

Our point is not that economies of scale do not serve a purpose, but rather that they represent a model that will increasingly be used in more confined settings rather than as the defacto business model of the future.

 Our point is not that economies of scale do not serve a purpose, but rather that they represent a model that will increasingly be used in more confined settings rather than as the defacto business model of the future.

Digital Twins

The second cornerstone of an economy of scope is the digital twin. Think back to the digital self we introduced in Chapter 6. A digital twin is a type of digital self that creates a virtual replica of a physical asset, process, or system, allowing real-time monitoring, simulation, and optimization. Most often these are machines or mechanical devices that are easier to test, simulate, and optimize in digital form rather than in the real world. Digital twins can help companies achieve economies of scope by providing deep insights into the performance and interactions of various products or services. They facilitate the identification of synergies and optimization opportunities, enabling companies to streamline processes, reduce costs, and improve overall efficiency. Additionally, digital twins can be used to test and simulate new product or service offerings without the need for costly physical prototypes or pilot projects. This includes the ability to understand how the behaviors of a physical object or organization will impact ecological impact.

In principle, digital twins aren't all that new. If you know anything about Apollo 13, you might recall how rookie astronaut Ken Mattingly, who had been bumped from the mission due to measles exposure, worked in the Apollo 13 simulator at mission control to identify the best way to repower the flight capsule for reentry. What he was doing is pretty much the essence of what a digital twin is supposed to do.

One of the most notable examples of recent digital twin technology is the design and manufacturing of Boeing's 777 aircraft. Boeing used digital twin technology to simulate various scenarios so that engineers were able to identify and address potential issues before they were discovered in real-world manufacturing. This approach led to a 40 percent increase in the quality of parts and well as a reduction in material waste and time and cost savings during the production process. While Boeing has not disclosed the cost savings of using a digital twin, estimates in the manufacturing of automobiles claim a 54 percent reduction in manufacturing costs as the result of digital twin technology.[5]

The digital twin is also not just limited to the design and manufacturing phases. Boeing uses it throughout the 777's lifecycle. By integrating real-time data from aircraft sensors, maintenance teams can predict and prevent potential issues before they escalate, further enhancing efficiency and reducing downtime.

Reusable Resources

The third cornerstone is reusable resources. These are simply assets, components, or systems that can be shared or repurposed across different products or services. In a digital context, reusable resources can include software modules, data, algorithms, and hardware components that can be easily adapted or reconfigured for different purposes. The idea is to design products, services, and systems in a way that promotes reuse, repair, refurbishment, and recycling, with the ultimate goal of creating a closed-loop system where waste is eliminated and resources are continuously cycled through the economy. One example that we've already covered in Chapter 5 is that of Autonomous Vehicles which are utilized 95 percent of the time as opposed to the 5 percent of today's owned vehicles.

Combining these resources with others in the cloud also allows companies to rapidly develop and deploy new offerings, leverage existing resources more effectively, and scale their operations more efficiently. Think of the example we used in Chapter 3 on the Hospital in the Cloud.

Shifting Gears

In his book *More from Less: The Surprising Story of How We Learned to Prosper Using Fewer Resources—and What Happens Next*,[6] Massachusetts Institute of Technology professor Andrew McAfee argues that hyper-dematerialization drives both profitability and economic growth, while reducing poverty levels and environmental impacts. We'd go further to suggest that without this shift to a hyper-dematerialized model that focuses on scope over scale, there is no way to build a global economy that will sustain eight to ten billion people.

 Without this shift to a hyper-dematerialized model that focuses on scope over scale, there is no way to build a global economy that will sustain eight to ten billion people.

The transition from physical to digital may sound simple in principle, but it can be incredibly difficult in practice. McAfee offers an example of the switch from traditional paper books to e-books. The transition resulted in significant cost savings for publishers, as they no longer needed to print physical copies and ship them out. Since less raw material was used, there was a reduced carbon footprint associated with printing processes, as well as emissions caused by shipping for distribution. However, none of this happened easily from within the publishing industry. It took the existential threat of Amazon to spur the industry towards a hyper-dematerialized model.

Perhaps an even better example, which speaks to why hyper-demateri-alization is so difficult, is that of Kodak and digital photography. If there's a poster child for how to get stuck in the past while the future drives by in the fast lane, in clear view, it would have to be Kodak, the iconic twentieth century company which invented both modern film emulsion photography and digital photography, and still found itself unable to move into the future. George Eastman, the founder and former CEO of Kodak, identi-fied one of his company's guiding principles as "mass production at low cost." This is precisely the mindset that had driven every company seeking economies of scale for the past two hundred years, because it worked. By 1976, Kodak had an unimaginable 90 percent share of the film market.

It's supremely ironic that the company which popularized one of the most disruptive technologies of the twentieth century was unable to take advantage of the switch to digital photography—especially given that Kodak invented digital photography in its own labs.

Steve Sasson, the engineer who built the first digital camera in 1975, and who went on to receive the National Medal of Technology and Inno-vation, the highest honor awarded by the US government to scientists, engineers, and inventors, recalled Kodak management's reaction in a 2008 *New York Times* interview:[7] "My prototype was big as a toaster, but the technical people loved it. But it was filmless photography, so manage-ment's reaction was, 'that's cute—but don't tell anyone about it...'"[8]

As the story is most often told, that lack of support from leadership was the reason for Kodak's ultimate failure. But Kodak's failure was not one of vision. The direction of photography was clearly understood by the company's executives. The culprit was an industrial era model whose ecosystem was built around the economies of scale of physical media, and not the economies of scope associated with a hyper-dematerialized product. The same investments and strategies that support economies of scale make transitioning to an economy of scope extraordinarily difficult, if at all possible.

Kodak's plight is hardly unique. In fact, we'd go so far as to suggest that some of the biggest failures over the last several decades—not only Kodak, but Borders, one of the world's largest booksellers, or Blockbuster, the company that built an empire of 9000 video rental stores—were not the result of an inability to innovate; each of these companies had innovated new products and services that recognized the future. Still, despite Kodak's invention of digital photography, Blockbuster having the on-demand streaming capability, and Borders being one of the first online booksellers, they could not squeeze the enormity of their industrial legacy through the doorway to the future.

 Despite Kodak's invention of digital photography, Blockbuster having the on-demand streaming capability, and Borders being one of the first online booksellers, they could not squeeze the enormity of their industrial legacy through the doorway to the future.

So, what does the inability of a Kodak or a Borders to evolve have to do with the other four billion and the transition from scale to scope? Companies that pursue an approach which relies strictly on an economy-of-scale business model will most likely be the earliest casualties of the next five decades. We realize this sounds heretical, but only because economies of scale have become such an immutable part of the way the industrialized world works.

Instead of rebuilding and repurposing their ecosystem in an increasingly hyper-dematerialized world, these businesses build physical fortresses around the past. As was the case with Kodak, tearing down these fortresses rarely, if ever, comes from an internal initiative. By the time these market threats become existential it's too late to respond and change. An economy of scope,[9] on the other hand, relies on the ability to quickly adapt to changing conditions with minimal friction, since much of that change is dependent on modifying digital assets rather than just physical assets.

Clearly, just making the changes we've described so far in this chapter will not solve many of the more basic challenges that the other four-billion face, such as the lack of housing, electrification, or food insecurity. For example, the materials that go into a building are only part of its environmental impact. As a general rule the materials (embodied energy and carbon) account for roughly 10 to 30 percent of the total lifecycle impact, while the operational energy consumption (heating, cooling, lighting, and other energy uses) account for the remaining 70 to 90 percent. Without solving these issues no economic model will be adequate to support even the most basic needs of the world's population.

Powering the Four Billion Left Behind

According to the U.N.'s International Energy Agency (IEA), at least 1.2 billion people are currently estimated to be living in "energy poverty," meaning they lack access to sustainable, reliable, and affordable energy services.[10] The IEA's current estimates are that it will cost $33 billion a year—or a total of $700 billion through 2030—to provide access to just this population alone, with the bulk of those costs attributed to the development of a new energy generation and transmission infrastructure. However, these numbers may significantly downplay the problem. According to one study[11] which looked specifically at the reliability of energy, the number of people without reliable electric services is as high as 3.5 billion. Since energy production and requirements are closely tied to economic growth, liberating marginalized populations from poverty (both economic poverty and energy poverty) will drive the need for more generation even further.

We should also emphasize that our focus in this chapter will be on energy technologies that can be easily scaled in remote geographies and countries with less than adequate infrastructure for energy delivery. For example, fusion energy has the potential to be a game changer for global energy production. However, it faces challenges in remote geographies and poorer countries due to factors such as high initial costs, technological complexity, limited energy infrastructure, maintenance and support requirements, political and social factors, and the suitability of some of the smaller-scale solutions we'll discuss. Developing and constructing a fusion power plant also requires significant financial investment—something that we would be foolish to ignore. Add to that the need for a skilled workforce to operate and maintain a fusion plant and you're looking at a much longer timeline for fusions acceptance in the less-developed parts of the world. These countries will benefit more from smaller-scale, decentralized energy solutions such as solar panels, wind turbines, or microgrids, which we'll discuss.

None of this is meant to downplay fusion. Companies such as Helion, which focuses on developing compact fusion energy technology, could potentially address some of the challenges undeveloped regions face. Helion's fusion process uses deuterium, a type of hydrogen found in water. The reaction gives off no external heat, but instead uses what's called the Faraday effect in a magnetic field to create electricity. Here's how it works according to Helion:[12]

> Deuterium and helium-3 fuel is heated to plasma conditions. Magnets confine this plasma in a Field Reversed Configuration Magnets accelerate two FRCs to 1 million mph from opposite ends of the forty-foot accelerator. They collide in the center.
>
> They are then further compressed by a powerful magnetic field until they reach fusion temperatures of 100 million degrees Celsius.
>
> At this temperature, the deuterium and helium-3 ions are moving fast enough to overcome the forces that would otherwise keep them apart, and they fuse. This releases more energy than is consumed by the fusion process. As new fusion energy is created, the plasma expands.
>
> As the plasma expands, it pushes back on the magnetic field. By Faraday's law, the change in field induces current, which is directly recaptured as electricity.

To give you an idea of how efficient the process is, one glass of deuterium replaces one million gallons of fossil fuel. To put it another way, that single glass could power the typical US home for 865 years. The goal is less expensive, smaller-scale, and modular fusion reactors that simplify the technology, to make it more accessible and affordable for remote geographies and poorer countries with varying energy demands. However, even if companies like Helion succeed in making fusion energy more accessible, other challenges like political, social, and environmental concerns, as well as the need for skilled labor and maintenance resources, will still need to be addressed. International cooperation, technology transfer, and capacity-building efforts will be crucial in helping remote geographies and poorer countries adopt and benefit from fusion energy in the future.

One thing that is clear, however, is that for the foreseeable future we cannot conserve our way out of energy poverty.

One thing that is clear, however, is that for the foreseeable future we cannot conserve our way out of energy poverty. Despite the longer-term promise of fusion and other on-going improvements in energy efficiency, there's a much more immediate and growing demand for more power, particularly in emerging markets, as a result of population growth and growing electrification. In India alone, the International Energy Agency projects the rate of electrification will likely increase five times faster than its population growth. Over the next twenty years India will need to add a power system the size of what the European Union has today.[13] This is consistent with the latest forecasts from U.S. Energy Information Administration (EIA), the statistical and analytical agency within the U.S. Department of Energy. Using the *World Energy Projection System*,[14] EIA's International Energy Outlook (IEO) presents an analysis of long-term world energy markets through 2050.[15]

In order to project the impact of economic growth on energy consumption, the International Energy Outlook applies regional factors of growth to project compound annual growth rates of global gross domestic product (GDP) for the period covering 2020 to 2050, with a range of 2.0 to 3.7 percent per year. The data we have used in this chapter is based on the 3.7 percent growth rate model. Although this may be high for developed markets represented in the OCED group (the thirty-eight member

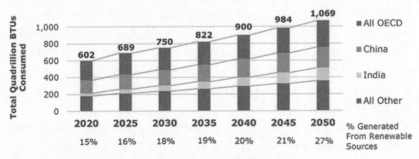

Figure 7.2: Global Energy Consumption 2020–2050
Global energy demands are conservatively expected to double by 2050.

nations who comprise the Organization for Economic Co-operation and Development[16]), this is a conservative growth rate for India and other developing markets we are more concerned with in this chapter.[17]

India has ambitious goals for both economic development and the expansion of its power capacity, which largely align with the International Energy Outlook projections of a roughly 500 percent increase in overall energy consumption and nearly 800 percent increase in the use of renewables. At the UN Climate Summit in 2021, Indian Prime Minister Narendra Modi announced their commitment to achieving net-zero emissions by 2070, which is anticipated to cost at least $10 trillion over the next thirty years.[18] To call that an aggressive goal, for a nation that today derives as much as 80 percent of its power from non-renewable sources,[19] would be a severe understatement

To meet a challenge of this magnitude, India is focused on increasing both generation capacity and efficiency. Part of this strategy is leveraging digital twins to create virtual replicas of power plants, which will be used to optimize their performance.[20] Both the National Thermal Power Corporation and Tata Power, India's two largest power producers, have implemented digital twin power plants which allow for real-time monitoring and analysis.

The Smart Grid

In Chapter 4 we introduced digital ecosystems with the example of a utility grid that connects business partners and their marketplaces. The smart grid is also a digital ecosystem. While connected to the national grid, both its architecture and operation is distinct from the brittle, vertically integrated model of the conventional grid, defined by the one-way flow of electricity from a centralized power plant. The smart grid is a decentralized model which leverages an ecosystem of sensors, AI, analytics, and automation to facilitate two-way communication among the various components of the grid.

This allows for a far more flexible model able to support distributed power generation, greater resiliency, as well as Demand Response[21] (the concept of enabling consumers to manage their own demand), to optimized consumption and leveraged dynamic pricing models. The smart grid is fast becoming a central tenant of energy modernization in emerging markets, with India's *National Smart Grid Mission*[22] as an example of the level of priority it's receiving. It's also a critical element in the integration of distributed generation capabilities, such as rooftop solar panels, allowing the monitoring and flow of electricity in and out of the grid.

 The origins of energy poverty among the other four billion are not limited to the lack of grid access, but rather the fact that most of the electricity supply systems they are connected to are unreliable and inadequate.

The origins of energy poverty among the other four billion are not limited to the lack of grid access, but rather the fact that most of the electricity supply systems they are connected to are unreliable and inadequate. But this isn't unique to this population; it's a flaw within conventional grids in developed economies as well.

The business model of electricity generation is one of the purest examples of supply and demand. Because storage capacity today represents only a fraction of electric power production capacity, it's critical for electric utilities to match power supply to consumer demand. If consumers demand more electricity than is generated, the strain on the power grid will result in brownouts—where frequency and voltage of the electrical current drops—or worse, the power grid may automatically shut itself down, resulting in a blackout.

On the other hand, generating too much electricity means not only that the excess power goes unsold, but leads to other problems across the power grid, such as a surge, resulting in an overvoltage that can fry electrical equipment, or a more dangerous form of surge called a transient, which can overwhelming the grid's infrastructure, again leading to a blackout.

To avoid these situations, electric utilities must continuously balance supply and demand. Instability of a given region's power grid is typically the result of a mismatch in supply and demand, yet, of the two, demand is the one utilities have the least control over. This creates the need for demand response or the ability to allow consumers to adjust their electricity usage in order to balance the supply and demand of electricity, reduce energy costs, and improve grid reliability.

Demand response illustrates a critical difference between conventional grids and smart grids, and the ability of electric utilities to continuously match supply with demand. In conventional grids, demand response programs are typically managed through manual intervention by utility companies, who ask customers to reduce their electricity usage during times of peak demand. But this process is often slow and inefficient, and if consumers do not comply it leads to involuntary service interruptions—rolling blackouts. This is especially common in developing nations, where they can occur weekly or even multiple times a week, such as in Sub Saharan Africa, which averages nine blackouts per month. Unlike the usual blackout, these are intentional shutdowns by the utility, leaving households, businesses, schools, and even hospitals without adequate power.

In contrast, smart grids use two-way communication and automation to effect real-time response to changes in electricity demand. One of the key enablers of this is smart meters, which allow utilities to gather real-time information on energy usage at the consumer level. Unlike traditional analog meters, smart meters can record and transmit energy usage data at regular intervals, allowing utilities to monitor and manage energy distribution more efficiently. This enables utilities to make faster and much more informed decisions about energy production and distribution by understanding consumer energy usage patterns.

Smart meters also enable utilities to offer new pricing models and programs, such as time-of-use pricing and demand response programs, which incentivize consumers to shift their energy usage to off-peak hours, when energy is cheaper and the grid is less stressed. This has a significant impact on cost in surprising ways. Work by the International Energy Agency (IEA) on the effectiveness of demand response programs has shown that a 5 percent reduction of use during peak demand periods can lead to a 50 percent price reduction in the consumer cost of electricity. A similar study, by Carnegie Mellon, demonstrated that even just a 1 percent shift in peak demand would result in a 3.9 percent cost savings.

Another advantage of smart grids is that they allow consumers to also be producers. Through the process of "net metering" consumers who generate their own electricity, through rooftop solar panels or wind turbines, receive credit for any excess electricity they produce and export to the grid. With net metering, smart meters track both consumption and production in real-time, which helps grid operators better balance supply and demand, allowing more stable and reliable operation of the grid.

Smart grids are categorized by energy generation capacity, from as low as one kilowatt for stand-alone *picogrids*, up to several Gigawatts for *macrogrids* scalable to meet the energy demands of large geographic regions, countries, or continents. Regardless of capacity, each category of smart grid leverages communication and control technologies to monitor and manage energy flows, via sensors and data analytics that optimize grid performance and respond to changing conditions. The degree to which automation and AI are leveraged generally increases with the number of consumer connections to a given grid, given the greater volume of data available from smart meters and other two-way communication. But it's also the case that at the far end of digitization are autonomous smart grids, which perform autonomically, leveraging AI and machine learning to self-optimize and operate with little to no human intervention. These today are microgrids, supporting target communities or large industrial applications. Examples include autonomous microgrids in Borrego Springs, California,[23] and the Miramar Marine Corp Airbase.[24] The five types of smart grids are defined and explained in Figure 7.3.

Macrogrids

A macrogrid is a large scale smart grid designed to handle energy supply for large communities with capacities from hundreds of kilowatts to gigawatts. It supports decentralized power generation and two-way communication between utilities and their customers, and uses sensors along transmission lines for real-time monitoring. Macrogrids are cost-effective for supplying the power to consumers near the grid infrastructure. They are owned by large commercial utilities or governments and by transmission system operators (TSOs) responsible for the control and monitoring of the operation of the electrical power system.

Mini-grids

A mini-grid is defined by renewable-based distribution (most commonly solar but also small wind turbine and or mini-hydro-based electricity generation) with a capacity in the range 10-600 kilowatts. Mini-grids are

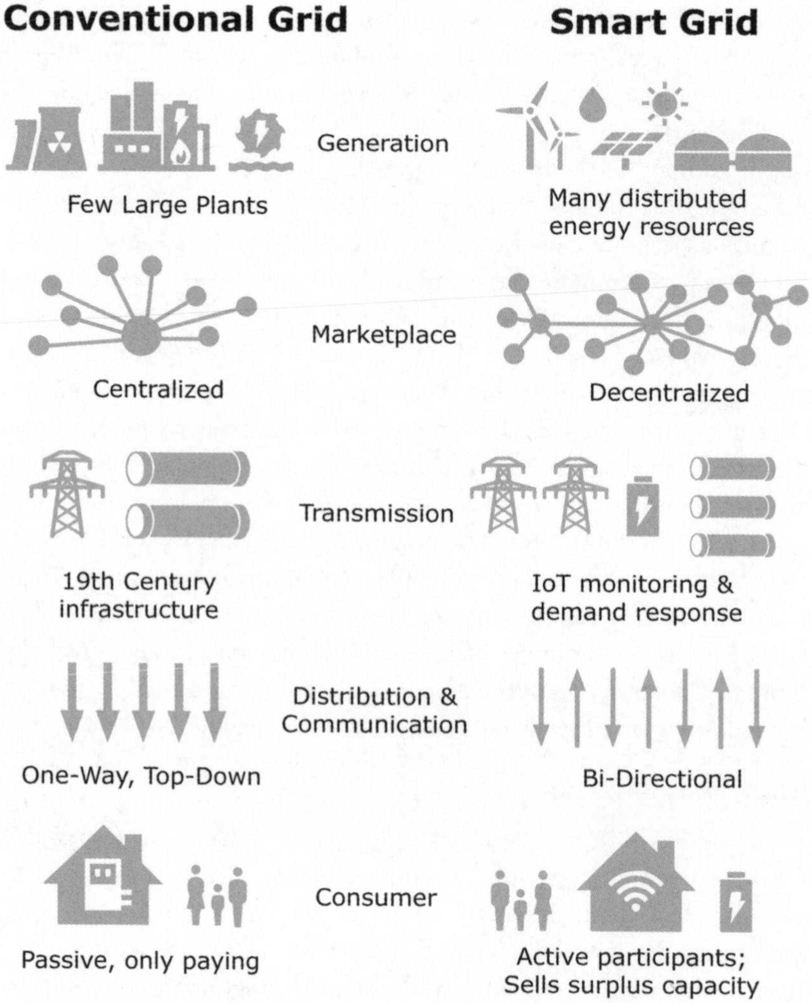

Conventional Grid

Smart Grid

Generation

Few Large Plants

Many distributed
energy resources

Marketplace

Centralized

Decentralized

Transmission

19th Century
infrastructure

IoT monitoring &
demand response

**Distribution &
Communication**

One-Way, Top-Down

Bi-Directional

Consumer

Passive, only paying

Active participants;
Sells surplus capacity

Figure 7.3: Comparing Smart Grids and Conventional Grids
Smart grids enable more efficient, reliable, and secure distribution of electricity
through greater integration of renewable energy sources and empowering
consumers with real-time data and control.

able to connect to a central grid to exchange power or otherwise operate
independently, and are increasingly used for rural electrification, such as
the Lolwe mini-grid in Uganda.[25] These are fully functioning smart grids,
leveraging communication between the digital ecosystem to optimize

generation and consumption through demand and energy management, grid measurement devices and remote operations. Mini-grids offer disconnected or "off the grid" communities greater resilience and reliability than conventional grids at a lower cost of infrastructure. They are typically owned by collaboratives and small for-profit operators, rather than larger commercial or national utilities.

Microgrids

A microgrid is another decentralized form of power generation, distribution and consumption with a capacity in the range 5-10 kilowatts. Where a mini-grid may supply an entire town, a microgrid could be used to support a small village, campus or even a single home. Microgrids often incorporate more complex energy systems with multiple sources of generation than nanogrids and generally leverage more advanced monitoring capabilities, such as digital twin functionality. An analog to microgrids, which is now emerging in some developing countries, such as India (as well as in OCED nations), are using Virtual Power Plants or VPPs. These follow a similar model to that of microgrids as decentralized, medium-scale interconnected power generating units. But unlike microgrids, VPPS operate merely as wholesalers and are not able to provide power directly to consumers. In markets such as India, they are being used to offset the power demands of large commercial enterprises, such as factories, to allow grid operators to better manage energy supply and demand.

Nanogrids

Nanogrids are less than 5 kilowatts, with more localized power generation and the ability to be self-sufficient systems with energy storage capability, while also allowing interconnection with larger grids. Within emerging market environments and other regions still reliant on conventional grids, utilities often do not have the means to store excess power. Mini-grids, Microgrids and Nanogrids typically include storage, which is necessary for the resiliency of the grid with variable renewable energy sources (such as solar power when the sun is down), as well as for storing excess energy generated during off-peak times. Although today lead-acid batteries are most commonly used, advances in digital technology such as AI, and in materials, are driving greater performance, efficiency and affordability.

Picogrids

Lastly, Picogrids are stand-alone smart grids—not connected to larger gridsable to handle up to 1kilowatt in power, connected in an ecosystem with sensors, as well as connectivity with remote management and data sharing. These are viable for supporting localized use cases such as an Electric Vehicle charging kiosk powered by solar panels or other nearby sources of power generation.[26]

Among the various smart grid types, mini-grids are generally viewed as offering the greatest potential to catalyze economic development and social progress in communities that lack access to reliable and affordable electricity. They offer a practical alternative where the costs of deployment are lower than for the extension of the national grid or stand-alone systems. Current research from the World Bank[27] estimates that by 2030 mini-grids can supply 50 percent of the power needs for half of the one billion people currently facing energy poverty. They also offer a platform for regional entrepreneurship by enabling the development of small-scale power generation and distribution businesses, enabling job creation and income-generating opportunities in areas where both are limited. But there are a number of considerations in evaluating whether or not the development of a mini-grid will be viable for a target market of energy consumers.

Evaluating Mini-grid Opportunities

 For many communities, the construction of mini-grids may offer the only viable option for power in remote areas where there is no access to a conventional power grid.

For many communities, the construction of mini-grids may offer the only viable option for power in remote areas where there is no access to a conventional power grid. However, the history of mini-grid development has shown that the costs of ongoing maintenance and infrastructure updates are often understated, with projects being pursued out of a sense for what a given community may need rather than prioritizing a viable business model.[28] Part of this consideration is determining the community of anticipated energy consumers' *willingness-to-pay*[29]—another way of describing the elasticity of demand. Compared to alternatives, what is the price they are willing and able to pay per kilowatt-hour for electricity? In developing markets, this comparison is typically made against candles and kerosene for lighting, and diesel for running generators. However, population density is a critical factor, as there needs to be sufficient aggregate demand to support even a small mini-grid, when compared against smaller scale solar alternatives, such as individually acquired plug-and-play, pay-as-you-go options.

The optimal application for mini-grids is typically smaller rural communities which are not accessible to, or otherwise not well-served by, conventional grids. High population density risks excess demand, resulting in problems of stability and reliability. Yet there needs to be a critical mass of demand to support the cost to set up and maintain, as well as to ensure long-term financial viability, of the business model supporting the mini-grid. There are also considerations which need to be made around the security of the mini-grid, especially in politically unstable areas where it may be impractical or infeasible to fully secure infrastructure. But grid operations should be able support the means for security personnel and

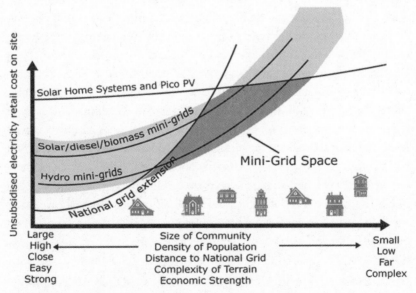

Figure 7.4: Prioritizing Mini-grid Target Opportunities

The optimal space for mini-grids is mid-density requirements outside of easy access to national grids.

surveillance systems, as well as backup systems to ensure continuity of power supply in the event of a security breach or other disruptions.[30]

Why Access to Electricity Is Especially Critical to Vulnerable Populations

The forecasts and predictions discussed earlier—such as those from the *International Energy Outlook*—project the total amount of energy required to meet the basic needs of a population for cooking, heating, transportation, as well as industrial processes, including electricity generation. For every nation, electricity is just one part, although a growing part, of their total energy consumption. For those facing energy poverty, access to electricity plays a far more significant role. The IEA estimates that around 2.6 billion people worldwide today rely on wood or charcoal for cooking, and that half of Africa—about 580 million people—rely on kerosene for lighting.

Both charcoal and kerosene represent significant health and environmental impacts, including indoor air pollution and carbon emissions. They also underscore the dual challenges of shifting vulnerable populations to rely more on electricity for basic needs, and meeting these needs with expanded access through rural electrification and greater supply of electricity in higher density urban areas. Access to clean and affordable electricity by vulnerable populations is not merely an issue of sustainability, but an economic imperative. During the instability and lack of reliability of conventional grid power in regions such as Sub-Saharan Africa, backup power sources such as diesel generators are used more than half the time, even by those with grid connections.[31] This puts an extraordinary burden on already challenged energy-impoverished regions. Even in Nigeria, which has the highest GDP in Africa, one study showed that the high cost of operating generators led nearly 800 firms to shut down between 2009 and 2011.[32]

 Even in Nigeria, which has the highest GDP in Africa, one study showed that the high cost of operating generators led nearly 800 firms to shut down between 2009 and 2011.

The Reliability-Adjusted Cost of Electricity is a measure increasingly used to provide a comparison of different power generation technologies based on their total cost of delivering reliable electricity, including factors such as the need for backup power or energy storage. For much of the developing world, the lack of reliability put the actual cost of electricity much higher than what is otherwise charged by the electrical grid utility. In Nigeria, for example, the more relevant comparison is the cost of diesel generation versus the cost of the next alternative—solar PV mini-grids. As of late 2022, this was $0.44 per kilowatt for diesel generation compared to $0.38 per kilowatt for solar PV mini-grids.[33]

This makes the two roughly comparable today, with a slight advantage for solar. But this gap is expected to only widen over time, as the cost of solar energy is projected to drop over the next decade to roughly $0.05 per kilowatt.[34] Compare this to diesel generation at $0.30 to $0.60 per kilowatt currently and likely to increase by 2030. As shown in Figure 7.5, solar PV mini-grids offer a far more compelling alternative for 580 million inhabitants of the African continent without any access to the conventional grid,[35] as well as millions more (two-thirds of the continent's entire population) who may be grid-connected, but otherwise face regular outages.[36]

In addition to the global effect of rising oil prices, emerging markets, and in particular rural populations, are more likely to see price shocks with diesel than developed markets. In Nigeria, the price more than

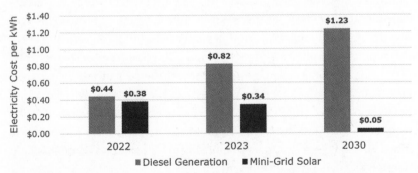

Figure 7.5: Per Kilowatt-hour Rates of Diesel-generated vs. Mini-grid Solar Power

The declining price of solar compared an increasing or otherwise unstable price of diesel makes off-grid solar power an increasingly advantageous option in areas with access to reliable grid power.

doubled 2022 over 2023, with other regions similarly affected over the last five years. Projecting the targeted cost of solar energy in 2030, compared against the cost of diesel with just a 50 percent increase by that time, the per kilowatt-hour cost of diesel-generated power will be nearly 2500 percent greater than mini-grid solar power.

Solar Power Will Continue to Decline in Cost

The continuous decline in the cost of solar power generation is both a real and predictable phenomenon. The obvious meaningful difference between renewable and non-renewable energy sources, in particular solar, is that the cost of power generation is concentrated almost entirely within the process of creating the means of generation (such as manufacturing and deploying solar panels), not acquiring the sources of energy used to fuel generation.

For non-renewable sources—notably coal, oil, natural gas, or nuclear energy—there are considerable costs resulting from the mining and refining the fuel used to generate energy, as well as the cost of transporting and storing fuel to the point of generation. However, in the case of solar, we are seeing the consistent and predictable decrease in costs associated with creating the means for generating power from solar energy (specifically photovoltaic panels).

The trend of decreasing costs observed in the solar energy industry is called Swanson's Law[37]. or the Swanson Effect, which states that the cost of solar photovoltaic (PV) modules decreases by 20 percent for every doubling of cumulative shipped volume. This law implies that as solar technology becomes more widely adopted, the cost of producing solar energy decreases, making it more accessible and cost-effective. This trend has been observed since the 1970s and has continued to hold true as solar technology has improved. The result is that the more we produce, the more we are able to improve manufacturing efficiency and quality, and develop thinner and more efficient panels.

By reducing the volume of materials required to deliver the same or better levels of energy, the generation cost of solar power continues to decrease over time, as do the materials needed to create solar panels and the cost of their manufacturing process. As a result, solar power will

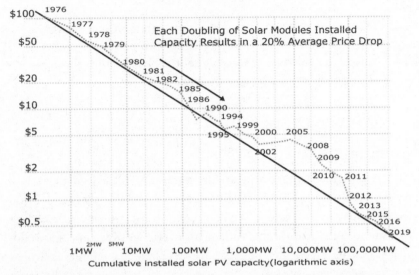

Figure 7.6: **History of the Cost and Production of Solar Photovoltaics**

The cost of solar panel manufacturing has consistently dropped year over year since introduction.[39]

become an increasingly attractive option for powering emerging market communities, in economic value as well as sustainability. How attractive? For both developed markets such as the U.S. and developing markets such as Sub Saharan Africa, the cost per kilowatt-hour is expected to drop below $0.05 by 2030—well below any other energy source.[38]

The declining price of photovoltaic (PV) panels has made utility-level solar production more cost-effective and competitive by reducing the cost of electricity generation. This has made solar not only economically competitive with other means for local elecitricy generation (such as diesel generators), but also increasingly cheaper large scale energy projects using non-renewable sources, including coal and natural gas.[40] This has led to greater consumer demand, on top of growing demand from governments for greater investment in solar power generation, which has led to increased investment in solar power production. That, in turn, has further reduced the cost of solar power according to Swanson's Law. As a result, solar power has become a mainstream energy source, and its adoption is expected to continue to grow, but may also lead to what otherwise seems like a counterintuitive notion: solar power energy exports.

Solar power has become a mainstream energy source, and its adoption is expected to continue to grow, but may also lead to what otherwise seems like a counterintuitive notion: solar power energy exports.

Exporting the Sun

Africa is a particularly good region for solar power due to its high levels of solar irradiation, expansive available land area, and the growing demand for electricity in the region. The continent receives some of the highest levels of solar radiation in the world, with an average of around 2,000 kilowatt-hours per square meter per year.[41] As technology continues to evolve, solar power may in the future become a significant economic driver for the region through energy exports.

Today there are no grid interconnections between Europe and Africa, but there has been an ambitious plan for several years, the Trans-Mediterranean Renewable Energy Cooperation (TREC), which would involve the construction of large-scale solar and wind power plants in North Africa and the Middle East, as well as the development of a high-voltage direct current (HVDC) transmission system to transport the electricity to Europe.

Through the use of concentrated solar power (focusing solar energy to drive electricity-generating turbines) as well as photovoltaic electricity generation, the TREC project has the potential to be a significant source of renewable energy for Europe, as well as providing significant economic benefits for the participating countries. The high upfront investment costs required to develop the necessary infrastructure have remained one of the hurdles, but these continue to decline, bringing the project closer to reality. Where this project was mostly fantasy considering the technology of the conventional grid, the smart grid will provide the necessary coordination and the automated maintenance necessary for interconnection at this scale. Again, what we're seeing here is the impact of hyper-dematerialization on the viability of options that would have simply been economically impossible in the past.

Another cornerstone to enabling TREC is blockchain. TREC represents a level of grid interconnectedness at an unprecedented scale, across a more complex ecosystem of power generators, grid operators, and consumers than what current models have supported. Blockchain provides a model capable of supporting this scope of cooperation through secure and transparent data-sharing, smart contracts, and immutable transactions. This would likely include peer-to-peer trading of renewable energy, as well as a tamper-proof and transparent record of energy transactions, ensuring that data is accurate and reliable. With energy flowing across multiple regulatory environments, it would provide the necessary traceability and transparency of renewable energy supply chains, by tracking the origin and certification of renewable energy certificates (RECs) and other renewable energy attributes, such as the source of generation.

One of the factors that makes Swanson's Law particularly relevant for the other four billion is that the continued decline in the cost of solar panels makes off-grid solar generation increasingly more affordable. Already equal to or cheaper than diesel generation or kerosene, the declining price of solar will help free up resources for other needs. For example, cheaper and more reliable energy will spur economic growth by lowering the cost of existing work, such as farming, where it will reduce the cost of electric-powered irrigation systems, refrigeration units, and other equipment.

Just as important will be the impact of cheaper energy in opening up new opportunities for entrepreneurs.

Energy Drives Growth and Entrepreneurship in Emerging Markets

The energy sector is a rich space for innovation and entrepreneurship across developing markets, helping to also foster economic development in other sectors such as farming, manufacturing, and services. This represents a pivot in the business of power generation towards economies of scope, with a growing number of value-added services and solutions, built on core capabilities such as access to smart grids and off-grid power generation.

Micro-scale power market generation for emerging market economies began roughly a decade ago with plug-and-play off-grid solar generation for lighting and other single-home use, available through pay-as-you-go and microfinance options. As capabilities have matured, Energy-as-a-Service (EaaS) has emerged as a business model, gaining traction in both developed and emerging markets, focused on delivering power through either off-grid microgrids or other grid-connected solutions, without the capital investment they would otherwise require. One of these, Azuri PayGo Energy[42], offers an off-grid pay-as-you-go (PAYGo) option for Sub-Saharan Africa for light use, such as lighting and mobile phone charging.

Other innovative PAYGo offerings are leveraging the same model, include Tanzania-based KopaGas, which offers a clean liquid-propane-based cooking platform that uses smart meters and micropayment via blockchain-stored digital wallets. In Uganda, ENGIE Energy Access[43] provides pay-as-you-go access to solar and wind-powered mini-grids in capacities of 10W to 200W. Their plans start at $0.19 per day, paid via mobile payments and financed through an "inclusive credit model" which leverages cryptocurrency traded globally as *Solar Loan Tokens* (SLTs)[44] to raise capital for upfront development and deployment costs.

While providing power is clearly among the most visible challenges in bringing the other four billion online, it may still be secondary to an even more fundamental need: overcoming food insecurity. This is precisely the right time to rethink this challenge in terms of economies of scope, tackling the solution to food insecurity with some of the same tools applied to energy poverty.

Our Last Mission

 Bringing online the other 4-billion who live on less than $6 per day is the defining mission of our era. For the majority of us, it will be our last mission.

Bringing online the other 4-billion who live on less than $6 per day is the defining mission of our era. For the majority of us, it will be our last mission—the final and most critical movement we will be a part of. To be clear, however, it is not an act of charity. It's not about an expanded welfare state, nor is it a public subsidy. It's an imperative for all eight billion of us. The solution for the population at the bottom of the pyramid is the same as the solution for the top. We need each other; we are equally interdependent, not just in a spiritual or humanist way, but with an economic interdependence which we often fail to consider. The forces of hyper-dematerialization effecting agriculture offer one of the most valuable leverage points for achieving this imperative.

Combating Food Insecurity: The Next Green Revolution

Over the last fifty years, agriculture has undergone a significant transformation, with advances in areas such as productivity-enhancing machinery, the cultivation of higher yielding crops, and crop-optimized fertilizers. We are now at the precipice of another agricultural revolution, this time fueled by technological innovation and the forces of hyper-dematerialization. By leveraging emerging technologies including AI, analytics, connected sensors, autonomous machines and other capabilities, farmers can boost yields while optimizing key inputs such as water, seeds, and fertilizer—driving resilience, sustainability, crop cultivation, diary production, and livestock management. This will be critical to growing agricultural output to the levels needed to meet the 70 percent increase in food demand that the World Bank projects by 2050. It will also be necessary to address competing goals of sustainability, threat of drought, and a global shortfall of drinkable water projected by 2040[45]—a problem already facing many nations.

 The challenge of feeding the other four billion can be summarized in three words: *yield per acre*.

The challenge of feeding the other four billion can be summarized in three words: *yield per acre*. Yield per acre offers an objective comparison between countries and regions that's not skewed by differences in the cost of living. In other words, it costs more to pay farm labor in higher wage regions, which translates to higher food prices. But the quantity of food

253

that can be produced with the same amount of farmland provides a more objective measure to compare the agricultural performance of one region versus another. For example, a farmer in 1800 could feed three to five people per year, whereas a farmer in 2020 could feed 166 people.[46]

Building on the agricultural productivity improvements described earlier, since 1948 farming in the U.S. has experienced expanded crop yields that have tripled production in agriculture, while simultaneously reducing the labor and land used by 75 percent and 22 percent, respectively.[47] This has certainly not been the experience of nations in Sub Saharan Africa, which have more than doubled land use for farming over the last thirty years, while yield only increased by 30 percent.[48] With an increase commensurate to its expanded land use, output should have at least doubled.

The low yields and low productivity in Sub Saharan African reflect where U.S. agriculture was in the mid twentieth century, only with ten times greater population. In the Introduction we discussed how Norman Borlaug revolutionized modern agriculture, launching the Green Revolution over the last fifty years through the development of far higher

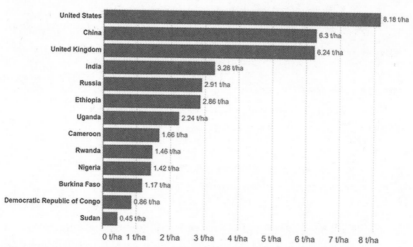

Figure 7.7: Comparison of Agricultural Yield Per Hectare Across Emerging and Developed Market Nations

Increasing crop yield is critical to addressing regional food insecurity and reducing the environmental impact of food production.

yielding and disease-resistant varieties of wheat, able to be grown in areas then on the verge of mass famine, notably Mexico and India. In order to the feed the other four billion—concentrated in areas most at risk of food insecurity—farmers in regions such as Sub Saharan Africa need a forth agricultural revolution, capable of transforming crop yields in the way the Green Revolution did in the last century. We believe this is within reach through better leveraging technologies such as mobile connectivity, sensors, and data analytics to expand agricultural yield with more precise crop monitoring, as well as reducing resource consumption and waste.

What makes Sub Saharan Africa a particularly important focus is that it faces the highest prevalence of food insecurity, at nearly 60 percent of its population, or 350 million people,[49] despite having the world's largest remaining areas of untilled land.[50] Farmable land is available, but agricultural productivity remains the issue. With low productivity, the cost of both inputs and farming labor put much of the land out of reach for the smallholder farms that comprise most of this impoverished region's agricultural sector.

Precision Agriculture

Part of the solution will be *precision agriculture*, which leverages an ecosystem of GPS, sensors, and in many cases drones, to collect data about soil conditions, weather patterns, and crop growth. This data is then used to create precise maps of a field, which are used to optimize the inputs such as water, fertilizer, and pesticides, driving greater crop yield by more accurately identifying and predicting deficiencies.

Precision agriculture is hyper-dematerialization at its best, since almost nothing new is needed other than the addition of intelligent automation. It's part of an evolving area of technology-enabled agriculture, which includes practices referred to as *site-specific management* and *smart-crop monitoring*. These are already common in developed markets, with their corresponding high rates of productivity and yield per acre. Precision agriculture allows reduction in the volume of inputs required (water, fertilizer, pesticides), with sensors monitoring soil conditions and then directing sprinklers to adjust water and nutrient application while delivering imagery and other data to more quickly identify and respond to threats such as drought conditions, pests or disease. With precise targeting and evidence-based decision making, farmers are also able to reduce their reliance on more labor-intensive methods of tending crops, by concentrating on more precisely defined areas of arable land.

These practices are touted for their benefits for sustainability, but what makes them more sustainable also makes them more cost-effective –improving crop yields, reducing waste, and optimizing resource allocation. The last point is critical to farmers in areas such as Sub-Saharan Africa, where the cost of fertilizer has increased by nearly 300 percent over the last three years,[51] with devastating consequences to farmers in the region. Given the many benefits we just listed, the obvious equation is: why has agricultural technology lagged in emerging markets?[52]

For smallholder farmers operating individually (typically family farms with less than five acres), integrating these technologies has been largely out of reach. But the emergence of digital ecosystems with regional farmer-tailored capabilities is driving adoption. One of these is AgroXchange,[53] an agriculture-specific "infomediary" platform for farmers in Sub Saharan Africa which provides a direct-to-buyer marketplace, along with a mobile-based payment system, which allow farmers to receive payment for their produce directly to their mobile phones.

The AgroXchange platform integrates market data, such as demand for different crops, assisting with informed decisions about what to plant and when to sell. It provides online training on modern farming practices, including crop rotation, pest control, and other agricultural techniques, to improve productivity and yield. Through a partnership with EOS Data Analytics it also provides access to satellite-based precision field monitoring, which enables farmers to model the development of crops, track surface moisture, assess vegetation health, and manage the condition of field. These capabilities are anticipate to deliver 30 percent productivity improvement for smallholder farms in the region.[54]

Another example is Hello Tractor, a tractor-sharing platform based in Kenya. Named to *Fortune*'s 2021 list of companies that change the world, the Hello Tractor[55] platform farm-equipment-sharing application connects tractor owners and smallholder farmers in Sub-Saharan Africa, allowing access to farm power and mechanization that is critical to raising the productivity and land yield. By *uberizing* tractors, owners are able to efficiently realize far greater utilization of their equipment, in addition to providing access to farmers for whom mechanization may otherwise be out of reach.

 By *uberizing* tractors, owners are able to efficiently realize far greater utilization of their equipment, in addition to providing access to farmers for whom mechanization may otherwise be out of reach.

Edge Case Innovations in Agriculture

The hyper-dematerialization of food—making it cheaper, more plentiful, and more sustainable through digital ecosystems—is not simply tweaking current farming practices. It involves other more exotic agricultural innovations. Technologies such as sensors, 5G, and mobile connectivity, paired with AI and data analytics, are part of the digital ecosystem that's revolutionizing traditional agriculture yields with technology-driven innovations.

One of these is *vertical farming*, which involves growing crops in vertically stacked layers, typically within precisely controlled environments, leveraging soilless techniques such as hydroponics, aquaponics, and aeroponics. Vertical farming at scale—larger than a single home environment—leverages a digital ecosystem of sensors, AI, robotics, and other automation, in order to ensure growing conditions, such as temperature, humidity, and lighting. Vertical farming has the potential to increase food production while reducing the environmental impact of agriculture. According to the USDA, "Beyond providing fresh local produce, vertical agriculture could help increase food production and expand agricultural operations as the world's population is projected to exceed 9 billion by 2050. And by that same year, two out of every three people are expected to live in urban areas."[56]

Paralleling this is another technology-enabled model of agriculture known as *cellular farming*. This practice is based on an emerging field of biotechnology focusing on producing food through cell cultures, without requiring traditional farming practices. Also known as "cultured meat" or "lab-grown meat" this process combines biotechnology, tissue engineering, molecular biology, and synthetic biology to "create" meat as well as milk, eggs, and even other animal products such as leather. *Steakholder Foods* has developed what it calls *Omakase Beef Morsels*, described as the "first-of-its-kind highly-marbled 3D-printed culture beef cut." The NASDAQ-traded firm is also partnering with Singapore-based UmamiMeats to develop 3D-printed seafood. Whether or not it sounds appetizing, the appeal is the combination of sustainable practices combined with hyper-customized foods, and "close-to-the-real-thing" equivalents of foods based on consumer preferences and dietary restrictions.

Manna from Heaven: Turning Air Into Food

 Rather than limiting options solely to extracting food from the ground, what about extracting it from the air?

There is another, much more exotic, dimension to feeding the populations facing food insecurity. Rather than limiting options solely to extracting food from the ground, what about extracting it from the air? Yes, it undoubtedly sounds far-fetched, bringing to mind images of the cafeteria onboard the USS Enterprise, but it is in fact the focus of a handful of biotech startups including Solar Foods, Air Protein, Deep Branch Biotechnology, and NovoNutrients.

While still an early-stage agricultural sector, it's based on work done by NASA dating back to the 1970s, to address the need for generating food during long space flights as well as scenarios such as the colonization of Mars. In both cases growing food would be impractical. Through a process called hydrogenotrophic methanogenesis, carbon dioxide is converted into a high-grade protein. This has the added benefits of advancing decarbonization while reducing our dependence on animal proteins (and the environmental impact they impose).

The "air-to-meat" sector is projected by market research provider Fact. MR to grow by 11.7 percent CAGR (compound annual growth rate) over the next decade to reach $100 million by 2032, although the much larger "alternative protein" market is expected to exceed $60 billion in roughly the same time frame.[57] Perhaps furthest along in this space is NovoNutrients, whose process focuses on CO2 and hydrogen captured from industrial exhausts, which is then upcycled[58] into protein suitable for both human and animal consumption. The approach leverages a digital ecosystem of machine learning and AI to optimize the current process, as well as to expand it into new areas such as renewable fuels.

NovoNutrients cites protein quality comparable to beef and superior to plant-based alternatives, but at far lower costs, as well as requiring very little water or land, and no pesticides or fertilizer for production. The resulting product from their fermentation process is 73 percent protein, with the same essential amino acids of naturally grown meat and little fat or fiber. Although the product is not currently on the market, trials conducted in the US and Japan have consistently shown high digestibility and palatability scores.

We have so far discussed two levers to improving the lives of the four billion existing on less than $6 per day: sustainable and affordable power generation and technology-enabled expansion of agricultural productivity. The third lever in this strategy is ensuring that both professional and childhood education is also accessible. There are several human capital dimensions to uplifting the population in poverty or otherwise existing at a basic level of subsistence. One is the need to provide them with the tools to participate in the global economy.

There are several human capital dimensions to uplifting the population in poverty or otherwise existing at a basic level of subsistence. One is the need to provide them with the tools to participate in the global economy.

Who will deploy and maintain the smart grids, solar power generation, and other aspects of energy transformation in the emerging sectors? How will farmers gain the tools necessary to leverage the new capabilities of digitally transformed agriculture? Building on the transformations underway in energy and agriculture, the third critical leverage point for realizing this mission is education.

A Global GI Bill: How Hyper-dematerialization Enables 1 Billion New Innovators and Entrepreneurs

"The postwar [WWII] GI Bill of Rights—and the enthusiastic response to it on the part of America's veterans—signaled the shift to the knowledge society. Future historians may consider it the most important event of the twentieth century. We are clearly in the midst of this transformation; indeed, if history is any guide, it will not be completed until 2010 or 2020. But already it has changed the political, economic, and moral landscape of the world."[59]

Management guru Peter Drucker was notoriously skeptical of the economic benefits of technology, famously stating in his 1973 book *Management: Tasks, Responsibilities, Practices* that "The technology impacts which the experts predict almost never occur." Instead, Drucker credited the U.S. GI Bill as the most critical driver for economic growth and productivity gains during the second half of the twentieth century—a belief he held even during the technological explosion that has lasted well into this century. From 1945 to 1956, nearly half of American WWII veterans took advantage of the GI Bill, which paralleled the expansion of US university instruction from a primary focus on liberal arts to business and other vocational studies, including science, agriculture, and engineering. Historian James T Patterson has called it "the most significant development in the modern history of American education."[60]

To clarify, however, while he spent most of his career in academia, it was learning and not universities themselves which Drucker credited. In fact, his expectations for the future of formal educational institutions was rather dim; according to Drucker in 1997, "Thirty years from now the big university campuses will be relics. Universities won't survive. It's as large a change as when we first got the printed book."[61, 62] Drucker may have been a few decades early, but it would appear the trajectory favors his prediction. Despite rising enrollments throughout the twentieth century, enrollments since 2009 have plateaued and are not expected to rise again through 2030.

Drucker described the "totally uncontrollable expenditures, without any visible improvement in either the content or the quality of education" as an untenable crisis, and instead looked to online education as the answer. Before he passed away in 2005, Drucker proposed that video delivery was the answer to the escalating costs of university education, "Already we are beginning to deliver more lectures and classes off campus via satellite or two-way video at a fraction of the cost. The college won't survive as a residential institution. Today's buildings are hopelessly unsuited and totally unneeded."

Drucker was making the case for the hyper-dematerialization of education. The industrial-era economies of scale model that has been foundational to campuses and the university experience is eroding.

 In the US, private university costs have skyrocketed, due almost exclusively to the facility, administrative, housing and food costs of the brick-and-mortar university. While we can endlessly debate the value of this model in the developed world, it is simply untenable in the developing world.

In the US, private university costs have skyrocketed, due almost exclusively to the facility, administrative, housing and food costs of the brick-and-mortar university. While we can endlessly debate the value of this model in the developed world, it is simply untenable in the developing world.

This is not just about university education and professional development. UNESCO estimates that 787 million school-age children lack access to education, and that by 2030 an additional 69 million teachers will be required to bridge this gap.[63] The rapid expansion of educational technology and digital platforms will undoubtedly be part of the solution, offering accessible education opportunities to emerging market populations who would otherwise lack access to high-quality learning resources. Yet we see this as just the beginning of educating marginalized populations. AI will revolutionize learning models, delivering individually-tailored guidance on-demand, without reliance on human instructors, while ensuring every student has equal access to knowledge. The latter is the subtle distinction which defines the inflection point for education that we are just now entering.

AI will serve both as an intermediary between student and teacher, but also increasingly as the teacher itself. Using AI, students will receive customized guidance to better understand their learning gaps and track their progress more effectively, with personalized suggestions on the best next steps to reach their learning goals. As a teacher, however, AI will deliver hyperpersonalized instruction, dynamically generated according to each student's skills gap, learning style, and pace of comprehension. Although currently in an early stage of maturity, these sorts of education options are already underway. Khan Academy recently announced it will use GPT-4 to power Khanmigo, an AI-powered assistant that functions as both a virtual tutor for students and a classroom assistant for teachers.[64] Another option, already in the classroom, is Cognii's AI-based teaching assistant for K–12 education.

Longer term, AI-enabled instruction will bridge the gap between educational inequality across countries and between different socioeconomic groups. With AI, students from disadvantaged backgrounds can access the same educational resources as those from wealthy backgrounds, regardless of their socioeconomic status. AI will also be leveraged for monitoring student performance, providing tailored feedback and resources that are individual learning trajectories

One quarter of the other four billion today live in Sub-Saharan Africa. By 2050 half this region's population will be under twenty-five years old. Today more than 60 percent of that region's workforce is employed with small-scale agriculture, with another 30 percent occupied with other subsistence-level activities, and all of them are part of the world's largest free trade area and a 1.2 billion-person market. Agricultural productivity in this region will improve dramatically over the next thirty years, reducing the 60 percent employed in agriculture to less than 6 percent by 2050.

What we also know is that by 2050, what they won't be doing is 90 percent of what we call knowledge work today, because that will be performed by digital workers. This includes many of the entry-level jobs created through the last few decades of labor globalization and offshore outsourcing. Nor can they subsist on the wages they earn today. It's not for us to determine what they choose to do, but we have more than a shared interest in determining what is available for them to do.

The Value of Increasing Returns

Hyper-dematerialization isn't faster dematerialization. It's the combined effect of multiple forces happening at once, simultaneously delivering multiple outcomes. It's realizing economies of scope, displacing an economy of scale. We introduced the concept with the example of the smartphone for two reasons: it is both relatable and meaningful. Today a mobile phone isn't free; it just costs a bit less than it once did. Is it realistic that feeding, powering, educating, sheltering, and caring for the other four billion could similarly be done, if not for free, at less cost than subsistence-level living costs today? Yes.

Consider the example of ENGIE Energy Access earlier in this chapter, levering the combination of solar power generation, smart grid technology, tokenization, and cryptocurrency—providing a service that previously required a significant capital investment.

Recall the example of NovoNutrients, which upcycles CO2, removing it from otherwise being an industrial pollutant, and converting it into a protein staple. While not yet at scale, having already created protein with "steak quality"[65] results, it should not be difficult to imagine it as input for products like Steakholder's Omakase Beef Morsels.

The combined value of these innovations illustrates the dynamics of hyper-dematerialization: the more the elements of things can be dematerialized through digitization, the more the creation of things becomes a function of digital processes, the faster things simultaneously become cheaper and better. Just over three decades ago, in his 1990 paper "Endogenous Technological Change," economist Paul Romer famously described increasing returns in the context of digital technologies:

> Digitized information is easy to store, easy to transmit, and easy to combine with other digitized information. These properties give rise to increasing returns: the more people use a digital technology, the more valuable it becomes, both because it becomes easier to use and because it can be combined with a wider range of other technologies.

This notion ages well. Romer's insights on digitization—then a much more novel and emerging concept—highlight the transformative power today of hyper-dematerialization and the ability to generate increasing returns. Just as with the smartphone example at the beginning of this chapter, hyper-dematerialization reduces the cost and increases the quality and capabilities of things, spurring emerging economies, and generating entirely new business models, products, and services that were previously unfeasible.

HYPER-DEMATERIALIZATION TIMELINE

2021–2030: Remote Work Revolution & the Rise of Green Energy

During this decade we see how the growing shift to "work from home" (while slower in the second versus the first half of the decade) has driven housing demand from traditional employment centers to smaller communities, both rural and planned developments. The growing availability and adoption of immersive environments and online education will further remove geographical boundaries and increasingly mitigate regional differences between real estate prices.

Digital twins will mirror an increasing number of physical environments, from businesses to homes, driving demand-side management of energy consumption. Global policy will push renewable energy to a series of new milestones over the course of the decade. Energy storage solutions such as batteries will become more efficient and affordable, driving adoption and smoothing out the quality of service challenges with decentralized intermittent energy sources.

2031–2040: Solar Dominance & Sustainable Agriculture

By 2030, driven by ongoing technological advancements, increased investment in clean energy infrastructure, and decarbonization policies, renewable energy surpasses fossil fuels as the primary sources of energy generation in the majority developed countries.

Obeying Swanson's Law, the price of solar photovoltaic modules drop to less than $0.25 per watt by the end of the decade, with the average cost of solar power now $0.05 per Kilowatt-hour. Sustainable sources will represent 60 percent of energy produced within emerging markets. Advances in grid storage capabilities shift from acid and rare earth materials to sustainable means that support both greater grid stability and cost-effective energy delivery.

The air-to-meat sector will exceed $100 million annually and be responsible for removing several tons of carbon from the air each year. 3D-printed steak will compete with Kobe Beef and A5 Waygu in taste, but at a fraction of the price. Digitization will become ubiquitous in agriculture, with farmers using precision agriculture techniques that incorporate real-time data from a variety of sources, including sensors, satellites, drones, and weather stations. This data will be used to optimize planting, fertilizing, and harvesting schedules, resulting in more efficient use of resources and higher yields.

2041–2050: Vertical Farming & Metaverse Economy

By 2040 vertical agriculture provides fresh farm-to-table options and sustainable agriculture to the majority of the population, without required soil, sunlight or water, in densely populated urban areas. The focus of agriculture increasingly shifts towards sustainability and resilience, with carbon sequestration, regenerative agriculture, and agroforestry common practices. Farmers in all regions rely on AI-powered models to optimize their practices for both productivity and environmental impact.

Energy generation has become more localized and decentralized, with smaller-scale systems ubiquitous, integrated into buildings and communities. Advanced energy storage technologies will be widely available and affordable, allowing for greater energy independence and resilience. Advancements in smart grid sensors and meters combined with AI enable more efficient and intelligent energy management systems. Sustainably generated, clean energy is available globally at $0.01 per Kilowatt-hour (KWh).

The metaverse is a significant part of the global economy, with virtual economies and businesses accounting for a sizable portion of global GDP. This could lead to new challenges and opportunities, such as the need for new regulations and standards for virtual transactions and digital currencies. The use of blockchain and other decentralized technologies could also become more prevalent, providing greater security and transparency for virtual transactions.

2051–2060: Autonomous Agri-Tech & Energy Storage

By 2050 the widespread adoption of autonomous vehicles, robotics, and drones will have revolutionized the way that crops are grown and harvested. These technologies will be used to perform tasks such as planting, weeding, and harvesting, with minimal human intervention. Advances in biotechnology such as CRISPR will enable farmers to grow crops that are more resistant to pests, diseases, and drought, resulting in greater yields and improved food security.

Large-scale batteries and pumped hydro-storage to balance the intermittency of renewable sources, as well as advancements in technologies such as carbon capture and storage (CCS), and nuclear fusion, help to address the intermittency and variability of renewables.

2061–2070: Agri-Tech Fusion & the Renewable World

Complex digital ecosystems driven by AI and robotics drive agricultural productivity to unprecedented levels. By this decade the lines between agriculture and technology will have become increasingly blurred. Meanwhile, advances in fields such as nanotechnology, synthetic biology, and artificial intelligence will open up new possibilities for improving crop yields and addressing global food security challenges.

The world has largely transitioned to a fully renewable energy system, with energy storage and distribution systems well-established and widespread, combined with advanced geothermal and ocean energy systems which further diversify the clean energy mix. Greater demand-side management is enabled by the widespread adoption of smart homes and buildings, as well as transportation systems powered by renewable energy sources.

By now 80 percent of the world's population lives in urban settings, with the majority in smart cities. What was previously known as "the metaverse" has become an integral part of human society, with virtual and physical environments seamlessly integrated into everyday life. This has fostered many new forms of creativity, innovation, and collaboration, as people are able to work and create together in immersive virtual environments.

The Dawn of a New Era

"… no human being can possibly predict the future,
let alone control it."

—PETER DRUCKER

At the start of the book we likened the future to a kaleidoscope, with its many pieces constantly in flux; each turn of the kaleidoscope revealing yet one more way to look at what might be. Are we being naive, somehow seduced by the pretty colors and shapes while they mask a dimmer view of tomorrow? As Peter Drucker used to say to us, "it's the wrong question." A better question might be, "why do we so often underestimate our power to positively shape the future?"

Part of the answer lies in the fact that humans have evolved with a deep cognitive bias that focuses on immediate concerns and threats rather than long-term possibilities. We're wired to see the danger, we gravitate to bad news, we are paralyzed by fear before we are drawn by opportunity. Eons of evolution have fine-tuned our brains to avoid threat and to focus on what we can see and experience with our five senses. That's not to say that civilizations haven't also spent considerable energy building longer term solutions and systems to sustain society. But that takes leadership and often a crisis to refocus us on the longer term. We're that not that case we wouldn't be staring down the barrel of a global ecological and climate catastrophe.

It's why our society and our economic systems most often prioritize short-term gains over long-term benefits. This focus can make it difficult for us to recognize and invest in the potential for long-term positive change. To use the metaphor in Chapter 4, the near future is easily measured in outputs while the long future is about much harder to measure outcomes. Clearly there has to be a balance between the two; without measurable positive performance in the short term, few businesses have the resources to survive long enough to realize visionary outcomes, and without vision fewer still will go on to change the world.

Since the future is inherently uncertain, it's difficult to predict the long-term impacts of our actions and decisions, especially when we feel overwhelmed by the enormity of the current challenges we are facing. In the several hundred pages so far it would appear that we've provided plenty of reason to be pessimists. We'd like to hope that we've also provided ample evidence for the reasons to be optimists.

Consider that from our vantage point today, what we have achieved in the past two-hundred years, during the industrial and information revolution, is so extraordinary that it would likely be harder to explain what 2020 would look like to someone from 1800 than it would be to explain what 1800 would look like to someone from two-thousand years ago.

Our sense is that we are in the midst of the next major global inflection point today. It certainly won't take 2000 years, nor 200 years. It may not even take twenty. But we can say with confidence that by 2050 the world will look much more different from today than today does from 1800. The other four billion—nearly half of humanity as we write this—need to be a part of this next phase of our evolution every bit as much as the other 98 percent of the workforce needed to be freed from tilling soil in order to create the extraordinary transformation we've undergone over the last 200 years.

There will be enormous challenges. In previous labor shifts of this magnitude—for example, moving factory workers out of manufacturing into knowledge worker roles—there was always a path for upward mobility. As productivity in manual labor increased through the use of automation, the economy also grew and more knowledge workers were needed. Automation and innovation create value, and value creates jobs.

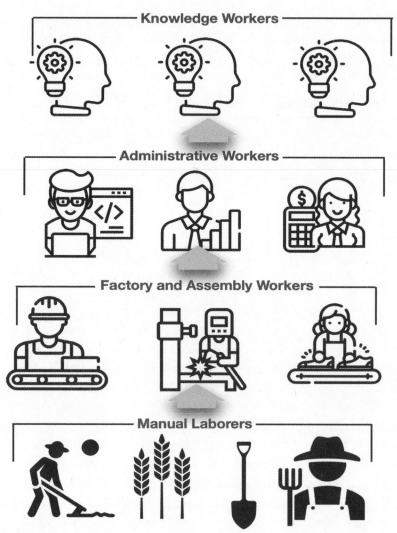

Figure E.1

Traditionally upward mobility existed from manual labor to factory and assembly work to administrative work to knowledge work. As robotics and automation became prevalent in farming and factories this allowed displaced workers to move into higher value jobs in new industries. Today, digital workers will create a similar migration of workers to higher value knowledge work and away from administrative positions. However, the longer-term challenge will be moving unskilled laborers directly to knowledge work, as automation, robotics, and digital workers eliminate the vast majority of jobs in both factories and administrative positions.

While there was always a period of disruptive unemployment, due to the time required to re-tool and re-educate the workforce, there was always ample opportunity to reemploy displaced workers on the other side of that transformation. However, in trying to do the same with the four billion people who today make their living primarily through low-value manual labor, AI creates a dangerously fascinating conundrum in that it can easily lure us into believing it is capable of much more than it is.

On the one hand, automation and AI will certainly soon displace these low-cost manual laborers due to both the productivity increases in using automation and AI and the increasing pressure on global organizations.

On the other hand, the overwhelming majority of the entry-level positions, which act as administrative or apprenticeship positions for knowledge workers, will no longer exist going forward. AI-powered digital workers will take on 90 percent of these administrative roles. This effectively shuts the door on entry-level knowledge work. Which leaves four billion people sandwiched between the proverbial rock and a hard place: they can't keep doing what they have been doing and they're locked out of entry-level knowledge to source labor responsibly work.

The question now becomes, "how do we provide an on ramp for the 4.5 billion people that we will have to re-educate, retrain, and re-tool? This single phenomenon could very well be the greatest challenge that we will face over the course of the next hundred years. The world has never seen an analogous situation, which is why measures such as Universal Basic Income as well as Universal Basic Services will be essential in order to provide access to critical services such as healthcare, education, and housing, regardless of employment status. This approach will reduce inequality and ensure a basic standard of living for all while we build new mechanisms for educating and retraining the other half of the world's future workforce. To be clear, these steps are inevitable if we are to reshape the workforce without a global revolution.

Terra Incognito

Let's offer a final piece of advice about the future; rather than focus all of our energy trying to predict what will change, perhaps we should spend more time thinking about what will *not* change. We've tried in this book to offer glimpses into how some of the world will change, and while we are confident in what we have described, we are only providing the palette of colors with which the canvas of tomorrow will be painted. The rest will unfold in ways more challenging and more magnificent than anything we can today imagine.

While we are confident in what we have described, we are only providing the palette of colors with which the canvas of tomorrow will be painted.

What will not change is the essential nature and purpose of humanity; our curiosity, our search for value and purpose, our need to connect as communities, our compassion and empathy for our fellow humans, and our unceasing curiosity and creativity.

We've had the future stolen from us before. What we thought our value was has repeatedly been replaced by machines. For the vast majority of human history our value was in our ability to labor. Machines slowly replaced us in the fields and the factories, which forced us to increasingly value human intellect. AI is the latest thief, promising to take that away from us as well. What will we have left? We could ask that question differently: what if there's more to being human than filling out rows in a spreadsheet? What if there were more to being human than plowing a field? In both cases the question is separated by decades from the answer.

Fifty years from now, AI will have unrecognizably transformed the landscape of knowledge work, having woven its intricate web of connections and augmentations throughout our lives—but the essence of humanity remains at the core of our future.

In this new world, the creative professions flourish like never before. Artists, writers, musicians, and designers push the boundaries of their crafts, guided by the unique spark of human ingenuity. Rather than replacing them, AI becomes an invaluable partner in the creative process, opening up new possibilities and inspiring new masterpieces.

Ethical decision-making and policy development take center stage as we grapple with the implications of AI's growing presence. Visionary leaders and thinkers emerge, ensuring that AI technologies align with our deepest values and contribute to a just and equitable society.

The call for human connection resonates louder than ever, so therapists, social workers, and counselors are in high demand, offering solace and guidance in an increasingly complex world. Their ability to empathize and understand the human condition is a skill that AI may be able to emulate, at least in how we perceive an interaction with AI, but we do not see that eliminating the importance of shared experiences between humans.

Scientists, engineers, and researchers—the torchbearers of innovation—tirelessly explore the frontiers of knowledge, while teachers, trainers, and mentors nurture the potential of future generations. In this world, AI becomes both a subject of study and a tool to vastly accelerated learning, but the passion and dedication of educators remains invaluable.

Meanwhile, experts maintain, troubleshoot, and customize AI systems, ensuring that the intricate web of technology remains functional and adaptable. As AI becomes more complex, the need for skilled human hands to navigate the delicate interplay of systems only grows.

Entrepreneurs seize the opportunity to create new ventures in the AI-driven world, their ambition and creativity driving the economy forward, creating new industries, jobs, and services. In this landscape, humans and AI collaborate harmoniously, each contributing their strengths and learning from one another.

And finally, we find ourselves in the realm of the unforeseen, the unpredictable waiting to be discovered. As technology and society continue to evolve, new professions will emerge, guided by human ingenuity and a desire to build a better future.

The future is a kaleidoscope of possibilities; always a journey into the unknown, filled with both promise and peril. Every one of the Gigatrends we've covered is an opportunity to shape that future, to architect a world where technology and human potential unite to unleash the extraordinary power of the human spirit. A future in which AI and humanity walk hand in hand, with the indomitable spirit of human creativity, curiosity, empathy, and determination; turning the kaleidoscope to reveal unimagined vistas, driving our collective journey forward into a future of limitless possibility.

GIGATRENDS

Gigatrend	2021-2030	2031-2040	2041-2050	2051-2060	2061-2070
Demographic Disruption	Aging Populations & Global Challenges	Declining Fertility & Labor Shifts	Population Skyscrapers & Technological Advancements	Below Replacement Fertility & Economic Adaptation	Stabilized Population & Africa's Global Impact
Ambient Care	Digital Disruption & Healthcare Transformation	Value-Driven Care & Global Health Challenges	Technological Integration & Personalized Medicine	Ambient Healthcare & Home-based Services	AI-Driven Healthcare & Universal Access
Digital Workers & Digital Ecosystems	Emergence & Early Adoption	Growth & Integration	Expansion & Optimization	Autonomy & Adaptability	Synergy & Symbiosis
Mobility as a Service	EV/AV Revolution & Acceptance	Mass Adoption of MaaS & Transportation Innovation	Integration & Optimization of MaaS	Ubiquitous MaaS Dominates Globally	Self-Optimizing AVs Deliver Mobile Meeting Spaces
Your Digital Self	The Rise of Trustless Digital Identity	Biometrics & Fluid Identity	The AI-Enhanced Digital Self	Identity-Driven Digital Economy	Seamless Identity Integration & Immortal Identities
Hyper-Dematerialization	Remote Work Revolution & the Rise of Green Energy	Solar Dominance & Sustainable Agriculture	Vertical Farming & Metaverse Economy	Autonomous Agri-Tech & Energy Storage	Agri-Tech Fusion & the Renewable World

Figure E.2: Summary Gigatrend Timeline

The table above summarizes the evolution of each of the six Gigatrends over the course of the next five decades by highlighting the central shift hat will occur with each Gigatrend during the corresponding decade.

Glossary

Ambient Care: This healthcare approach incorporates ambient intelligence and smart technologies to offer personalized and non-intrusive monitoring and assistance to individuals in their daily lives, as well as the ability to adapt and respond to individuals' behavior by providing personalized and relevant services and information. This method utilizes sensors, wearable devices, and Internet of Things (IoT) technologies to collect real-time data, analyze health patterns, and provide proactive support for managing chronic conditions, promoting overall well-being, and ensuring safety.

Ambient Intelligence: Creating intelligent environments that are sensitive to the presence and needs of individuals through sensors, pervasive computing, and machine learning, to create smart environments that can perceive, understand, and interact with humans in a seamless manner.

Autonomic Innovation: The concept of autonomic innovation pertains to the development of self-regulating and self-managing systems. This involves the creation of intelligent software, technologies, or systems that possess the capability to autonomously adapt, optimize, and make decisions based on real-time data and changing circumstances.

Autonomous Vehicles (AVs): Vehicles equipped with advanced sensors, artificial intelligence, and automation technologies that enable them to navigate and operate without direct human input. AVs have the capability to perceive the environment, interpret sensory data, and make informed decisions to control acceleration, braking, and steering.

Bitcoin: A digital currency that operates on a peer-to-peer network and uses cryptographic principles to secure transactions and regulate the creation of new units. It allows direct transactions without intermediaries, resulting in fast and low-cost transactions. Bitcoin is recognized as the first cryptocurrency and has potential as a store of value and a medium of exchange, as well as for its underlying blockchain technology. (also see "Blockchain")

Blockchain: Digital ledger technology (DLT) that is decentralized and distributed, thus not controlled by a single entity and is spread across a network of numerous computers. Blockchain records transactions in a transparent and immutable manner, which means that once the data is recorded, it cannot be altered or deleted, providing a secure and tamper-proof way to store data, ensuring that it is transparently verified and held accountable. The most common example of blockchain is the Bitcoin cryptocurrency network, where participants on the network verify and record transactions using consensus mechanisms like proof-of-work.

Cloud-based: Cloud-based as well as "cloud-native" refers to the delivery of IT services, applications, or systems Internet through remote servers and data centers. It means that users can store, process, and access data, applications, and resources remotely, without the need for local hardware or infrastructure. Cloud-based services offer scalability, flexibility, and cost-efficiency, allowing users to leverage computing power, storage, and software on-demand through subscription-based models.

Cone of Possibility: The Cone of Possibility suggests that as one explores and expands their knowledge, the space of potential options widens, leading to increased opportunities and innovation. Visual metaphor depicting a cone-shaped space, where the base represents the known or existing options, and the apex represents the unknown or yet-to-be-explored possibilities.

Cryptographically-secure: A cryptographic technique is employed by a system, algorithm, or protocol to guarantee the confidentiality, integrity, and authenticity of data, ensuring its authenticity as well as enabling non-repudiation between parties exchanging the data.

DARPA's LifeLog: Project of the Information Processing Techniques Office of the Defense Advanced Research Projects Agency (DARPA) of the U.S. Department of Defense which aimed to create a comprehensive database of an individual's daily activities and experiences, for the purpose of predicting future actions and behavior (see also "Pattern of Life).

Dall-E: Artificial intelligence program developed by OpenAI that generates images from textual descriptions. The name DALL-E is a blend of Salvador Dali, the famous artist, and Pixar's WALL-E movie

Decentralized Autonomous Organization (DAO): An organizational model established through the utilization of smart contracts on a blockchain, effectively eliminating the requirement for centralized control, relying instead on transparent and autonomous decision-making as well as governance by enabling stakeholders to actively participate, vote, and influence the operations of the organization, without dependence on conventional hierarchical structures.

Decentralized Identifiers (DIDs): A globally unique identifier is a means by which an entity can be identified in a manner that is verifiable, persistent (for as long as the DID controller wishes), and does not necessitate the utilization of a centralized register.

Deepfake: Artificially manipulated videos or images created using deep learning techniques to convincingly alter or superimpose someone's appearance or actions.

Deeptrace: Amsterdam-based cybersecurity company providing deep learning and computer vision technologies for the detection for detecting deepfakes and other forms of synthetic media manipulation.

Digital Business Ecosystem: An extension of the traditional business ecosystem, leveraging digital technologies and platforms to create a virtual network of interconnected organizations, individuals, and resource, which collaborate and interact digitally to create value, deliver products and services, and gain.

Digital Identity: The distinct information and characteristics that distinguish an individual in the digital world, comprised of personal information, authentication credentials, and other personally identifying metadata. For example, or email addresses, usernames, browsing history, and often even biometric information may comprise our digital identity.

Digital Self: The virtual representation or persona of an individual that is created through various digital interactions, activities, and data. It includes the online presence of a person, their social media profiles, digital footprints, and the data generated from their digital interactions. A person's digital self can be exemplified by their social media profiles and online accounts that collectively form their digital identity.

Digital Twin: The computerized replica of a physical entity, such as a process, system, or object which captures and reflects the entity's unique attributes, behavior, and performance in real-time, providing a comprehensive and dynamic view of the entity's operations. For instance, a digital twin of an industrial machine can simulate its functionalities, track its health status, and enhance maintenance schedules to improve efficiency and reliability.

Digital Worker: AI-powered software agent that can perform work autonomously in the same capacity as and/or in collaboration with human workers. Digital workers may be leveraged to perform repetitive tasks and others predefined functions, typically by signing into the same systems and applications, as well as following the same rules and instructions as with human workers.

Distributed Ledger Technology (DLT): Distributed Ledger Technology (DLT) is a digital system that allows multiple participants to maintain a synchronized and decentralized record of transactions or data across a network of computers, by use of hashing to secure and link blocks of data, ensuring immutability and integrity within the chain.

Electric Vehicles (EVs): Vehicles that run on electric motors powered by rechargeable batteries instead of internal combustion engines, and therefore deemed more environmentally friendly than traditional gasoline-powered vehicles.

Economy-of-Scale: Cost advantages for industries and companies that arise from producing goods or services in large quantities, allowing companies to reduce their per-unit costs as well as to compete on the on the basis of production capacity.

Economy-of-Scope: Cost savings can be achieved by producing multiple products or services together and utilizing shared resources and capabilities. Through diversification of production and sharing inputs, companies can enhance efficiency, decrease costs, and create synergies, ultimately resulting in improved profitability and a competitive edge.

Federated Identity: Federated identity refers to the use of single sign-on (SSO) technologies to allow users to access multiple systems using a single set of credentials. It enables users to authenticate themselves once and access multiple systems without having to log in again.

Generation Alpha: Generation Alpha refers to the demographic group who were born entirely in the 21st century, following Generation Z. This cohort typically includes individuals born from the mid-2010s to the mid-2020s. As the first generation to grow up entirely in the digital age, Generation Alpha is also known as "Digital Natives. They are highly familiar with technology and have grown up using smartphones, tablets, and other digital devices as part of their daily lives. Due to their exposure to technology, Generation Alpha is expected to exhibit distinct characteristics such as increased digital literacy, adaptability to emerging technologies, and a strong preference for digital communication and media consumption.

Generative AI: AI algorithms which use deep learning techniques like neural networks to create new content such as images, videos, and music. The algorithms analyze existing data patterns to produce coherent and realistic outputs that resemble human-created content. By combining and transforming existing data or extrapolating from examples, these models can produce novel and creative content. Generative AI has applications in art, design, content creation, and simulation. It has the potential to change how we generate and interact with digital content.

Generative Pretrained Transformers (GPT): A family of generative language models developed by companies such as OpenAI. They are based on transformer architecture and can be fine-tuned for various natural language processing tasks such as text classification or question answering.

Hashing: The method of converting input data into a hash, which is a fixed-size output, using a mathematical function, commonly used for password storage, digital signatures, data integrity checks, and cryptographic protocols. Hash functions are designed to be one-way, ensuring that the original data remains protected.by producing a fixed-size output (hash) that is unique to the input data. Once data is hashed, it cannot be converted back to its original form. (also see "Tokenization")

Hospital in the Cloud: Cloud-based healthcare services that allow patients to receive medical care remotely using telemedicine technologies, for the purpose of enable doctors to diagnose and treat patients without having to be physically present with them.

Hyper-Dematerialization: The combination of dematerialization and demonetization has led to an increase in utility at a reduced cost. Dematerialization refers to the absorption of capabilities that were previously delivered through a separate product or system into another system. Demonetization, on the other hand, refers to the provision of capabilities that were previously paid for at no cost. A good example of this is the modern smartphone which now provides capabilities such as a digital camera, GPS unit, and media player at no additional cost, whereas in the past, these capabilities would have required the purchase of separate devices.

Internet of Things (IoT): A network of physical devices, vehicles, home appliances, and other items that are equipped with sensors, software, and network connectivity. These objects can collect and exchange data using various technologies, bridging the gap between the digital and physical worlds. Sensors within these objects can monitor factors like temperature or motion, as well as other changes in their environment.

Machine Learning (ML): A branch of statistical AI which enables digital systems to determine actions or functions by extracting patterns from historic data ("training data") in order to make predictions or execute actions, such as the training of a model to categorize emails as spam or not by leveraging past email data.

Metaverse: The collective digital universe comprising interconnected virtual and augmented reality experiences that are accessible to users through immersive technologies. It allows for the creation of shared digital spaces where individuals can interact, collaborate, and engage in various activities. A popular instance of the Metaverse is the virtual world of "Roblox," where users can create, play, and socialize in a shared online environment.

Mobility as a Service (MaaS): The transportation concept based on common access rather than individual ownership of transportation vehicles, through user-centric services which integrate on-demand access to various modes of transportation, such as ride-hailing services, bike-sharing, car-sharing, and in the future both ground-based and VTOL autonomous vehicles.

Non-Fungible Tokens (NFTs): Non-Fungible Tokens are unique digital assets that are stored on blockchain technology, often used to represent immutable ownership of digital items such as art, music, or videos.

Non-repudiation: Mechanisms such as digital signatures combined with cryptographically-secure data which ensure that no involved party in a transaction or communication can deny their participation.

Pattern of Life: A comprehensive record of an individual's life can be created through the digital representation of various sources of data. This includes GPS location information, location-based sensors, emails, social media activity, web browsing history, phone calls, photos, and other personal records. Advanced technologies such as natural language processing, data mining, and machine learning can be utilized to analyze and interpret the collected data, allowing for a deeper understanding of the individual's life (see also "Ambient Intelligence").

Prelytics: Also known as "Predictive Analytics" this specialized field of advanced analytics leverages past data, statistical algorithms, and machine learning techniques to make informed predictions about future events or outcomes. The process entails analyzing patterns, trends, and relationships from historical data to forecast or estimate what is likely to occur in the future.

Precision Agriculture: Approach to farming that uses technology to optimize crop yields and reduce waste. It involves using sensors, GPS mapping, and other technologies to collect data about soil conditions, weather patterns, and other factors that affect crop growth. This data is then used to make more informed decisions about planting, fertilizing, watering, and harvesting crops.

Self-Sovereign Identity (SSI): Model for managing digital identities in which individuals or businesses have sole ownership over the ability to control their accounts and personal data. SSI is an approach to digital identity that gives individuals control over the information they use to prove who they are to websites, services, and applications over the Internet.

Singularity: Theoretical future moment in time where artificial intelligence exceeds human intelligence in all domains. This notion is commonly linked to the concept of technological singularity, which proposes that once AI reaches this stage, it will swiftly enhance itself and generate more sophisticated forms of intelligence.

The Other 4-Billion: The bottom half of the world's population, the major of whom according to sources such as the World Bank subsist on less than $5.50 per day, as well as lack access to critical resources such as clean drinking water and Internet connectivity.

Tokenization: Tokenization is a process that involves converting sensitive data, such as payment card information or personal identifiers, into a unique identifier called a token which cannot be reverse-engineered to reveal the original data. Tokenization's primary purpose is to replace sensitive data with non-sensitive tokens while preserving the data's referential integrity. It is commonly used to protect data during storage or transmission, tokenization focuses on data substitution with reversible tokens to protect sensitive data, while hashing transforms data into irreversible and unique hash values which cannot be reversed or retrieved to its original form.

Turing Test: Test proposed by the English mathematician Alan M. Turing to determine whether a computer can "think." The test involves a human evaluator who judges natural language conversations between a human and a machine designed to generate human-like responses. If the evaluator cannot reliably differ computer from human, computer is considered to have passed the test.

Verifiable Credentials (VCs): An open standard has been developed for digital credentials that can encompass various types of information. These credentials are capable of representing data typically found in physical documents like passports or licenses, as well as intangible assets such as ownership of a bank account.

VTOL and **eVTOL:** Vertical Takeoff and Landing (VTOL) transportation is a type of mobility service that can operate without a runway or long takeoff/landing space, which as part of Mobility as a Service has the potential to improve urban and regional mobility by offering faster point-to-point travel, greater flexibility, efficiency, and accessibility. Electric-powered VTOL (eVTOL) aircraft are being developed by companies such as Uber Elevate, Joby Aviation, and Volocopter to provide quieter, electric-powered, and more environmentally friendly transportation solutions for short to medium-range flights in urban areas.

Web3: The next generation of the Internet built on decentralized protocols, blockchain technology, and the concept of ownership (of user generated content and personal data) with the goal creating a more open, transparent, and user-centric web experience. An example is the Ethereum blockchain, enabling decentralized applications (dApps) and smart contracts that operate without intermediaries, offering new possibilities for digital interactions and trustless transactions.

Zero Trust: A security strategy that operates under the assumption of zero trust within a network is implemented, which necessitates rigorous authentication, ongoing monitoring, and restricted access privileges. This approach ensures that every user, device, and network request is thoroughly verified, irrespective of their location, in order to prevent unauthorized access and mitigate potential threats, thereby bolstering the overall cybersecurity measures.

Endnotes

Introduction

1 Frank H. Knight, *Risk Uncertainty and Profit* (Boston: Houghton Mifflin, 1921).
2 Gary Arndt, "Norman Borlaug: The Man Who Fed the World," Everything Everywhere, accessed March 27, 2023, https://everything-everywhere.com/norman-borlaug-the-man-who-fed-the-world/.
3 Thomas Koulopoulos, "Paul Romer's Nobel Prize In Economics Marks A New Era Of Innovation Driven By Ideas," *Inc.*, October 9, 2018.
4 "Total Installed Based of Data Storage Capacity in the Global Datasphere from 2020 to 2025," Statista, accessed March 27, 2023, https://www.statista.com/statistics/1185900/worldwide-datasphere-storage-capacity-installed-base/.
5 Chris Mellor, "Storing 25 Exabytes in a 2-Inch Kenzan Diamond Wafer," Blocks & Files, May 3, 2022.
6 Bill Kovarik, "Radio and the Titanic," Revolutions in Communication, accessed March 27, 2023, https://revolutionsincommunication.com/features/radio-and-the-titanic/.
7 Ibid.

Chapter 1

1 "Agriculture," Digital History, accessed March 27, 2023, https://www.digitalhistory.uh.edu/disp_textbook.cfm?smtID=11&psid=3837.
2 UBS Editorial Team, "Let's Chat About ChatGPT," UBS, February 23, 2023.
3 Cade Metz, "How Smart Are the Robots Getting?" *New York Times*, January 20, 2023.
4 "Welcome to Podcast.ai," Podcast.ai, accessed March 27, 2023, podcast.ai.
5 Anthony Kalamut, "AT&T - 1993 'You Will' Ad Campaign," YouTube Video, May 18, 2021, https://www.youtube.com/watch?v=RvZ-667CEdo.
6 Adapted from Thomas M. Koulopoulos and George Achillias, *Revealing the Invisible: How Our Hidden Behaviors Are Becoming the Most Valuable Commodity of the 21st Century* (New York: Post Hill Press, 2018).
7 Based on an iPhone Max 3.23 GHz Bionic chip and 1TB of memory.
8 Future of Life Institute. "An Open Letter to Pause Giant AI Experiments." Future of Life Institute. Accessed March 30, 2023. https://futureoflife.org/open-letter/pause-giant-ai-experiments/.

9 Thomas M. Koulopoulos, *The Innovation Zone: How Great Companies Re-Innovate for Amazing Success* (Boston: Nicholas Brealey, 2011).

10 Georgette Kilgore, "Carbon Footprint of Data Centers & Data Storage Per Country (Calculator)," 8 Billion Trees, March 28, 2023.

Chapter 2

1 U.S. Census and Minnesota Population Center, "U.S. Census Population Pyramid, 1850–2000," accessed March 27, 2023, http://vis.stanford.edu/jheer/d3/pyramid/shift.html.

2 Portions Adapted from Thomas M. Koulopoulos and Dan Keldsen, *The Gen Z Effect: The Six Forces Shaping the Future of Business* (Brookline, MA: Bibliomotion, Books + media, 2014).

3 "Historical Estimates of World Population," U.S. Census Bureau, accessed March 27, 2023, https://www.census.gov/data/tables/time-series/demo/international-programs/historical-est-worldpop.html.

4 Institute of Medicine Committee on the US Commitment to Global Health, The US Commitment to Global Health: Recommendations for the New Administration (Washington, DC: National Academies Press, 2009).

5 Victor Oluwole, "China Ranks ahead of America as the Largest Investor in Africa Since 2010," *Business Insider Africa*, February 20, 2022.

6 Deborah Hardoon, Sophia Ayele, and Ricardo Fuentes-Nieva, "An Economy For The 1%: How Privilege and Power in the Economy Drive Extreme Inequality and How This Can Be Stopped," Oxfam International Briefing Paper, January 18, 2016.

7 Virginia Yans-McLaughlin, "Mead, Margaret," American National Biography," https://a.co/d/8IDcE0o page 99 9.

8 Thomas M. Koulopoulos and Dan Keldsen, *The Gen Z Effect: The Six Forces Shaping the Future of Business* (Brookline, MA: Bibliomotion, 2014).

9 "Fact Sheet: Aging in the United States," Population Reference Bureau, accessed March 27, 2023, https://www.prb.org/resources/fact-sheet-aging-in-the-united-states/.

10 G. A. Mensah et al., "Decline in Cardiovascular Mortality: Possible Causes and Implications," Circulation Research 120, no. 2 (2017): 366–80.

11 "Cardiovascular Disease: A Costly Burden for America Projections Through 2035," American Heart Association Office of Federal Advocacy, n.d., accessed March 27, 2023, https://www.heart.org/-/media/Files/About-Us/Policy-Research/Fact-Sheets/Public-Health-Advocacy-and-Research/CVD-A-Costly-Burden-for-America-Projections-Through-2035.pdf.

12 Jared Ortaliza, Matthew McGough, Emma Wager, Gary Claxton, and Krutika Amin, "How Do Health Expenditures Vary Across the Population?" Peterson-KFF Health System Tracker, November 12, 2021.

13 R. Navickas, V. K. Petric, A. B. Feigl, and M. Seychell, "Multimorbidity: What Do We Know? What Should We Do?" Journal of Comorbidity 6, no. 1 (2016): 4–11.

14 P. Boersma, L. I. Black, and B. W. Ward, "Prevalence of Multiple Chronic Conditions Among US Adults, 2018," Preventing Chronic Disease 17 (2020).

15 N. Shehab et al., "US Emergency Department Visits for Outpatient Adverse Drug Events, 2013–2014, JAMA 316, no. 20 (2016): 2115–25.

Chapter 3

Portions adapted from Koulopoulos, Thomas. 2020. *Reimagining Healthcare.* Post Hill Press.

1 Tolentino v. Health Care Service Corp., 3:14-cv-00017 (5th Cir., Tex. S.D. 2016), https://www.courtlistener.com/recap/gov.uscourts.txsd.1147247.22.0.pdf.
2 Bernd Rechel, Yvonne Doyle, Emily Grundy, and Martin McKee, How Can Health Systems Respond to Population Ageing? (Copenhagen: WHO Regional Office for Europe, 2009).
3 G. C. Brown, "Living Too Long: The Current Focus of Medical Research on Increasing the Quantity, Rather Than the Quality, of Life Is Damaging Our Health and Harming the Economy," EMBO Reports 16, no. 2 (2015): 137–41.
4 Ibid.
5 UN Department of Economic and Social Affairs, World Population Ageing 2019: Highlights (New York: United Nations, 2019).
6 Half the World Lacks Access to Essential Health Services: UN-Backed Report," United Nations, accessed March 27, 2023, https://news.un.org/en/story/2017/12/639272-half-world-lacks-access-essential-health-services-un-backed-report.
7 Richard Bruns and Nikki Teran, "Weighing the Cost of the Pandemic," Institute for Progress, April 21, 2022.
8 Gabriela Flores et al., Tracking Universal Health Coverage: 2017 Global Monitoring Report (Geneva: World Health Organization; Washington, DC: World Bank, 2017).
9 "Social Security History," Social Security Administration, accessed November 11, 2019, https://www.ssa.gov/history/lifeexpect.html; "Survival to Age 65, Male (% of Cohort)—United States," World Bank, accessed November 11, 2019, https://data.worldbank.org/indicator/SP.DYN.TO65.MA.ZS?locations=US.
10 Ibid.
11 "New Hope for Patients Living with Cystic Fibrosis after Scientists Unveil Therapy," All Thing Considered (NPR), November 1, 2019
12 Berkeley Lovelace Jr., "A New Alzheimer's Drug Will Cost $26,500 a Year: Who Will Be Able to Get It?" NBC News, January 9, 2023.
13 Peter Long et al., eds., Effective Care for High-Need Patients: Opportunities for Improving Outcomes, Value, and Health (Washington, DC: National Academy of Medicine, 2017), 31.
14 Ibid.
15 Penelope Dash et al., How Prioritizing Health Could Help Rebuild Economies (New York: McKinsey Global Institute, 2020).
16 "Global Health Expenditure Database," World Health Organization, accessed March 27, 2023, https://apps.who.int/nha/database.
17 "The Digitization of the World From Edge to Core," International Data Corporation (IDC), accessed July 12, 2023, https://www.seagate.com/files/www-content/our-story/trends/files/idc-seagate-dataage-whitepaper.pdf.
18 "Latest Trends in Medical Monitoring Devices and Wearable Health Technology (2023)," Insider Intelligence, January 13, 2023.
19 "Blood Pressure Anytime, Anywhere," Omron, accessed March 27, 2023, https://omron-healthcare.com/products/heartguide-wearable-blood-pressure-monitor-bp8000m/.

20 Chris Welch, "Apple and Stanford's Apple Watch Study Identified Irregular Heartbeats in over 2,000 Patients: Only 0.5 Percent of Participants Received the Notifications," *The Verge*, March 16, 2019.

21 Wired Staff, "Know Thyself: Tracking Every Facet of Life from Sleep to Mood to Pain," *Wired*, March 22, 2009.

22 Brian Dolan, "Carolinas HealthCare Monitors Fitbit Data to Intervene with CHF Patients," *Mobi Health News*, March 1, 2016.

23 Chris Notte and Neil Skolnik, "Where to Go with Wearables," *MDedge*, October 31, 2018.

24 Brian Dolan, "Prediction: Health Wearables to Save 1.3 Million Lives by 2020," *Mobi Health News*, December 16, 2014.

25 Marcia Frellick, "Doctors, Nurses Give Lifestyle Advice But Are Skeptical It's Heeded," Medscape, March 29, 2018.

26 M. Viswanathan et al., "Interventions to Improve Adherence to Self-Administered Medications for Chronic Diseases in the United States: A Systematic Review," Annals of Internal Medicine 157, no. 11 (2012): 785–95.

27 Aurel O. Iuga and Maura J. McGuire, "Adherence and Health Care Costs," Risk Management and Healthcare Policy 7 (2014): 35–44.

28 Jeffrey C. Greene et al., "Reduced Hospitalizations, Emergency Room Visits, and Costs Associated with a Web-Based Health Literacy, Aligned-Incentive Intervention: Mixed Methods Study," Journal of Medical Internet Research (October 2019).

29 "Why Health Insurance Is Important," HealthCare.gov, accessed March 27, 2023, https://www.healthcare.gov/why-coverage-is-important/protection-from-high-medical-costs/.

30 Alyssa Corso, "Emergency Room Visit Cost Without Insurance in 2023," Mira, December 19, 2022.

31 "Fast Facts on U.S. Hospitals, 2022," American Hospital Association, accessed March 27, 2023, https://www.aha.org/statistics/fast-facts-us-hospitals.

32 "What is Public Health?" American Public Health Association, accessed November 11, 2019, https://www.apha.org/what-is-public-health.

33 David Talbot, "Cell-Phone Data Might Help Predict Ebola's Spread," MIT *Technology Review*, August 22, 2014.

34 "Ebola Outbreaks: 2014," HealthMap.org, accessed March 27, 2023, https://healthmap.org/ebola/#timeline.

35 Susan Hall, "Digital Data Makes Real-Time Flu Tracking a Reality: Smart Technology and Tracking Tools Make Delivering Flu Resources and Information a More Current Endeavor for Public Health Officials," *HealthTech*, March 19, 2018.

36 Howard Brody et al., "Map-Making and Myth-Making in Broad Street: The London Cholera Epidemic, 1854," *The Lancet* 356 (July 2000).

37 American Hospital Association, Trendwatch Chartbook 2018: Trends Affecting Hospitals and Health Systems (Washington, DC: American Hospital Association, 2018), 31.

38 Ibid, 30.

39 "Cost of Older Adult Falls," Centers for Disease Control and Prevention, accessed March 27, 2023, https://www.cdc.gov/falls/data/fall-cost.html#:~:text=Each%20year%20about%20%2450%20billion%spent%20related%20to%20fatal%20falls.

40 Robert Holly, "Home Health Spending Rate Projected to Surpass All Other Care Categories," *Home Health Care News*, February 20, 2019.

41 National Alliance for Caregiving (NAC) and AARP Public Policy Institute, 2015 Report: Caregiving In the U.S. (Washington, DC: National Alliance for Caregiving; Washington, DC: AARP Public Policy Institute, 2015).

42 Lynn Feinberg, Susan C. Reinhard, Ari Houser, and Rita Choula, Valuing the Invaluable: 2011 Update; The Growing Contributions and Costs of Family Caregiving (Washington, DC: AARP Public Policy Institute, 2011).

43 Richard Schulz and Jill Eden, eds., "Economic Impact of Family Caregiving," in *Families Caring for an Aging America*, ch. 4 (Washington, DC: National Academies Press, 2016).

44 R. Schulz and S. R. Beach, "Caregiving as a Risk Factor for Mortality: The Caregiver Health Effects Study," *Journal of the American Medical Association* 282, no. 23 (1999): 2215–19.

45 Andree LeRoy, "Exhaustion, Anger of Caregiving Get a Name," CNN Health, accessed November 11, 2019, http://edition.cnn.com/2007/HEALTH/conditions/08/13/caregiver.syndrome/index.html.

46 Judy Mathias, "AHRQ Releases Stats on Outpatient, Inpatient Surgeries," OR Manager, June 2, 2017.

47 Ateev Mehrotra, Christopher B. Forrest, and Caroline Y. Lin, "Dropping the Baton: Specialty Referrals in the United States," Milbank Quarterly 89, no. 1 (2011): 39–68.

48 "Survey: Patients See 18.7 Different Doctors on Average; Practice Fusion Surveys Patients, Highlights the Inefficiency of Paper Records and the Need for Electronic Medical Records in the US," Cision PR Newswire, April 27, 2010.

49 Tom Sullivan, "Why EHR Data Interoperability is Such a Mess in 3 Charts," *Healthcare IT News*, May 16, 2018.

50 MyHealthEData is an initiative announced under the Trump administration that aims to empower patients by ensuring that they control their healthcare data and can decide how their data is going to be used.

51 "CMS Advances Interoperability & Patient Access to Health Data through New Proposals," CMS.gov, February 8, 2019.

52 Christopher Jason, "Epic Systems Advises Hospital Execs Against Interoperability Rule," HER Intelligence, January 23, 2020.

53 Center for Individualized Medicine, "Pharmacogenomics In Patient Care," Mayo Clinic, accessed March 27, 2023, https://www.mayo.edu/research/centers-programs/center-individualized-medicine/patient-care/pharmacogenomics.

54 The Geneticure test did not require a prescription as of the writing of this book. However, that is expected to change and will require it to be ordered through a provider.

55 "Historic Cost of Sequencing a Human Genome.svg," Wikimedia Commons, last modified June 6, 2022, https://commons.wikimedia.org/wiki/File:Historic_cost_of_sequencing_a_human_genome.svg.

56 "The Cost of Sequencing a Human Genome," National Human Genome Research Institute (NHGRI), accessed October 7, 2017, https://www.genome.gov/27565109/the-cost-of- sequencing-a-human-genome/.

57 Dawn McMullan, "What Is Personalized Medicine?" *Genome*, August 3, 2014.

58 "Hospital Consolidation: Trends, Impacts & Outlook," NIHCM, January 1, 2020, https://nihcm.org/publications/hospital-consolidation-trends-impacts-outlook.

59 "2018 M&A in Review: The Year in Numbers," Kaufman Hall, 2018.

60 Cristin Flanagan, "U.S. Hospitals Shut at 30-a-Year," Bloomberg, August 21, 2018.

61 According to the AHA: "A System is defined by AHA as either a multihospital or a diversified single hospital system. A multihospital system is two or more hospitals owned, leased, sponsored, or contract managed by a central organization."

62 "Fast Facts on U.S. Hospitals, 2020," American Hospital Association, 2020, https://www.govstar360.com/article/fast-facts-on-u-s-hospitals-2020.

63 Traci Prevost, Ion Skillrud, Wendy Gerhardt, and Debanshu Mukherjee, "The Potential for Rapid Consolidation of Health Systems: How Can Hospitals Use M&A to Innovate for the Future?" Deloitte Insights, December 10, 2020.

Chapter 4

1   Robert Shackleton, Total Factor Productivity Growth in Historical Perspective (Washington, DC: Congressional Budget Office, 2013).

2   Daniel Menaker, "'The Glass Cage,' by Nicholas Carr," New York Times, November 7, 2014.

3   Koulopoulos, Thomas M. 1997. Smart Companies, Smart Tools. Van Nostrand Reinhold Company.

4   James Flanigan, "The Reckoning by David Halberstam," Los Angeles Times, November 23, 1986.

5   David Halberstam, The Reckoning (New York: Avon Books, 1987), 205.

6   David Halberstam, The Fifties, (New York: Villard Books, 1993), 123.

7   Ibid, 241.

8   Willem Roper, "Productivity vs Wages: How Wages in America Have Stagnated," World Economic Forum, November 10, 2020.

9   Real Wage Trends, 1979 to 2019 (Washington, DC: Congressional Research Service, 2020).

10 Susan Fleck, John Glaser, and Shawn Sprague, "The Compensation-Productivity Gap: A Visual Essay," Monthly Labor Review (January 2011).

11 Wikimedia Commons, "Median Real Wages by Educational Attainment.png," last updated September 23, 2020.

12 Robby Brumberg, "Study: Workers Waste 32 Days Per Year Juggling Tech, App Overload," Ragan PR Daily, March 21, 2018.

13 Assumes 100,000,000 knowledge workers at $38/hour and an 8-hour workday.

14 "US Agriculture [keyword search]," Our World in Data, accessed March 27, 2023, https://ourworldindata.org/search?q=us+agriculture.

15 Pablo Illanes, Susan Lund, Mona Mourshed, Scott Rutherford, and Magnus Tyreman, "Retraining and Reskilling Workers in the Age of Automation," McKinsey & Company, January 22, 2018.

16 "The Talent Challenge: Harnessing the Power of Human Skills in the Machine Age," PwC, 2017.

17 "'I'm Outta Here': Korn Ferry Survey Reveals Reasons Behind Great Resignation," Korn Ferry, August 12, 2021.

18 "Turnover and Retention (Quick Take)," Catalyst, April 16, 2020.

19 Shane McFeely and Ben Wigert, "This Fixable Problem Costs U.S. Businesses $1 Trillion," Gallup, March 13, 2019.

20 Jack Zenger and Joseph Folkman, "Quiet Quitting Is About Bad Bosses, Not Bad Employees," *Harvard Business Review*, August 31, 2022.

21 Jim Harter, "Is Quiet Quitting Real?" Gallup, September 6, 2022.

22 Parts of the section on Digital Workers adapted from and used with permission from "The Digital Worker Mandate" Hybrid Global Publishing 2023 by Marco Buchbinder.

23 Fritz Machlup and Trude Kronwinkler, "Workers Who Produce Knowledge: A Steady Increase, 1900 to 1970," Weltwirtschaftliches Archiv 111, no. 4 (1975): 752–59.

24 "A Visual History of the U.S. Workforce, 1970 to 2012," Marketplace, October 11, 2012.

25 Gabe Luna-Ostaseski, "Announcing The Knowledge Work Demand Index," Braintrust, July 28 2021.

26 "Monthly Employment Level of the United States from February 2021 to February 2023," Statista, accessed March 27, 2023, https://www.statista.com/statistics/209123/seasonally-adjusted-monthly-number-of-employees-in-the-us/.

27 Matthew Herper, "MD Anderson Benches IBM Watson in Setback for Artificial Intelligence in Medicine," Forbes, February 19, 2017.

28 Steve Lohr, "What Ever Happened to IBM's Watson?" *New York Times*, July 16, 2021.

29 Brennon Slattery, "Apple iPad Reviews: The Critics Weigh In," *PCWorld*, January 28, 2010.

30 James Manyika et al., "Jobs Lost, Jobs Gained: What the Future of Work Will Mean for Jobs, Skills, and Wages," McKinsey & Company, November 28, 2017.

31 Louise B. Andrew, "Physician Suicide," *Medscape*, August 1, 2018.

32 Tawfik, Daniel S., Jochen Profit, Timothy I. Morgenthaler, Daniel V. Satele, Christine A. Sinsky, Liselotte N. Dyrbye, Michael A. Tutty, Colin P. West, and Tait D. Shanafelt. 2018. "Physician Burnout, Well-Being, and Work Unit Safety Grades in Relationship to Reported Medical Errors." *Mayo Clinic Proceedings. Mayo Clinic* 93 (11): 1571–80. https://doi.org/10.1016/j.mayocp.2018.05.014.

33 Daniel S. Tawfik et al., "Physician Burnout, Well-Being, and Work Unit Safety Grades in Relationship to Reported Medical Errors," Mayo Clinic Proceedings 93, no. 11 (2018): 1571–80.

34 "Creating the Future of Human Resources," IBM, accessed March 27, 2023, https://www.ibm.com/case-studies/ibm-human-resources-watson-orchestrate.

35 Ibid.

36 Jonathan Webb, "How Many Suppliers Do Businesses Have? How Many Should They Have?" *Forbes*, February 28, 2018.

37 Ibid.

38 Tom Sullivan, "Why EHR Data Interoperability Is Such a Mess in 3 Charts," *Healthcare IT News*, May 16, 2018.

39 "Explosive Internet of Things Spending to Reach $1.7 Trillion in 2020," *IDC* [press release], June 2, 2015.

40 Ray Kurzweil, "The Singularity is Near," accessed March 27, 2023, http://www.singularity.com/.

41 Nicholas Negroponte, "5 Predictions, from 1984," TedTalk, accessed March 27, 2023, http://www.ted.com/talks/nicholas_negroponte_in_1984_makes_5_predictions?language=en.

42 Paul Daugherty, "The Rise Of Digital Ecosystems In The 'We Economy,'" *Forbes*, March 9, 2015.

43 Gil Press, "Internet of Things By The Numbers: Market Estimates And Forecasts," *Forbes*, August 22, 2014.

44 Fiona Jackson, "Chinese Tech Company Appoints an AI-Powered Virtual Humanoid Robot as CEO," *Daily Mail*, September 8, 2022.

45 Miklos Dietz, Hamza Khan, and Istvan Rab, "How Do Companies Create Value from Digital Ecosystems?" McKinsey Digital, August 7, 2020.

46 Lucy Handley, "Lego CEO Says Toymaker's Digital Future Is a 10-Year Journey," CNBC, September 2, 2020.

47 "Build, Render, and Create Instructions," BrickLink, accessed March 27, 2023, https://www.bricklink.com/r3/studio/download.page#xlink.

48 Apple's first year royalty for an app sold on the Apple store is 30% but it drops to 15% in the second and subsequent years.

49 Aleksandra Gjorgievska and Spencer Soper, "Amazon to Lease 20 Boeing 767s to Build Its Own Delivery Network," Bloomberg, March 9, 2016.

50 Covisint, *Creating a Frictionless Automotive Ecosystem, A Connected Experience* (Detroit, MI: Covisint, 2015).

Chapter 5

1 "2016 Production Statistics," International Organization of Motor Vehicle Manufacturers, accessed October 2, 2017, http://www.oica.net/category/production-statistics/

2 Assuming 100 million vehicles at an average length of 10' / 5280' per mile / 24,000-mile distance at the equator = 7.89.

3 "Achievements In Road Safety," International Organization of Motor Vehicle Manufacturers, accessed October 2, 2017, http://www.oica.net/category/safety/global-safety/.

4 Daniel Tencer, "Number Of Cars Worldwide Surpasses 1 Billion; Can The World Handle This Many Wheels?" *Huffington Post*, August 23, 2011.

5 Andrew Gross, "More than 80 Percent of Older Drivers Aren't Talking About Driving Safety," AAA Newsroom, August 14, 2018.

6 Zachary Shahan, "NASA Says: Automobiles Largest Net Climate Change Culprit," *Clean Technica*, February 23, 2010.

7 American Automobile Association, American Driving Survey, 2020–2021 (Heathrow, FL: American Automobile Association, 2022).

8 "A Brief History of Drones," Imperial War Museums, accessed March 27, 2023, https://www.iwm.org.uk/history/a-brief-history-of-drones.

9 412th Test Wing Public Affairs, "DoD Artificial Intelligence Agents Successfully Pilot Fighter Jet," Edwards Air Force Base, February 13, 2023.

10 The Road to Autonomy adapted from Koulopoulos, Thomas M, and George Achillias. 2018. *Revealing the Invisible: How Our Hidden Behaviors Are Becoming the Most Valuable Commodity of the 21st Century*. New York: Post Hill Press.

11 Son, Khansari, Shastrula, Jarrahi, and Tomko v. Tesla, Inc., 8:16-cv-02282 (C.D. Calif. 2016), https://assets.documentcloud.org/documents/3534570/Teslaamendedcomplaint.pdf.

12 By saying the claim is convoluted we are not passing judgment or implying anything about the merits of the lawsuit, but simply pointing out that AVs create all sorts of legal and even ethical challenges.

13 "The State of Level 3 Autonomous Driving in 2023: Ready for the Mass Market?" *Autocrypt*, January 13, 2023.

14 "SAE J3016 Levels of Driving Automation," SAE International, 2021, accessed March 27, 2023, https://www.sae.org/binaries/content/assets/cm/content/blog/sae-j3016-visual-chart_5.3.21.pdf.

15 John Paul, "Cars Crashing Into Buildings," WHIO-TV, November 4, 2014.

16 Abdul, "How Many Moving Parts In An Electric Car," OSVehicle, October 30, 2022.

17 "Electric Vehicle Battery Costs Soar," Institute for Energy Research, April 25, 2022.

18 "Electric Vehicles Are Forecast to be Half of Global Car Sales by 2035," Goldman Sachs, February 10, 2023.

19 Coral Davenport, Lisa Friedman, and Brad Plumer, "California to Ban the Sale of New Gasoline Cars," *New York Times*, August 24, 2022.

20 "Federal Vehicle Fleets: Observations on the Transition to Electric Vehicles," US Government Accountability Office, October 20, 2022.

21 "Societal Costs," National Safety Council, accessed March 27, 2023, https://injuryfacts.nsc.org/all-injuries/costs/societal-costs/.

Chapter 6

1 Shoshana Zuboff, *The Age of Surveillance Capitalism: The Fight for a Human Future at the New Frontier of Power* (New York: PublicAffairs, 2020).

2 Reuters, "Pentagon Explores a New Frontier In the World of Virtual Intelligence," *New York Times*, May 30, 2003.

3 "Baby Monitoring with Intelligent Audio Cueing Based on an Analyzed Video Stream," Google Patents, accessed March 27, 2023, https://patents.google.com/patent/US20190272724A1/en.

4 Peter H. Diamandis, "Metatrend #9: Trillion-Sensor Economy; The Ability to Sense and Know Anything," Peter H. Diamandis, December 8, 2022.

5 "Demystifying web3: What Does web3 Mean for Your Business?" PWC, accessed March 27, 2023, https://www.pwc.com/us/en/tech-effect/emerging-tech/what-is-web3.html.

6 McKinsey Global Institute, "Digital Identification: A Key to Inclusive Growth," McKinsey Digital, April 17, 2019.

7 "Facts + Statistics: Identity Theft and Cybercrime," Insurance Information Institute, accessed March 27, 2023, https://www.iii.org/fact-statistic/facts-statistics-identity-theft-and-cybercrime.

8 "Global Cybersecurity Awareness Survey Reveals 33 Percent of U.S. Respondents Have Experienced Identity Theft, More than Twice the Global Average," *Proofpoint*, October 11, 2018.

9 "Office of Personnel Management Data Breach (2015)," Cyber Law Toolkit, last modified June 4, 2021, https://cyberlaw.ccdcoe.org/wiki/Office_of_Personnel_Management_data_breach_(2015).

10 Josh Fruhlinger, "The OPM Hack Explained: Bad Security Practices Meet China's Captain America," CSO, February 12, 2020.

Endnotes

11 "2012 Linkedin Breach Had 117 Million Emails and Passwords Stolen, Not 6.5M," *Trend*, May 18, 2016.

12 Wikipedia, "2012 LinkedIn Hack," last modified November 17, 2022.

13 Julia Carrie Wong, "Facebook Says Nearly 50m Users Compromised in Huge Security Breach," *Guardian*, September 28, 2018.

14 Lily Hay Newman, "A New Google+ Blunder Exposed Data From 52.5 Million Users," *Wired*, December 10, 2018.

15 Patrick George, "Ford's Self-Repossessing Car Patent Is a Nightmare of the Connected-Car Future," *The Verge*, March 3, 2023.

16 "Permanent suspension of @realDonaldTrump," Twitter, January 8, 2021, https://blog.twitter.com/en_us/topics/company/2020/suspension.

17 Alex Preukschat and Drummond Reed, "Why the Internet Is Missing an Identity Layer: And Why SSI Can Finally Provide One," Manning, accessed March 27, 2023, https://livebook.manning.com/book/self-sovereign-identity/chapter-1/v-1/.

18 "The Laws of Identity," The Laws of Identity … as of 5/11/2005, accessed March 27, 2023, http://www.identityblog.com/stories/2005/05/13/TheLawsOfIdentity.pdf.

19 Ibid.

20 "Identification For Development (ID4D) Global Dataset," World Bank, last updated January 19, 2023, https://datacatalog.worldbank.org/search/dataset/0040787.

21 Alexander Preukschat et al., *Self-Sovereign Identity: Decentralized Digital Identity and Verifiable Credentials* (Shelter Island, NY: Manning, 2021).

22 Satoru Hori, "Self-Sovereign Identity: The Future of Personal Data Ownership?" World Economic Forum, August 12, 2021.

23 G. Aarti, B. Pramod, and K. Vineet, *Employment Screening Services Market Outlook 2028* (Portland, OR: Allied Market Research, 2021).

24 M. Shuaib et al., "Immunity Credentials Using Self-Sovereign Identity for Combating COVID-19 Pandemic," *Materials Today:* Proceedings (2021, March 22).

25 Simeon Tegel, "COVID Test Forgery Schemes Are Popping Up Around Latin America," *Vice*, February 11, 2021.

26 Jamie Grierson, "Fake Covid Vaccine and Test Certificate Market Is Growing, Researchers Say," *Guardian*, May 16, 2021.

27 Emily Gee and Topher Spiro, "Excess Administrative Costs Burden the U.S. Health Care System," Center for American Progress, April 8, 2019.

28 Sarah Yates Abigail O'Leary, "'Fake' Doctor Earned £1m in Two Decades after 'Tricking NHS with False Degrees,'" *Mirror*, January 11, 2023.

29 "Statistics," Blue Cross Blue Shield of Michigan, accessed March 27, 2023, https://www.bcbsm.com/health-care-fraud/fraud-statistics.html.

30 "Background Press Call by a Senior Administration Official on a U.S. Counterterrorism Operation," White House [press release], August 1, 2022.

31 "Department of Defense DEERS Enrollment and ID Card Issuance," US Department of Defense, updated June 2020, https://www.cac.mil/portals/53/documents/required_docs.pdf.

32 "Hashcat," OpenBenchmarking.org, accessed March 27, 2023, https://openbenchmarking.org/test/pts/hashcat-1.1.1.

33 Dan Arias and Sam Bellen, "What Are Refresh Tokens and How to Use Them Securely," auth0 [blog], last updated October 7, 2021.

34 Department of the Army, "Every Soldier Is A Sensor [video]," Internet Archive, accessed March 27, 2023, https://archive.org/details/every_soldier_is_a_sensor.

35 Pablo Ferrezuelo, "Why Deepfake Fraud Losses Should Scare Financial Institutions," Finextra, November 14, 2022.

36 Matt Burgess, "A Deepfake Porn Bot Is Being Used to Abuse Thousands of Women," *Wired*, October 20, 2020; Daniel Dominguez, "Microsoft Unveils VALL-E, a Game-Changing TTS Language Model," InfoQ, January 27, 2023.

37 Dominguez, Daniel. 2023. "Microsoft Unveils VALL-E, a Game-Changing TTS Language Model." InfoQ. January 27, 2023. https://www.infoq.com/news/2023/01/microsoft-text-to-speech-valle/.

38 Todd Kuhns, "Electronic Signature Law of the People's Republic of China," AppInChina, April 23, 2019.

39 White, Olivia, Anu Madgavkar, James Manyika, Deepa Mahajan, Jacques Bughin, Mike McCarthy, and Owen Sperling. 2019. "Digital Identification: A Key to Inclusive Growth." McKinsey & Company.

40 "Total Identity Fraud Losses Soar to $56 Billion in 2020," *Business Wire*, March 23, 2021.

41 Seth Goldfarb, "A Report on the Digital Identity Session at Seattle Devcon," *Evernym*, July 2, 2019.

42 "Data Protection: Federal Agencies Need to Strengthen Online Identity Verification Processes," US Government Accountability Office, May 17, 2019.

43 "Medicare Program & Improper Payments," US Government Accountability Office, accessed March 27, 2023, https://www.gao.gov/highrisk/medicare-program-improper-payments.

44 Nicholas Rossolillo, "A Complete Guide to Minting NFTs (Using OpenSea as an Example)," The Motley Fool, June 29, 2022.

45 Brooke Becher, "Did the NFT Bubble Burst?" *Built In*, February 7, 2023.

46 Wikipedia contributors. 2023. "HTTP Cookie." Wikipedia, The Free Encyclopedia. March 30, 2023. https://en.wikipedia.org/w/index.php?title=HTTP_cookie&oldid=1147401366.

47 "How Self-Sovereign Identity Might Impact Payments and Customer Experience," Barclaycard, accessed March 27, 2023, https://www.barclaycard.co.uk/business/accepting-payments/corporate-payment-solutions/news/self-sovereign-identity.

48 "SK Telekom, KT, LG U+ Launch Blockchain Identity App for Driving License Authentication," *Ledger Insights*, June 23, 2020.

49 Millennium, "Millennium Hotels and Resorts Launches M Social Decentraland," *Hospitality Net*, April 27, 2022.

50 "Why the Metaverse (Really) Matters for Travel," Miafrica, accessed March 27, 2023, https://miafrica.net/why-the-metaverse-really-matters-for-travel/#/.

Chapter 7

1 "How Much Did the Stuff on Your Smartphone Cost 30 Years Ago?" WebFX, accessed March 27, 2023, https://www.webfx.com/blog/internet/how-much-did-the-stuff-on-your-smartphone-cost-30-years-ago/.
2 Dennis Peng, "Cell Phone Cost Comparison Timeline," *Ooma*, September 16, 2019.
3 Jed Friedman and Ruth Hill, eds., *Shared Prosperity 2022: Correcting Course* (Washington, DC: World Bank Group, 2022).
4 "'What a Waste' Report Shows Alarming Rise in Amount, Costs of Garbage," World Bank, June 6, 2012.
5 Carlos Miskinis, "Digital Twin Genie Case Study: 54% Reduction in Automotive Manufacturing Costs," *Challenge Advisory*, March 2018.
6 Andrew Mcafee, *More from Less: The Surprising Story of How We Learned to Prosper Using Fewer Resources—and What Happens Next* (London: Simon & Schuster, 2020).
7 "Obama Awards the National Medal of Science and National Medal of Technology and Innovation Ceremony: Speech Transcript," *Washington Post*, November 17, 2010.
8 Claudia Deutsch, "At Kodak, Same Old Things are New Again," *New York Times*, May 2, 2008.
9 Joel D. Goldhar and Mariann Jelinek, "Plan for Economies of Scope," *Harvard Business Review*, November 1983.
10 International Energy Agency (IEA), *Tracking SDG 7: The Energy Progress Report 2021* (Paris: IEA, 2021).
11 John Ayaburi, Morgan Bazilian, Jacob Kincer, and Todd Moss, "3.5 Billion People Lack Reliable Power," *Energy for Growth Hub*, September 8, 2020.
12 "Our Technology," Helion Energy, accessed April 1, 2023, https://www.helionenergy.com/our-technology/.
13 International Energy Agency (IEA), India Energy Outlook 2021 (Paris: IEA, 2021).
14 "World Energy Projection System (WEPS) Module Documentation," US Energy Information Administration, accessed March 27, 2023, https://www.eia.gov/outlooks/ieo/weps/documentation/
15 "International Energy Outlook 2021," US Energy Information Administration, October 6, 2021, https://www.eia.gov/outlooks/ieo/.
16 "Who We Are," Organisation for Economic Co-operation and Development, accessed March 27, 2023, https://www.oecd.org/about/.
17 PricewaterhouseCoopers, *The World in 2050: The Long View; How Will the Global Economic Order Change by 2050?* (New York: PWC, 2017).
18 Niharika Sharma, "These Are the Biggest Hurdles to India Achieving Its Net Zero Goals," *Quartz*, September 22, 2022.
19 "India: Country Commercial Guide," US Department of Commerce, International Trade Administration, accessed March 27, 2023, https://www.trade.gov/country-commercial-guides/india-energy.
20 Ahmad K. Sleiti, Jayanta S. Kapat, and Ladislav Vesely, "Digital Twin in Energy Industry: Proposed Robust Digital Twin for Power Plant and Other Complex Capital-Intensive Large Engineering Systems," *Energy Reports* 8 (2022): 3704–26.
21 "Demand Response," US Department of Energy, accessed March 27, 2023, https://www.energy.gov/oe/demand-response.

22 "Smart Grid," Ministry of Power, Government of India, accessed March 27, 2023, https://www.nsgm.gov.in/en/smart-grid.

23 Josh Rasmussen, "NREL, SDG&E Collaboration Expands Resiliency in Borrego Springs, Yields Nationally Scalable Results," National Renewable Energy Laboratory, October 22, 2018.

24 Caitlin Dorsey, "Marine Corps Air Station Miramar and NREL: Allies in Energy Efficiency, Systems Integration, and Resilience," National Renewable Energy Laboratory, April 6, 2021.

25 "Uganda: Engie Commissions a 600 kWp Solar Mini-Grid on Lolwe Island," Africa Energy Portal, January 18, 2022.

26 Julian Conzade, Hauke Engel, Adam Kendall, and Gillian Pais, "Power to Move: Accelerating the Electric Transport Transition in Sub-Saharan Africa," McKinsey & Company, February 23, 2022.

27 Energy Sector Management Assistance Program, *Mini Grids for Half a Billion People: Market Outlook and Handbook for Decision Makers* (Washington, DC: World Bank, 2022).

28 Bin Xu et al., "A Case Study of Digital-Twin-Modelling Analysis on Power-Plant-Performance Optimizations," *Clean Energy* 3, no. 3 (2019): 227–34.

29 "How Does Willingness to Pay Influence Mini-Grid Economics?" USAID, https://www.usaid.gov/energy/mini-grids/economics/willingness-to-pay.

30 "Electric Grid Security and Resilience," https://energy.gov/epsa/downloads/electric-grid-security-and-resilience-establishing-baseline-adversarial-threats.

31 Energy for Growth Hub, "The Reliability-Adjusted Cost of Electricity (RACE): A New Metric for the Fight against Energy Poverty," Energy Metric Working Group, October 2019.

32 Electricity Supply and Output in Nigerian Manufacturing Sector, *Journal of Economics and Sustainable Development* www.iiste.org ISSN 2222-1700 (Paper) ISSN 2222-2855 (Online) Vol.7, No.6, 2016.

33 Ezeh Matthew Chinedum and Kenneth U. Nnadi, "Electricity Supply and Output in Nigerian Manufacturing Sector," *Journal of Economics and Sustainable Development* 7, no. 6 (2016).

34 SunShot 2030, U.S. Dept of Energy, Solar Energy Technologies Office, https://www.energy.gov/eere/solar/sunshot-2030

35 Africa Energy Outlook 2019, November 2019, International Energy Agency, https://www.iea.org/reports/africa-energy-outlook-2019

36 "Powering Sub-Saharan Africa – A fresh take on an old problem," World Bank, Masami Kojima, OCTOBER 26, 2016, https://blogs.worldbank.org/energy/powering-sub-saharan-africa-fresh-take-old-problem.

37 Ed Crooks, "Swanson's Law Provides Green Ray of Sunshine for PV," *Financial Times*, January 17, 2016.

38 "2030 Solar Cost Targets," U.S. Dept of Energy, Solar Energy Technologies Office, August 13, 2021, https://www.energy.gov/eere/solar/articles/2030-solar-cost-targets.

39 Max Roser, "Why Did Renewables Become So Cheap So Fast," Our World in Data, December 1, 2020, https://ourworldindata.org/cheap-renewables-growth.

40 "Solar Is Now 'Cheapest Electricity in History,' Confirms IEA," *CarbonBrief*, October 13, 2020.

41 "Download Solar Resource Maps and GIS Data for 200+ Countries and Regions," Solargis, accessed March 27, 2023, https://solargis.com/maps-and-gis-data/download/world.

42 "Life Changing Technology," Azuri, accessed March 27, https://www.azuri-group.com/.

43 "ENGIE Energy Access," ENGIE, accessed March 27, https://engie-energyaccess.com/.

44 Jonathan Spencer Jones, "New Blockchain Crowdfunding Platform to Launch for Solar in Africa," Smart Energy International, April 29, 2022.

45 Strategic Futures Group, "The Future of Water: Water Insecurity Threatening Global Economic Growth, Political Stability," National Intelligence Council, March 2021.

46 "Food and Farm Facts" (2021 edition), American Farm Bureau Foundation for Agriculture, https://www.agfoundation.org/resources/food-and-farm-facts-2021.

47 Sun Ling Wang, Richard Nehring, and Roberto Mosheim, "Agricultural Productivity Growth in the United States: 1948–2015," US Department of Agriculture Economic Research Service, March 5, 2018.

48 "Data," Food and Agriculture Organization of the United Nations, accessed March 27, 2023, https://www.fao.org/faostat/en/#data.

49 Ned Rauch-Mannino, "Rising Inflation Forces Greater Attention to Food Insecurity in Africa," Foreign Policy Research Institute, November 3, 2022.

50 Louise Fox and Landry Signé, "Overcoming the Barriers to Technology Adoption on African Farms," Brookings, June 28, 2022.

51 Global Market Analysis Modeling Team, "Impacts and Repercussions of Price Increases on the Global Fertilizer Market," US Department of Agriculture Economic Foreign Agricultural Service, June 30, 2022.

52 Aslihan Arslan et al., "A Meta-Analysis of the Adoption of Agricultural Technology in Sub-Saharan Africa," PLOS Sustainability and Transformation, July 1, 2022.

53 "Welcome," AgroXchange, accessed March 27, 2023, https://agroextech.com/.

54 "EOS Data Analytics Partners Up With AgroXchange," EOS Data Analytics, October 2, 2021.

55 "Technology for Smarter, Better Maintained and More Profitable Tractors," Hello-Tractor, accessed March 27, 2023, https://hellotractor.com/.

56 Sarah Federman and Paul M. Zankowski, "Vertical Farming for the Future," US Department of Agriculture, August 14, 2018.

57 Ahuja, Kunal, and Sarita Bayas. 2022. "Global Alternative Protein Market Size, Share and Industry Analysis Report by Source Industry Analysis Report, Regional Outlook, Growth Potential, Competitive Market Share & Forecast, 2022–2028." Global Market Insights Inc.

58 Wayne Labs, "How NovoNutrients Upcycles CO2 into Alternative Proteins for Human and Animal Food," *Food Engineering*, March 4, 2022.

59 Peter F. Drucker, *Post-Capitalist Society* (New York: Harper Business, 1993).

60 James T. Patterson, *Grand Expectations: The United States, 1945–1971* (New York: Oxford University Press, 1996).

61 Natalie Robehmed, "Seeing Things As They Really Are," *Forbes*, March 10, 1997.

62 Paul Jones, "Drucker Says 'Universities Won't Survive,'" ibiblio [original post to ils310@listserv.oit.unc.edu], accessed March 27, 2023, https://www.ibiblio.org/pjones/ils310/msg00140.html.

63 UNESCO, "The World Needs Almost 69 Million New Teachers to Reach the 2030 Education Goals," UIS Fact Sheet 39, October 2016.

64 "Khan Academy: Khan Academy Explores the Potential for GPT-4 in a Limited Pilot Program," OpenAI, accessed March 27, 2023, https://openai.com/customer-stories/khan-academy.

65 Jim Lane, "Breakthrough for Cows: NovoNutrients Achieves 'Beef-Quality' Protein from CO2 Instead of Cattle," *The Digest*, May 16, 2022.

Acknowledgments

The journey that led to *Gigatrends* was a long one having traversed nearly a decade of thinking about the trends that will most shape our future. However, as any author will tell you, there is a moment when the essence of a book takes shape; the aha moment when the book's title, message, and purpose all come into focus.

As authors we are constantly scanning the horizon looking for something worth writing about. As futurists, we are constantly overwhelmed by the many possibilities of the future while we struggle to synthesize them into simple and easily understood frameworks. That moment came from a conversation one of us had with a dear friend, Andrew Winston during the very early weeks of the COVID 19 pandemic.

Andrew, whose work in sustainability is legend, mentioned the term gigatrends in a conversation we were having about his view of the impact that dramatic changes, such as those we are experiencing in global weather patterns, would have on the future. In that instant *Gigatrends* came into focus.

We owe an enormous debt of gratitude to the dedicated staff at Post Hill Press. From our very first conversations with Anthony and Michael, who saw the potential of *Gigatrends*, to our editor, Ashlyn, who kept us on track and on message, you believed in our vision for *Gigatrends* from day one, and your steadfast commitment and support throughout this journey have been indispensable.

Thanks also to the incredibly talented design team at Post Hill Press, whose skillful interpretation of the book has given *Gigatrends* a visual identity as compelling as its ideas.

We are deeply grateful for the team of researchers and colleagues who helped refine the concepts in *Gigatrends*. Acacia James, Dr. Tim Mcgee, and Obafemi Fawibe, your intellectual rigor and curiosity were invaluable in expanding and challenging our thinking.

We would like to extend a special acknowledgement to the late John Naisbitt, whose profound insights have had an immeasurable impact on our world. His legacy continues to thrive within the pages of this book.

Thanks to Marco Buchbinder for introducing Tom to the idea of digital workers and their potential to radically alter the way we work. Marco's groundbreaking work in the field and with his startup Ampliforce, is paving the way for unimaginable advances that will elevate the human condition and challenge some of the most fundamental notions of what it means to work. We have no doubt that his efforts and insights will be a cornerstone of how we measure the value and contribution of human capital in the future.

Sunil Malhotra has been a dear friend for nearly two decades. His work with Tom on the future of autonomous vehicles, which is included in the chapter on the future of transportation, has been prescient in charting the course for AVs. More importantly, his constant support as both friend and muse has been invaluable in helping to shape much of the thinking that went into *Gigatrends*. Big ideas need conversation, they need challenge, and ultimately, they need time, patience, and encouragement to take shape. Sunil has provide all of these in abundance.

Many thanks to Jim Hays who introduced us to the work of Sir Karl Popper whose theories about emergent systems formed a cornerstone for how we think about the future and the way in which all of the Gigatrends will take shape. Jim's adventurous spirit and encouragement to think differently about the world are a constant source of inspiration.

To the numerous industry leaders and visionaries who offered their insights and experiences in our interviews, your generosity with your time and knowledge has enriched this book immensely. We hope that *Gigatrends* does justice to your contributions to our understanding of the future.

Most of all we are indebted to the love and support of our families. To our forward scouts into the future who have taken on the roles of sherpas and mentors into a future that they will ultimately shape much more that we can ever imagine; Mia, Adam, Nathaniel, and Amelia, we are forever grateful for all that you have taught and will continue to teach

Acknowledgments

us. To Nathaniel's wife Heather, for her unyielding support and patience in this and her instrumental role in so many endeavors over the past three decades.

To Joyce for her endless energy, enthusiasm, and encouragement while sharing the often unpredictable, but always exciting, journey of an author's restless mind.

Finally, a special note of gratitude to the tens of thousands of attendees at our many keynotes and to the countless readers of our prior books. Your encouragement, engagement, challenge, insights, and insatiable appetite for exploring the future is what fuels our passion for writing.

The journey to *Gigatrends* was complex, rewarding, and demanding. Still, every late night, every rewrite, every challenging concept, was worth the effort. To all of those who every small and large way contributed, this book is as much a product of your support, belief, and contributions as it is ours.

Thank you.